HEALTH AND SOCIETY IN
TWENTIETH-CENTURY BRITAIN

THEMES IN BRITISH SOCIAL HISTORY

edited by Dr J. Stevenson

This series covers the most important aspects of British social history
from the Renaissance to the present day. Topics include education,
poverty, health, religion, leisure, crime and popular protest, some of
which are treated in more than one volume. The books are written
for undergraduates, postgraduates and the general reader, and each
volume combines a general approach to the subject with the primary
research of the author.

HEALTH AND SOCIETY IN TWENTIETH-CENTURY BRITAIN

Helen Jones

LONGMAN
London and New York

Longman Group UK Limited,
Longman House, Burnt Mill,
Harlow, Essex CM20 2JE, England
and Associated Companies throughout the world.

Published in the United States of America
by Longman Publishing, New York

© Longman Group UK Limited 1994

First published 1994

ISBN 0 582 004594 PPR

British Library Cataloguing-in-Publication Data

A catalogue record for this book is
available from the British Library

Library of Congress Cataloging-in-Publication Data

Jones, Helen, 1954–
   Health and society in Twentieth-century Britain / Helen Jones.
      p.   cm. —(Themes in British social history)
      Includes bibliographical references (p. 00) and index.
      ISBN 0–582–00459–4 (P/B)
      1. Social medicine—Great Britain—History—20th century.
2. Public health—Social aspects—Great Britain—History—20th
century.   3. Medical care—Great Britain—History—20th century.
I. Title. II. Title: Health and society in 20th-century Britain.
III. Series.
   RA418.3.G7J65   1994
   362.1′0941′0904—dc20   93–25751
                                                                                            CIP

Set by 5 in 10 on 11 Times Roman
Printed in Malaysia by TCP

CONTENTS

Health and society in twentieth-century Britain

ACKNOWLEDGEMENTS

I am grateful to Longman Higher Education and John Stevenson for their support. I should also like to thank John Stevenson for his helpful comments on the manuscript. My thanks go to the following friends and colleagues for their comments on various chapters: Pat Ayers, Andrew Davies, Fiona Devine, Kevin Jefferys, Philippa Levine and Kenneth Roberts.

The publishers would like to thank the following for permission to reproduce copyright material: Macmillan Press Ltd for tables 1, 2, 4 and 5 from McPherson K, Coleman D, 1988 Health. In Halsey A. H. *British social trends since 1900: A guide to the changing social structure of Britain*; HMSO for tables 3, 6 and 7 from Central Statistical Office *Social Trends* (1993).

LIST OF ABBREVIATIONS

ARP	Air Raid Precautions
BMA	British Medical Association
CCHE	Central Council for Health Education
CCPR	Central Council for Physical Recreation
DGH	District General Hospital
DHSS	Department of Health and Social Security
DORA	Defence of the Realm Act
EHS	Emergency Hospital Service
EVW	European Volunteer Workers
FANY	First Aid Nursing Yeomanry
FPA	Family Planning Association
GHS	General Household Survey
GP	General Practitioner
HEC	Health Education Council
HMWC	Health of Munition Workers' Committee
IMR	Infant Mortality Rate
IWS	Industrial Welfare Society
JBG	Jewish Board of Guardians
MMR	Maternal Mortality Rate
MOH	Medical Officer of Health
MRC	Medical Research Council
NASL	National Anti-Sweating League
NCWP	New Commonwealth and Pakistan
NHI	National Health Insurance
NHS	National Health Service
PAI	Public Assistance Institution
SEN	State Enrolled Nurse
SMS	School Medical Service
SRHS	Sick Rooms Help Society
SRN	State Registered Nurse
SSFA	Soldiers' and Sailors' Families Association
TB	Tuberculosis

TUC	Trades Union Congress
UAB	Unemployment Assistance Board
VD	Venereal Disease (sexually transmitted disease)
VAD	Voluntary Aid Detachment
WAAC	Women's Auxiliary Army Corps
WCG	Women's Co-operative Guild
WRNS	Women's Royal Naval Service
WVS	Women's Voluntary Service
WWC	Well Woman Clinic

For my mother

Chapter 1

INTRODUCTION: A PICTURE OF HEALTH

'Health' is difficult to define and measure. Individuals know when they feel well or ill, but perceptions of health change over a lifetime; they also vary between generations as well as between individuals or groups at any one time. Even within the relatively short compass of the last hundred years, ideas about health have changed. Notions of basic minimum standards of housing and working conditions are significantly higher, and we all expect more of health services. Disease and an early grave affect fewer of us, and our ideas about what it means to be healthy are couched in far more positive terms than at the beginning of the century. 'Health' is relative to one's age and expectations. In 1948 the World Health Organisation offered a comprehensive definition of health as 'Not merely the absence of disease and infirmity but complete physical, mental and social well-being.' This definition suggests that an individual's health is multi-dimensional, and intimately linked with the social and economic environment. When people talk about tension headaches and nervous stomachs they are acknowledging that their health is affected by social situations and relationships.[1] 'Health' cannot be siphoned off and analysed in isolation from other aspects of our daily lives.

Social relationships – those relationships between men and women, between classes, between ethnic groups and between the medical profession and the rest of the population – all mesh together to create changing patterns of health experiences and standards of health.[2] Material factors, such as income, housing and the environment, along with cultural influences, which shape our attitudes and beliefs, all affect the ways in which those relationships are negotiated and fractured. Power relations in the home are gendered, and economic relationships are affected by an individual's or a group's position in the labour market. Relationships between ethnic groups are affected by power coupled with prejudice (racism).

Both material and cultural influences have been brought to bear on the strategies which different groups have developed to promote their

1

health and well-being. Throughout the twentieth century women have played a crucial role as formal and informal health promoters and carers. In turn, it is impossible to understand women's experiences without exploring the ways in which ideas about the family and motherhood impacted on gender relationships.

The way in which social relationships affect our health is the subject of this book. Such an approach is in contrast to those studies which treat the health of women, or a particular class, or an ethnic group, in isolation; none of these categories are 'optional extras' to be tagged on to a discussion of the health of society.

The approach of this book means that many of the conventional 'history of medicine' subjects, such as the history of the medical and nursing professions, medical institutions, health policies, diseases and how medical knowledge has been applied to them, are only dealt with in passing, if at all.[3] Instead, the book discusses the ways in which the social history of twentieth-century Britain has affected the health of differing groups in society. It focuses on the ways in which relationships between social groups have affected inequalities in standards of health. Such an approach is not politically uncontroversial.

In the 1970s and 1980s arguments over the causes of health inequalities led to major political rows between health researchers and politicians. *The Black Report*, commissioned by a Labour government and presented to a Conservative one in 1980, received a hostile reception from the Secretary of State, Patrick Jenkin. He refused to endorse the report, and warned in its foreword 'I must make it clear that additional expenditure on the scale which could result from the report's recommendations . . . is quite unrealistic in present or any foreseeable economic circumstances.' The report was not published in the usual fashion; only 260 duplicated copies of typescript were made available. No press release or press conference was called when copies were sent to a few journalists, on the Friday before the August bank holiday. This apparent attempt to bury the report provoked a backlash: an alternative press conference was called; the press reviewed the report enthusiastically; it was taken up in health circles around the country, and a Penguin edition of the report was produced, so ensuring a wide readership.

In 1986 the Health Education Council (HEC) commissioned an update of the *Black Report*. Its findings, published as *The Health Divide*, found increasing class inequalities in standards of health. In its preface, Dr David Player, Director General of the HEC, drew out the political implications of the report, and commented, 'Such inequality is inexcusable in a democratic society which prides itself on being humane.' The launch of *The Health Divide* in 1987 followed a similar pattern to that of *The Black Report*. An hour before the press brief was due to start it was cancelled by the chair of the HEC, Sir Brian Bailey. An alternative press briefing was quickly arranged and intense media interest was aroused, both in the contents of the report and the means of its launch. In contrast to its frosty reception from the Government, health researchers and those involved in health issues at grassroots level took up the report's findings. Most accepted the report's conclusions, and in many parts of the country they led to plans for action.[4] The attitude of governments in the 1980s is not untypical of those in earlier decades. In the 1930s research findings which were embarrassing to governments were ignored or belittled.[5] Even when governments have recognised the relevance of social and economic circumstances and relationships for people's health, they have done little to change them.

A NOTE ON SOURCES

This book relies heavily on published secondary work; a range of primary sources, many of them published, have also been used. No one source is entirely reliable; and it is best to regard each source as part of a jigsaw, with some pieces chipped or tarnished and with other pieces missing altogether.

Contemporary publications by social reformers and investigators usually rely on personal predilections and insight. They are more haphazard for the early part of the century, but all depend on what the investigators' subjects 'allow' them to see; and they paint their subjects as saints or sinners, depending on the purpose of their project. For instance, between 1909 and 1913 the Fabian Women's Group compiled a dossier on the daily lives of working-class families in Lambeth, London. *Round about a Pound a Week* (1913) aimed to show how well working-class families coped in overcrowded homes with too little money. In 1989 it was criticised by Mary Chamberlain for offering a sanitised version of working-class life. In an attempt to portray the working class as skilful and careful household managers, Chamberlain argues that they were thereby rendered merely a dim reflection of the middle class. In reaction, she wrote *Growing up in Lambeth* to provide an insight into the richness of working-class life – warts and all.[6]

Annual Reports of Medical Officers of Health and other governmental publications are useful as a guide to what was important to governments at a particular point, but they must be seen as political documents expressing the views of officials and politicians, rather than as reliable guides to the attitudes and experiences of differing groups of the population. Charles Webster has revealed that in the 1930s the Chief Medical Officer of Health wrote politically inspired reports with considerable economy of truth.[7] Other non-governmental organisations, such as the Women's Co-operative Guild (WCG), also wrote with a specific audience and goal in mind. All these sources may shed as much light on the investigator as those under the microscope.

Autobiographies and diaries tend to be patchy, and even when unpublished they may have been written with an audience in mind. Oral histories can provide information and colour not available from other sources, but they are not necessarily any more reliable – memories fade or are influenced by subsequent events; interviewees tell the interviewer only what they want the world to know. Jocelyn Cornwell interviewed twenty-four people in the East End of London. She found that some of them gave substantially different accounts of events when they were reinterviewed. Cornwell did not believe that the discrepancies were tricks of memory; rather, they occurred because of a changing relationship between her and the interviewees. What people say will vary according to whom they are saying it, the circumstances in which they are being interviewed and the interview techniques employed.[8]

Archival sources, such as the Imperial War Museum, the Bradford Heritage Recording Unit or the National Sound Archive all contain material which throws light on people's health and well-being. However, the material was not normally collected with the express purpose of finding out about people's health. Such information has emerged as a by-product, which means that people may have written or spoken comments without the same forethought that they gave to other subjects. People caught off their guard may utter revealing comments, or misleading and simplistic ones. At the very least these sources provide 'human interest', but this is again problematical, as a balance has to be achieved between failing to make explicit the horrors of domestic violence, racist attacks and poverty on the one hand, and avoiding a prurient voyeurism on the other hand.

Official statistics of morbidity and mortality offer us a picture of broad trends. Morbidity statistics are only partial as much illness goes unreported. Mortality figures are more comprehensive but there are various methodological problems in their use; for instance, during the course of the twentieth century there have been changes in the way in which information is collated and categorised.

Changes have also occurred during the twentieth century in the main causes of death and the age at which death normally takes place (see Table 1 p. 195). More and more people now die in old age; cancers and circulatory diseases pose a greater threat than in the past, but rarely are people struck down in the prime of life by the old infectious diseases, such as smallpox, chicken-pox, croup, tuberculosis, scarlet fever, diphtheria, whooping cough, polio and measles. In the first decade of the century the death-rate per million of the population at ages under fifteen years was 271 for scarlet fever, 571 for diphtheria, 815 for whooping cough and 915 for measles. Now, as the century draws to a close, only whooping cough and measles appear in the figures; the former is down to one per million and the latter to two per million (see Table 2, p. 196). During the course of the century life expectancy for the young has increased by over twenty years. The most impressive improvements have occurred in the infant mortality rate. For every 1,000 live births, 154 babies died in 1900, thirty died in 1950 and nine died in 1985 (See Table 3, p. 196). Unfortunately, TB has again raised its ugly head in various parts of the country. The death of babies has plummeted as a result of an entire raft of changes which include rising incomes, improved nutrition, better housing, a decline in family size, the growth of state welfare, and medical improvements which are now more widely available than at the beginning of the century.[9] Stark inequalities in standards of health and health experiences nevertheless remain: broad trends conceal enormous variations within a class, a region and even a family (See Table 4, p. 197).

NOTES

1. For a full examination of definitions of health see **Blaxter M.** 1990 *Health and lifestyles*. Routledge, pp. 2–4, 16, 30, 35–6, 42 and *passim*.
2. See Chapter 8 for use of the terms class and ethnicity.
3. Some useful histories are: **Dingwall R., Raffety A. M., Webster C.** 1988 *An introduction to the social history of nursing*. Routledge; **Bryder L.** 1988 *Below the magic mountain: A social history of tuberculosis in twentieth-century Britain*. Clarendon; **Webster C.** 1988 *The health services since the war. Volume I. Problems of health care: The National Health Service before 1957*. HMSO. For a list of recently commissioned institutional histories see **Cantor D.** 1992 Contracting cancer? The politics of commissioned histories *Social History of Medicine* **5**: 131. This article is a warning beacon against the ethical problems which the author argues are inherent in commissioned histories.
4. Inequalities in health 1988 *The Black report: The Health divide*. Penguin, pp. 3–4, 8, 13.
5. See Chapter 4.
6. **Chamberlain M.** 1989 *Growing up in Lambeth*. Virago, pp. 9–11.
7. See Chapter 4.
8. **Cornwell J.** 1984 *Hard-earned lives: Accounts of health and illness from East London*. Tavistock, pp. 1, 11–12.
9. **McPherson K., Coleman D.** 1988 Health. In **Halsey A. H.** *British social trends since 1900: A guide to the changing social structure of Britain*. Macmillan, pp. 39, 408.

Chapter 2

THE RACE FOR HEALTH: EDWARDIAN BRITAIN

INTRODUCTION

In this chapter we discuss the ways in which social and economic conditions influenced standards of health. Health experience was usually far removed from the influence and control of the medical profession. For example, women of all classes developed their own health strategies, independently of the medical profession. Similarly, the Jewish community developed health services (some of which led the field) to meet its cultural requirements. All levels of society perceived health issues as intimately linked with power, either between groups within the country or, in the case of official policies, as part of Britain's relations with continental Europe. The competitive strength of continental Europe was considered a threat to the future of the British race and caused 'health' to become a prominent feature of British social policy. At the same time, Britain adapted a number of continental health strategies: continental Europe concurrently posed a threat and offered a role model.

POVERTY, HOUSING AND THE ENVIRONMENT

In Victorian Britain the connection between poverty and disease was well recognised.[1] Health and well-being were regarded as closely linked with economic and social position. John Benson has argued that while one cannot determine the precise relationship between ill health and poverty, the former certainly contributed to the latter. Labourers with a poor physique found it more difficult to obtain and retain work, while those with a disability were harder hit than

6

other workers in periods of high unemployment. Poor Law statistics show a link between poverty and ill-health with nearly one-third of all paupers receiving medical treatment. Charles Booth, in his pioneering study of the East End of London poor, claimed that 10 per cent of the 'submerged one-tenth' had been impoverished by sickness or infirmity. In 1910 Rowntree and Lasker claimed that in their sample of the unemployed in York, roughly 10 per cent of 'regular workers' were in some way physically disqualified from work.[2] Poverty was a cause of ill health which in turn pushed individuals and families into greater poverty. Poor housing played a major part in the ill health of the poor.

The home could be a source of tension, disease and illness, or of contentment and satisfaction. Family income, class position, gender, age and ethnic origin were all key variables in determining home and environment. Contemporaries were not slow to recognise the relationship between standards of health and standards of housing. Back in 1842 Edwin Chadwick had recognised the link between poor housing and disease.[3] In 1903 it was argued that the height, weight and nutrition of children in Aberdeen reflected their housing.[4]

One of the most graphic contemporary descriptions of housing comes from Seebohm Rowntree's survey of York (published in 1901), which found that although a sewage disposal system existed, many of the house drains were defective. Of 11,560 houses investigated, 3,130 had no sole use of a lavatory, and in working-class districts most lavatories were midden privies which were unhealthy even when frequently cleaned. Until January 1901 the corporation had charged roughly 1s every time an ashpit or midden privy was cleared, a great inducement to the poor to allow sewage to accumulate. In 1900 the Medical Officer of Health found that the majority of typhoid fever cases were associated with midden privies, which were usually 'foul' or leaking, polluting the adjacent soil, with dilapidated and uncemented walls and floors. According to Rowntree, 'no housewife with any remnant of an olfactory nerve will open her window if it be 15 feet from [the privy]'. Personal cleanliness must have been impeded when 15 per cent of all the houses had no separate water supply, and many water taps were some distance from the houses. Some of the houses were built around common yards which, according to Rowntree, were 'unhealthy, dirty, smelly, filthy'.[5]

Poor housing conditions were made worse by overcrowding. Family relationships were intimately affected by home conditions. People living in overcrowded homes were more likely than those living in spacious accommodation to rub alongside each other with increasing friction and thence violence and abuse. Shared facilities between families were a source of difficulty with rows erupting over who last used the lavatory or cleaned the stairs.[6]

The burden of the ubiquitous slums of Britain fell not only on their inhabitants, but also on the better-off who foresaw in them the seeds of their own potential downfall. Contemporary commentators and social reformers feared that the huddled urban masses posed a threat to the moral fibre of society and to social and political stability. As Anthony Wohl observed, overcrowding was thought to breed drunkenness, crime and sexual immorality, to destroy families, to concentrate the masses in a politically dangerous way, to dispose the mind to socialism or nihilism, to encourage atheism and to help spread disease.[7]

To a certain extent, as Martin Daunton has pointed out, the level of overcrowding was determined by the relationship between the size of the wage packet and the cost of rent. The wage-rent relationship was less favourable in Scotland than in England, which helps to explain the extensive overcrowding, tenement blocks and poky homes of the Scots. In England, Londoners suffered the worst wage-rent relationship, followed by inhabitants of Plymouth who tended to live in rambling subdivided houses.[8] Housing location and environment varied not only between cities and regions but also reflected class and ethnic origin (immigrants and ethnic minorities tended to congregate in the least desirable areas).

Damp and badly constructed homes meant heavy and time-consuming housework for women and girls. Such conditions were likely to be aggravated in times of illness, for as one observer noted 'illness brings more for the housewife to do, unaccustomed duties, more trouble . . . everything is bound to be even more uncomfortable than it was before'.[9] Women tended to be the ones worst affected by poor housing.

DOMESTIC STRATEGIES

The domestic environment and women's work in that environment was central to health and well-being. Elizabeth Roberts has studied Barrow and Lancaster where the indigenous population, despite earnings near or below the poverty line, enjoyed above-average health and a relatively low infant death-rate. Roberts's explanation lies in the way mothers developed strategies to improve their families' health and well-being. Although few married women were in full-time employment, a number of them undertook casual work, such as taking in lodgers, cleaning, helping with their husbands' work or dressmaking. The extra cash meant standards of living could creep up and a few extra shillings jangled in the purse to spend on food. Money was then spent wisely. Mothers put healthy food, such as a wide range of vegetables, on the table. Some families had allotments, gathered fruit in the countryside or went fishing. In years of depression soup kitchens provided a vital element in working-class diets. Many families lived on credit, never paying for their food in full.[10] Although Roberts focuses on the important role played by mothers in raising standards of health, it is clear from her own account that community services (such as soup kitchens) were important, and that the mothers benefited from a range of local resources. This latter explanation is supported by the research and arguments of Lara Marks.

The wide-ranging maternal and other welfare services which the Jewish community provided for itself offers the most likely explanation, according to Marks, for a surprisingly low infant death rate among East End Jews. She challenges the contemporary view that the low death-rate among Jews was due to a combination of healthy behaviour, and the parents, especially the mothers, taking good care of the children. Rather, Jewish community services enabled pregnant women to give up paid work and to enjoy relatively good diets. Moreover, it was Jewish custom to breast-feed and this reduced the risk of infection.[11] It is unlikely that the infant welfare centre's sewing and educational work could have reduced the infant death-rate, but it did provide the icing on the cake. It would seem that community services could contribute to reduced infant mortality and, where local resources allowed, women might be able to devise strategies for improving their families' health. For some women the range of options available to them in the kitchen was undergoing something of a transformation.

From the turn of the century the shelves of grocers' shops carried a wider range of foods than ever before. Tinned foods, imported food and chocolate all whetted the appetite. Changes were also taking place in the consumption of more traditional foods: more meat and sugar were eaten at the expense of potatoes and bread. However, not everyone was able to indulge in the wider choices. Those who lived in the country continued to eat a starchier diet and drink more milk than city dwellers. Large sections of the population remained too poor to benefit from the wide range of foods for sale.[12] This lack of choice was not only a matter of class differences or family income but also of the way food was apportioned within a family. It was recognised by contemporaries (and current researchers are discovering anew) that the diets of women and children were frequently inferior in quality and quantity to those of the men.[13] The evidence in *Round about a Pound a Week* suggests that husbands consistently received more food than the rest of the family. A random example shows that in the course of a week one husband (a carter) was given various tasty additions to his meals, kippers, eggs, fried potatoes and fish, corned beef and bacon,[14] which the rest of his family did not enjoy. Women's and children's diets were elastic, whereas the quality and quantity of men's meals tended to be maintained.[15] Women's diets often suffered most when they were pregnant or breast-feeding – the very times when they needed an improved diet – as they skimped on food in order to make savings for the additional cost of a new baby.[16]

Ideas about an equitable distribution of food within a family were superficially wedded to the notion of a male breadwinner bringing in a family wage: the man had to be given the best diet the family could afford in order to keep him healthy and in work. In fact, the distribution of food within a family was part of a complex web of power relations which were not purely determined by rational family economics. While it may or may not have made economic sense for the male producer rather than female reproducer (and often producer as well) to receive the lion's share of the food, the motivation was also culturally specific. The food on a man's plate reflected his tastes; he was given what he fancied: 'It is he who has to be satisfied in the long-run, and if he desires pickles, pickles there will be.'[17] Thus diet contributed to and reinforced power relations within the family.

The nature of relationships within the family directly affected not only the standard of living of family members, but also the quality of their life and general well-being. Many a woman suffered years of spousal abuse because she feared that if she left her husband he would wreak his revenge by seeking her out and inflicting yet further violence on her.[18] Divorce was out of the question for most people; and in any case before 1923 divorce laws were structured to women's disadvantage. A man only had to prove that his wife had committed adultery, whereas a woman had to prove additional aggravating factors, such as cruelty or desertion. There were, however, Separation Orders which were much cheaper than a divorce and could require the husband to maintain the wife. Women's organisations, such as the Women's Co-operative Guild (WCG), conscious of the hazards to health caused by the difficulty of women obtaining a divorce, demanded equal moral standards under the law for men and women. A wife's economic dependence on her husband meant that she was unable to leave a husband who might have given her venereal disease (VD) or abused her in some other way. It was hard, too, for poor people to live together if they did not get along because they did not have the space to get away from each other under the same roof. The WCG demanded that cruelty (including the transmission of VD) alone, without adultery necessarily having taken place, should be grounds for a divorce.[19]

As well as the fear of a man's revenge, and the legal and economic barriers to a woman leaving a man, society's quick condemnation of a woman separated from her husband meant that women stayed in unhappy and hazardous relationships. While there is some evidence that in certain neighbourhoods a battered wife would be given shelter for the night by neighbours,[20] censorious attitudes towards women were widespread. For instance, a man who did not give his wife enough housekeeping money was not censored by society (often of course such behaviour would be well hidden); however, public opinion readily condemned a divorced woman without regard to the circumstances, so that the disgrace of separation was dreaded even if (as the WCG argued) a husband made sexual demands to the destruction of a wife's body and soul.[21]

POVERTY, SEX AND LABOUR

Historians' investigations into a whole range of issues around reproduction have exposed the yawning gender gap between lay and professional opinion. Angus McLaren has suggested that up until the First World War working-class women practised abortion as their chief means of birth control; their approach to fertility control flew in the face of medical and ecclesiastical opinion. Although abortion was illegal, lay opinion and practice would not have drawn a distinction between birth control and abortion. Women learnt about fertility control, usually from friends, neighbours or midwives, independently of a medical profession overwhelmingly hostile to artificial contraception. Middle-class women also procured abortions, but probably not on the same scale as working-class women, and then only as a last resort.[22]

There is, too, evidence of upper-class women's independence from the iron grip of medical orthodoxy. Pat Jalland's study of 500 upper-class families has shown that upper-class women frequently rejected medical advice. Medical check-ups during pregnancy were rare; labour and pregnancy were both seen as natural processes not normally requiring medical intervention; births took place at home (even when complications were expected) and almost always with the husband at the bedside to provide emotional support.[23]

Since the mid-nineteenth century some women had been organising themselves to promote their health quite independently of the medical profession. In Scotland women organised schools for mothers; infant welfare centres; dinners for pregnant and nursing mothers; holidays; milk for babies; crèches, and nursery schools.[24] After a WCG visit to 'consultations for mothers' in Ghent, a similar school for mothers was started in Bolton.[25] Mothers' meetings, first organised by middle-class women in the nineteenth century to bring women of all classes together, increasingly turned their attention to health-related matters. Talks were given on infant and child health; there were instances of district nursing growing out of the mothers' meetings, and indeed infant welfare centres and schools for mothers, which were later taken on board by local authorities, were pioneered by these women.[26] As well as organising services themselves, women campaigned for state-provided facilities. In the early twentieth century largely middle-class groups demanded anaesthesia in labour and mainly working-class groups called for hospitalisation at childbirth.[27]

Women's organisations regarded 'health' as a deeply political issue. They recognised that when politicians and social reformers confined themselves to creating infant welfare clinics and hectoring women about the importance of cleanliness, self-sacrifice, and looking after the family, they diverted attention from their own failures; attacks on vested interests were thereby deflected.[28] Both middle-class and working-class women linked improvements in their health with obtaining the vote. Margaret Llewelyn Davies, of the WCG, argued that women should be able to influence protective legislation, working conditions, child labour, temperance, education, health and divorce laws. 'Who knows so well as a woman how she is hindered in her work as a "homemaker" by badly lit houses, ill-lighted streets, defective drains, and general insanitary conditions.'[29]

Even the most ardent campaigners were, however, reluctant to grasp the nettle of birth control. There were two main reasons why many feminists were inhibited from campaigning publicly for birth-control information to be made widely available. Family limitation was considered a vulgar subject for polite and public discussion, and without the possibility of procreating it was feared that men would demand even more sex, without let or hindrance. What hope then of raising men's morality to the level of women's propriety? Such questions were especially pertinent at a time of growing concern about men's vice and disease. The problem was not simply a moral one, for it was assumed that the spread of VD was causing widespread sterility and was, therefore, contributing to the falling birth-rate, a matter of considerable worry in Edwardian Britain.[30]

The immorality of men fuelled a public 'purity' campaign by women. Most historians distinguish between feminist and non-feminist purity strands. As Frank Mort has pointed out, not all historians see the purity campaigns as being fired by feminist convictions. Jeffrey Weeks, for instance, views the campaign as yet another peak in perennial moral panics. Mort, however, convincingly argues that there was much cross-membership between women in suffrage organisations and women involved in parts of the purity movement. Millicent Fawcett, as President of the National Union of Women's Suffrage Societies (NUWSS) and a prominent member of the National Vigilance Association, personified the overlap.[31]

Reform of male sexual behaviour was part of the early twentieth-century feminist project. Whereas in the early nineteenth century men were thought of as a biological 'norm' from which women deviated, by the late nineteenth century feminists had turned the argument on its head, and argued that women's restrained, monogamous behaviour was more natural, and men should adapt their lifestyles accordingly. The health of individuals and the nation was under threat unless men's sexual behaviour rose to women's standards. Gender relations were, therefore, central to the future health of the race.[32]

Women's duty, as in the past, was to ensure the protection of the race. If women did not behave as moral guardians they were 'unnatural'. As Lucy Bland has argued, the categories of health and ill-health were superimposed on those of virtue and vice. If a woman risked her health by catching VD she was undermining her duty to the nation. Morals were not only a personal matter but also a public one with implications for national security.[33] As we will see below, there was widespread concern over the quality of the British race. Carol Dyhouse has pointed to a mass of strident imperialistic advice offered to women and girls, urging them to preserve their health as a moral duty to the empire and the race (illness was equated with moral weakness). Similarly, Lord Baden-Powell, founder of the scouting movement, rallied his young recruits to the pennant of clean thoughts and self-discipline.[34]

Carol Dyhouse has explained why the question of whether married women should undertake paid work outside the home became an increasingly contentious moral issue with implications for the reproduction of the race. The Infant Mortality Rate (IMR) had been high throughout the ninetieth century, averaging 149 deaths for every 1,000 live births. When the birth-rate and the general death-rate had both been high, the high infant death-rate was accepted. Between the 1860s and 1900 there was an overall fall in death-rates of about 15 per cent, but no comparable fall in the infant death-rate. As the new century opened, the birth-rate was falling, from 35.5 in 1871–75 to 29.3 in 1896–1900; between 1867 and 1907 the death-rate for children aged between one and five years had fallen by 33 per cent, and yet as big a proportion of babies were dying in their first year of life as in the 1860s.[35]

The ideal of mothers staying at home permeated all classes of society; the middle class and upper working class viewed it as a sign of respectability; and male trade unionists saw women workers as competitors, undermining male wages. Three health-related reasons were also posited against married women's paid work: it reduced their physical capacity for childbearing; it made breast-feeding more impractical if not impossible (bottle-feeding was closely linked with infant deaths), and it was detrimental to the moral fibre of society for mothers not to be at home with young children. May Tennant, an ardent campaigner against the sweated trades, feared that if mothers worked they would be too tired and too busy to learn from the health visitor in the evenings.[36]

An enquiry carried out during 1909–10 by the Women's Industrial Council found that women in Glasgow were compelled by poverty to work almost up to the hour of childbirth, so ruining their health and sending the babies to a premature grave. (Such evidence was nothing new; in the early nineteenth century similar concern had been expressed over women miners). Older women worked as chars, younger ones in blouse factories or restaurants. The work was not necessarily injurious in itself, but the scandalously low wages drove the women into overwork.[37] Following the rapid wage rises in the late nineteenth century, for many groups of workers in the Edwardian period real wages were either stagnant or actually falling. Even among those who opposed married women working outside the home, there was a recognition that the women worked as a result of their social and economic circumstances which were not immediately alterable.[38] The extra money which wages brought into the home was thought by many commentators actually to improve women's health.[39] In areas such as the textile districts of the West Riding of Yorkshire, where women traditionally worked outside the home, the infant death-rate was lower than in Durham and South Wales where women tended not to work outside the home, and where it was believed overcrowding and insanitary conditions killed the infants. A Birmingham survey carried out between 1909 and 1910 found that babies had a better chance of celebrating their first birthday if their mothers went out to work. A mother's wages contributed significantly to the family's standard of living.[40]

Poor women who were not in paid work outside the home often took in work. Home work was a menace to the entire family. Cramped homes were piled high with matchboxes, shirts, trousers or paper bags; sewing machines rattled remorselessly throughout the day and evening; meals were eaten alongside glue or paste pots; the smell of new cloth, dust and fluff or flannelette pervaded the rooms of 'finishers'; damp paper bags or cardboard boxes were stacked up on beds.[41]

While there was much moralising and wringing of hands over the evils of (low) paid work, especially for pregnant women and mothers, often the heaviest toll on women's health came from the unpaid work they did in the home. It was claimed that domestic labour, not paid work outside the home, was largely responsible for the loss of women's robust health.[42]

Small children in poor homes also contributed to the family economy, to the detriment of their health. 'Our milk, our news-papers, our green grocery are brought to us by small boys; young boys are out at all hours and in all weathers with parcel-delivery vans.'[43] Many schoolchildren worked 'part-time', although this was something of a misnomer as the hours were frequently very long indeed. Boys and girls ran errands, or plied their trade as street hawkers. Girls also worked as domestic servants. Girls from poor families worked in neighbours' or relatives' homes, receiving food, clothes or odd pennies. Little girls might have to take food to their parents at work, work in the home or look after siblings.[44] From the age of twelve, children were permitted to work half-time and attend school half-time. Such children tended to be employed in unskilled 'blind-alley' jobs which they were thrown out of when they became adults.

The 'boy labour problem', as it was known, was criticised on the grounds that it denied children a childhood, condemned them to dead-end jobs and, more importantly, posed a moral and social threat to society. It was feared that these children lived undisciplined lives, roaming the streets and falling into bad company. Children were a national resource and should be treated as such. In fact, although there was great concern about the boy labour problem, the ratio of boy to adult workers was actually falling at this time.[45] (Like the nation's health the problem was perceived to be getting worse when in fact a long-standing problem was coming to light and causing concern.)

Special concern also surrounded those workers (mainly women) outside the Factory Acts who worked in appalling conditions with long hours and low pay, in what were known as the 'sweated trades'. Women were at the forefront of the campaign against the sweated trades.

Sporadic pressure had been put on governments since the mid-nineteenth century, but in the winter of 1905–06 an exhibition of products of home workers held in Berlin provided a spur to action; the following year the *Daily News* arranged a similar exhibition of the 'sweated trades' in London which was followed by a House of Commons select committee on homework (although it also received evidence about wages and conditions in factories and workshops); a special commissioner was sent out to Australia to study its system of wage regulation. In 1908 the newly formed National Anti-Sweating League (NASL) organised a conference in London which included speakers from France and Belgium; pressure was maintained on the Government to introduce minimum wage rates in notoriously badly paid trades with calls for Britain to learn from the examples of Australia and New Zealand.[46] Critics and supporters alike pored over every scrap of evidence about the working of the minimum wage system in Victoria, Australia.

Support for legislation was widespread. It was assumed that minimum wages in the sweated trades would improve the efficiency of the workforce by raising their standard of health, discouraging home work and stimulating good management practices.[47] Large employers feared shoddy goods would ultimately lose British firms much needed foreign contracts. John Rickard has highlighted the way in which German, but more especially Australian, precedents were drawn on. He points out that it is hardly surprising that those who saw Australian practice as relevant to Britain should be those with an interest in the empire. Imperialists were fascinated by the impact of pioneers on their new countries; a pioneer spirit supposedly brought out the best in the British race. Rickard argues that the abolition of the sweated system evoked colonial comparisons because it gelled with Britain's self-image of a country with a history of humanitarian endeavour going back to the age of Shaftesbury. Germany was of interest to British social reformers because it was thought to be coping so successfully with similar industrial and economic problems.[48]

The 1909 Trade Boards Act set a minimum wage in a number of sweated trades. Its relatively limited scope reflected the hostility to a minimum wage of some trade unionists who feared that it would undermine free collective bargaining, and in practice be taken as a maximum wage. The NASL, for its part, favoured a national minimum wage, but did not press for one, for fear of alienating the House of Lords and wealthy patrons of the League.[49] There was in fact no dramatic improvement in the wages of those covered by the Act; there were evasions of the law, and great disparity in negotiating skills between the employers' and workers' representatives.[50] Over the years more and more trades were brought under the wing of the Trade Boards Act, but no government would ever brook a universal application of the minimum wage principle. For instance, during the First World War it was argued that no 'scientific' rate could be set because conditions between trades and areas varied too greatly and consequently any level set would be based on political rather than economic considerations.[51]

While conditions in the sweated trades were notorious, working conditions in the rest of industry were not necessarily much better. Under the 1901 Factory and Workshop Act women and children were permitted to work up to sixty hours a week (fifty–five and a half hours in textile factories), exclusive of meal times; they could work for periods up to twelve hours at a stretch, less one and a half hours (two hours in textile factories) for intervals; no children under twelve could be employed and a certificate of employment for children and young people could be qualified by the conditions under which they could work. However, doctors were under great pressure to issue certificates of fitness when poor families were desperate for their children to bring home a wage packet. Sufficient means of ventilation, adequate temperatures, drainage and fire escapes had to be maintained. Finally, the Home Secretary could make special regulations where there were particular dangers.[52]

For many workers, conditions fell well below the legal minimum. In numerous factories, trade refuse and dirt collected on the floors, benches and ledgers, with the result that vast clouds of dust were constantly billowing up into the air. In some factories cleaning was only undertaken when rubbish actually obstructed the floors and benches, or reduced the efficiency of tools and machines. The Factory Inspector for North-East London commented sourly that standards were highest in factories where the employers themselves had to spend a lot of time in the workrooms.

Factory Inspectors, first appointed in the 1840s, had given industrial diseases relatively high priority since the 1870s. In the last quarter of the nineteenth century special rules to regulate work in dangerous trades developed, along with an ever-lengthening schedule of notifiable industrial diseases. In 1906, twenty-four occupational diseases were scheduled for compensation. Until the mid-1930s lead poisoning was by far and away the most commonly reported industrial disease.

In one important area the activities of governments and the Factory Inspectorate narrowed over the course of the twentieth century, for women's health and safety at work was increasingly marginalised. Nineteenth-century Factory Acts had originally only covered the hours and conditions of women and children. (That women and children were lumped together in one category says much about the way women were viewed as indistinguishable from children.) In 1893 the first two women Factory Inspectors were appointed, in the teeth of opposition from many male Factory Inspectors, to deal specifically with women's health at work. Although the women inspectors were popular with working women there were only a handful of inspectors to cover 1,500,000 women workers, which must call into question the effectiveness of the women inspectors.[53] After the First World War the men's and women's branches of the Inspectorate were amalgamated and women's health no longer received the Inspectors' special attention.

Whereas policies relating to women's working conditions were primarily motivated by a concern over the alleged degeneracy of the race and a desire to promote national efficiency (see below), men's health and safety at work was tackled largely in order to parry both industrial unrest and the infant Labour Party.

ETHNICITY

Immigrants were often seen both as the perpetrators and victims of poor working conditions, although in many ways the problems of poor East End Jewish immigrants mirrored those of the indigenous majority population. Poverty, poor housing and bad working conditions were common problems, but they were compounded for the Jews by hostility, either violent or subtle, from the host community. In 1903 violence against Jews flared up around the country. In 1911 a coal and rail strike brought hardship in its wake which it was thought the Jews and Chinese were exploiting – a suspicion which led to racial attacks in South Wales. Hostility varied from one area to another. According to Jerry White, children shouted anti-Semitic taunts at each other in the area around the Rothschild buildings, built for Jewish immigrants in Spitalfields, East London, yet a violent racial incident was rare; in contrast, neighbouring Bethnal Green had a permanently threatening reputation.[54]

Throughout the Edwardian years there was a hostile climate of opinion towards immigrants, graphically depicted in the 1903 Report of the Royal Commission on Alien Immigration: a battery of complaints were hurled at new immigrants who were allegedly impoverished, destitute, dirty and insanitary and, as there was no medical examination on arrival, they were thought to bring infectious diseases into the country. Complaints were made to the Royal Commission that a high percentage of the immigrants were anarchists, prostitutes or criminals. Immigrants congregating in the East End of London allegedly worsened the housing shortage and so contributed to overcrowding and rising rents; they worked for wages which the indigenous population could not survive on, and local businesses lost trade as the new immigrants, who did not assimilate, traded exclusively with those of their own race and religion.[55] Between 1891 and 1901 the Jewish community increased by nearly 60 per cent (from 101,189 to 160,000); and between 1901 and 1905 by more than 40 per cent (from 160,000 to 227,166). A concerted campaign against Jewish refugees from Russia and Poland culminated in the 1905 Aliens' Act which aimed to keep Britain free from 'undesirable and destitute aliens'. Between 1905 and 1911 the Jewish population in Britain increased by less than 5 per cent.[56]

More subtle hostility permeated supposedly 'caring' institutions. One doctor at the London Hospital spoke of Jews making it a custom to visit the hospital 'whenever they felt like it'; they would get 'very excited' and 'pour out torrents of words in Yiddish . . . . Even their diseases did not always resemble those suffered by Gentiles.'[57] Jewish patients were stereotyped as neurotic and prone to exaggerate symptoms and pain. Despite the London Hospital's official policy of not discriminating against Jews (and indeed a number of Jewish facilities were provided), local Jews believed that some of the administrators and low-grade staff were anti-Semitic.[58]

Lara Marks and G. Black have shown that the specific needs of the Jewish community were not always catered for by the wider community. In order to meet Jewish needs, the Jewish Board of Guardians (JBG) provided a plethora of welfare and medical aid facilities. In 1895 the JBG established the Sick Rooms' Help Society (SRHS) in the East End of London which offered a range of partly means-tested services, such as a home help service, home nurses for the sick poor, and midwives. The inspiration for the scheme came from a similar Jewish one in Frankfurt. It was many years before the home help scheme was implemented more widely in Britain. The home helps, themselves widows or deserted mothers, were in turn helped by the wages they received. In 1911 the SRHS opened a maternity home in Whitechapel. The following year it started an infant welfare centre with classes for mothers in thrift, hygiene and sewing. Milk supplements and vitamins were provided free of charge for those mothers who had difficulty breast-feeding. Other facilities included a JBG scheme for medical attendance; sanitary inspectors; health visitors; a Tuberculosis (TB) sanatorium and after-care committee; various dispensaries for those suffering from TB, and mothers' meetings. In 1897 a day nursery was started which was about half the price of other nurseries. It was hoped that, if mothers could leave their children at a cheap nursery where they would be properly looked after, the mothers would be able to go out to work and not be a burden on the rates. The late nineteenth century saw the rapid growth of numerous long-established Jewish Friendly Societies, almost exclusively for men, which provided quick access to doctors, specialists and nurses as well as a convalescent home.[59]

Partly as a result of anti-Semitism, Jews took their formal health care into their own hands. Other immigrant groups had taken similar action in the past. Since 1845 there had been a German hospital, with three dispensaries in different parts of London. In 1900 kosher kitchens were added to the German hospital which caused some irritation, but they were grudgingly accepted in order to hold on to Jewish patients and their money. In the early years of the new century a German convalescent home was opened.[60] Since 1884 there had been an Italian hospital in London. East London and Manchester Jews favoured the establishment of local Jewish hospitals. First and foremost, the language difficulties faced by first generation immigrants made a hospital stay particularly unnerving. Second, cultural differences, relating to kosher food, childbirth, death and circumcision, could create problems unless Jewish medical or nursing support was available. However, hostility from long- established, and especially wealthy, Jews to a Jewish hospital on the grounds that Jews should assimilate and make use of existing facilities, meant that there was a tough fight before a Jewish hospital opened in Manchester in 1904; and it was not until 1919 that the London Jewish Hospital opened its doors.[61]

FORMAL HEALTH SERVICES

With the bulk of the population living and working in unhealthy conditions what formal health care was generally available to contain or repair the damage? Many working men, if they did not have a chronic illness which rendered them uninsurable, belonged to Friendly Societies which covered them for hospital or General Practitioner (GP) treatment, and payments in time of sickness. David Green argues that a surprisingly high proportion of working men were covered by Friendly Societies or Medical Institutes. Moreover, the working class enjoyed great power over the medical profession because if a doctor was not thought to be up to scratch he could be dismissed from a Friendly Society's employment. Thus patients were guaranteed a good service. Green dismisses the needs of those not covered by such schemes on the grounds that the poor had recourse to the Poor Law.[62] However, only a minority of the population could benefit from Friendly Societies as women and children were not normally covered. It is impossible, therefore, to accept the optimistic view of Green that the working class was well served by the system they ran among themselves.

For the majority of the population a visit to a GP cost money and was, therefore (unless *in extremis*) out of the question, even though some doctors charged what they thought patients could afford. Regional disparities in the distribution of GPs operated to the disadvantage of poor areas: as GPs were small businessmen they tended to work where the financial rewards were greatest. The treatment offered by GPs was not so different to that offered in hospitals as minor surgery was performed in people's homes.

Hospitals were a last resort, especially for working-class families. Two types of hospitals ran alongside each other: voluntary hospitals, supported by voluntary contributions, and workhouses (in 1913 renamed Poor Law Infirmaries), supported by local taxes. From the late nineteenth century, standards of care rose in both types of hospital, although a higher standard was normally found in the voluntary hospitals. Poor Law infirmaries struggled along with limited resources with patients suffering from 'passive cruelty' as staff were too busy to give adequate individual attention. Voluntary hospitals normally demanded payment, so were used either by those who could afford to pay directly for their services or by those who belonged to a hospital insurance scheme, perhaps run by a Friendly Society. Most hospitals ran out-patient clinics or dispensaries where the poor could receive free treatment. However, parents were inhibited from taking their children to hospital for a range of reasons: hospitals were too far away; the travelling costs were too high, there were long waits, and parents lost wages if they took time off work.[63]

Irrespective of the suspect quality of care or the inconvenience, there was a terrible stigma attached to using Poor Law Infirmaries. A patient entering such hospitals required an Admission Order from a Poor Law Receiving Officer which automatically labelled the patient a pauper. In 1929 when Poor Law institutions were transferred to local authorities there was a name-change but otherwise the system appeared intact to its users. In order to receive free treatment a patient was forced to undergo the indignity of a means-test conducted by a Lady Almoner. For many this was an appalling intrusion and severe blow to their pride. To guard against such an eventuality, the bulk of the working class made a weekly contribution towards an industrial life assurance, or burial insurance, as it was popularly known. In an age when a decent burial counted for a great deal, families went to enormous lengths to insure against a pauper's funeral.[64] This rudimentary formal health-care system offered great scope for expansion.

SOCIAL REFORMS AND THE FEAR OF NATIONAL DECLINE

Some members of the 1905–15 Liberal governments saw social legislation as an antidote to socialism, whereas others saw the need to 'civilise' the Labour Party rather than combat it. Piecemeal social legislation gave the Liberal Party a strategy. In 1905 the party had entered office under Campbell-Bannerman with a list of complaints about the previous Conservative administration, rather than with its own list of policy proposals. Clutching a bundle of social reforms the Liberals could claim a *raison d'être*. Roy Hay has argued that this was a time when the relationship between the state and the citizen was being redefined, when attitudes towards poverty were undergoing a change, and when new statistical techniques were providing more accurate information than in the past. There was a growing recognition that major social problems could no longer be left to local authorities to deal with and that central government would have to take a stronger lead than in the past. In spite of this, much legislation remained permissive rather than obligatory for local authorities.[65] Individual reforms were introduced for a variety of motives; nevertheless, there was one primary concern that dominated health reforms, and that was the fear of the decline in the health of the British nation.

From the 1880s concern was expressed over the alleged deterioration (physical, mental and moral) of the British race, but around the turn of the century a number of influences came together to transform this concern into an obsession. There was evidence from various sources that large sections of the population were in poor health: the infant mortality rate remained high – in 1900 154 babies died out of every 1,000 live births. The publications of Charles Booth and Seebohm Rowntree detailed extensive poverty and poor health, and the poor physical standard of recruits to the Boer War resulted in the rejection of 38 per cent of potential soldiers. They suffered from heart complaints, poor sight, inadequate hearing and rotten teeth. From this evidence of poor health developed a common asssumption (although not one generally held by the medical profession) that the quality of the British race was actually deteriorating.[66]

It was the supposedly vicious circle of deterioration as much as the actual standards of health discovered which prompted scare-mongering among a broad cross-section of the middle class. First and foremost, a decline in the birth-rate was more pronounced in the middle class than working class, which caused alarm as it was assumed that the middle class was intellectually, physically and morally the strongest section of society. Second, emigration to the empire was thought to be draining Britain of some of its healthiest stock while the immigrants it took in were supposedly far weaker. Third, it was thought that the strength of the country required building up so that Britain could meet her commercial, military and colonial competitors – in particular Germany – on level playing fields. Throughout the early years of the century there was a sense that Britain and Germany were hurtling towards a head-on collision which only the tougher of the two national machines would survive.[67] The need was for national efficiency at home and abroad.

Fears of national decline were fed by eugenicists, who in turn drew succour from these fears. Eugenicists argued that it was possible to improve the quality of the racial stock (and this is the language they used) by negative or positive eugenics. Negative eugenics meant preventing the reproduction of 'low grade' human stock by, for instance, segregation or sterilisation. Positive eugenics meant encouraging the 'better stock' to breed. One favoured means of achieving positive eugenics involved altering the tax system to the advantage of married couples with dependent children. (As broadly speaking only the middle class paid direct taxes, this policy would not encourage breeding among the poorer sections of society.) Whether eugenicists fell into the positive or negative camp, their solutions revolved around intervention in the reproductive process, and as such there were direct implications for all women.[68]

Fears of racial decline influenced some health strategies directly, and others indirectly, but all health initiatives bore the hallmarks of international developments, either in the sense that they were prompted by fears of international competition or that they consciously borrowed ideas from policies and services already up-and-running abroad. (The cases of the Trade Boards Act and the Jewish home help scheme have already been mentioned.) The middle class had long looked to the Continent as the font of good health, but for very different reasons. German spas were a magnet for the British, while a Mediterranean climate, along with exercise and fresh air far removed from the sources of stress and fatigue, was thought to be the perfect prescription for those suffering all manner of ills.[69] Now the Continent, cast as the villain of international peace and Pax Britannica, posed a threat to the empire's security.

The 1904 Inter-Departmental Committee on Physical Deterioration (hereafter Physical Deterioration Committee), set up as the country reeled from the shocking revelations during the Boer War about the poor health and therefore inability of so many young men to defend Britain and the empire, reported that standards of health and morals were not genetically inherited and therefore environmental and behavioural changes could improve standards of health. The committee did not believe that there was a progressive deterioration of the race taking place, and indeed a rapid improvement in standards of health was possible if there were changes in food, clothing, overcrowding, cleanliness, drunkenness and home management.[70] A range of policy initiatives already tentatively emerging were thereby given a boost.

COMPETITIVE STRATEGIES AND HEALTH INITIATIVES

The model for promoting clean milk came from France, where there was a long-standing concern about the declining birth-rate and the supposed difficulty France would face in raising a large enough army in any future war, particularly one against Germany. (American pioneers were not known about in Britain quite as early as the French ones.) French efforts to increase the birth-rate came to nothing, so an alternative tack was tried; that of reducing the infant death rate so that more babies would survive into adulthood. Infant diarrhoea, caused by infected milk, was a terrible scourge of babies, and in order to supply clean milk to those mothers who could not breast-feed their babies, milk depots were opened.

In 1899 the first British milk depot opened in St Helens. Publicity at conferences and through the *British Medical Journal* led to the opening of other depots around the country. The Battersea milk depot, which opened in 1902, branched out three years later offering consultations to mothers about their babies' health. At milk depots it was emphasised that if a baby could not be breast-fed, it should be given cow's milk and not cheap condensed milk. The depots aroused awareness about one important cause of infant deaths and provided one cheap and easy partial solution.[71]

The Board of Education had already shown an interest in the way other countries provided domestic training, especially in hygiene, for working-class girls, and the Physical Deterioration Committee spurred the Board into action. The committee argued that schools, continuing education classes and philanthropic and municipal agencies should offer 'social education' so that the foundations of 'maternal competence' could be laid.[72] To be a good working-class mother was not only a moral duty but also a national one; and to be a good mother required instruction.[73] School Boards duly began laying greater emphasis on cookery, household management and child care.[74]

For those mothers who had not been caught young enough at school to be taught about the best way to bring up their children, the infant welfare movement was to provide the solution. In 1907 the first School for Mothers opened its doors in St Pancras; others were quick to follow. Working-class mothers were exhorted, by health visitors or at infant welfare clinics, to breast-feed their babies and to maintain an hygienic home in order to avoid a baby's death. Infant welfare centres (also known as schools for mothers, babies' welcomes and infant consultations) combined classes and health talks for mothers with individual consultations where the baby was weighed and the mother advised on feeding and looking after her baby. Some centres also organised baby shows, sewing meetings, cookery demonstrations and provident clubs. Up until the First World War the majority of clinics were run by voluntary organisations, rather than by local authorities.[75]

A broad pincer movement of education, material improvements (in housing and income) or medical treatment to attack the ferocious onslaught of infant death and disease was not attempted, even though this was what numerous women demanded. The Fabian Women's Group called for mothers' endowment (later known as family allowances), while Anna Martin, a suffragist and Settlement worker, argued that a husband should be bound by law to give a proportion of his income to his wife. Medical treatment was no more forthcoming, indeed health visitors and infant welfare centres were explicitly banned from offering treatment. In Jane Lewis's view, the movement offered a cheap and apparently easy way of dealing with a complex problem: that of an unacceptably high infant death-rate. Although there were real dangers to babies from domestic dirt, Lewis argues that one cannot jump to the conclusion that the mothers were to blame for this dirt. Frequent pregnancies, poor living conditions, urban pollution, poor nutrition and overwork also contributed to the high infant and maternal mortality rates, but these problems were not tackled.[76] (Similarly the keynote of the campaign against TB was personal responsibility and a change in behaviour, not the importance of improving economic and social conditions, or of reducing the stigma associated with the disease.)[77]

Deborah Dwork has mounted a spirited defence of educational work on the grounds that it was a last resort and the only possible tactic given Britain's economic and social structure. As the economic and social structure influenced power relations between politicians, the medical profession and mothers, this is an implicit recognition by Dwork that the death and sickness rates of infants were connected with the social and economic structure: in order to save the babies it was necessary to do more than tinker with the education and advice given to mothers; rather, economic and social changes were required. She quotes the WCG as enthusiastically embracing the work of health visitors, although she fails to record that while the WCG did indeed welcome health visitors, it wanted far more in the way of birth control information and financial assistance.[78]

Women's groups demanded free medical treatment for women and children, but to no effect. Assumptions about the inadequacies of working-class mothering and the sanctity of the family (which should not be intruded upon) meant that calls for financial assistance fell on deaf ears, while calls for educating working-class girls and women were laced with highly judgemental attitudes. The pages of the Physical Deterioration Committee are littered with references to 'lazy', 'improvident, idle and intemperate' parents; mothers' 'indifference' to the feeding of their children; women stinting on food and other basic necessities in order that they might 'adorn' themselves; parents eating pickles and vinegar for a cheap sensation; and babies dying not through poverty but because mothers gossiped in the street with their ill-clad babies exposed to the cold.[79]

The early twentieth century did witness a steep decline in the IMR, from 154 deaths per 1,000 live births in 1900, to 105 in 1910 and 80 in 1920. There is no direct evidence that changes in working-class women's behaviour, brought about by education, played any part in the improved rates. The reasons for the welcome improvement were complex, but Lewis suggests that they must have included the wider availability of pure milk, better sanitation, a rising standard of living and improved medical attention for premature babies.[80]

The establishment in 1906 of a school meals service (inspired by the French), and in 1907 of the School Medical Service (SMS) for the whole of the country were the most obvious results of the 1903 Royal Commission on Physical Training (Scotland) and the 1904 Physical Deterioration Committee. Building on developments which had been underway since the 1890s (greatly influenced, according to Bernard

Harris by a scheme in the German town of Wiesbaden), the SMS involved the inspection and treatment of elementary schoolchildren (and from 1918 secondary schoolchildren as well).[81]

Peter Hennock has argued that between the 1880s and the outbreak of the First World War, German social policies loomed large in the minds of British social reformers who were not behind in embracing, and at times improving, those German measures thought most appropriate for Britain. The 1897 Workmen's Compensation Act had adopted two key legal principles of 1880s German legislation: it gave the worker injured in the course of his employment the right to compensation from his employer, irrespective of negligence, and it defined the limits of that compensation in advance. In the shift towards the adoption of compulsory state-supported insurance for unemployment and ill-health, the advantages of the German state insurance scheme played no small part in British reformers' minds. The Chancellor of the Exchequer, David Lloyd George, not only wanted to learn from the German national insurance system, but also to improve on it. Hennock has detailed how, when Lloyd George discovered that his plans did not provide women with any payment during their confinement but Germany paid a minimum of six weeks' maternity benefit at normal sickness rates for women contributors, he ensured that women received a one-off 30s maternity grant. This was more generous than the German scheme as husbands could also make a claim on the confinement of their wives. Similarities to German law were highlighted when the National Insurance Bill was presented to Parliament.[82]

Under National Health Insurance (NHI) all manual workers aged over sixteen and earning below £160 a year were covered for medical, sickness, disablement, maternity and sanatorium benefits. Cash benefits were administered through Approved Societies, and medical and sanatorium benefits through Local Insurance Committees.

For a contribution of 4d a week from men and 3d a week from women there were three types of NHI cover. First, there were cash payments of 10s a week for men and 7s 6d for women. Roughly 90 per cent of married women were not part of the formal economy at this time and were, therefore, excluded from the scheme. The disparity between men's and women's rates of benefit increased over the years. In 1915, and again in 1932, women's cash benefits were cut. Married women who were covered by NHI were subject to strict surveillance by Health Insurance visitors, on account of their unexpectedly high insurance claims. Alice Foley was appointed a sick visitor by her union, the Weavers' Association. She recalls that the most disagreeable aspect of her work was 'keeping an eye' on suspected malingerers. Married women tended to continue with their housework while registered as 'incapacitated' for work. A sick visitor was expected to report such cases. Poorer families usually left the front door on the latch, so it was much more likely that a poor woman would be caught unawares then a better-off one who would have time to clear away tell-tale signs of housework before opening the door.[83] There was also a weekly 5s disablement benefit, and a one-off 30s maternity benefit, although the latter was gobbled up by the midwife's fee, leaving nothing for additional food and basic extras for mother or baby. (Married women in paid work could, in addition, claim maternity benefit in their own right, which meant that they received £3 instead of 30s).

Second, there were medical benefits provided by NHI, such as GP consultations, drugs and appliances. Specialist treatment was not included, and a visit to a GP could be of only limited benefit. In 1914 one doctor claimed that on average he saw seventy-six cases in the morning and ninety-two in the evening, which worked out at three and a quarter minutes per patient, one and a quarter minutes of which he spent writing. As poorer patients could not afford the fees of a consultant, GPs had to rely on their own diagnosis and judgement during a hasty consultation. An appointment followed an average wait of two and a half hours, unless the patient was present when the surgery opened.[84]

Third, there were additional benefits which the Approved Societies offered, but it was difficult to know before joining a scheme where the best deals were to be found. NHI did not cover either the better-off or large sections of the poorest in society, that is the dependants of the insured, or young workers between the ages of fourteen and sixteen. The self-employed, even if they earned under £160 a year, were not covered. Medical services were limited even for those covered by NHI: there was no cover for specialist advice and many could not get ophthalmic, dental or other treatment through NHI. Still others were not covered for convalescent homes.[85] Inability to pay a doctor was not the only deterrent to seeking professional medical advice. There were few women doctors and many women were too embarrassed to discuss personal problems with a male doctor.

Lloyd George's main concern was to maintain the physical efficiency of the male breadwinner and to avoid pauperism, rather than to prevent ill-health. Consequently, NHI did nothing for most married women, young workers between the ages of fourteen and sixteen or children when they were ill (presumably on the assumption that the man of the family would bring home a family wage sufficient to provide for their medical needs).[86]

Full-blooded eugenicist thought failed to exert a major impact on health policies. The 1913 Mental Deficiency Act came closest to embodying unadulterated eugenicist views, but even here the devil did not have it all his own way. In 1908 the Royal Commission on the care and control of the feeble-minded struck a chord with Edwardian

Britain when it called for more control (including detention and separation) over those whose 'wayward and irresponsible' lives were leading to crime and misery.[87] Harvey Simmons has detailed the history of the Act. It was assumed that mental deficiency was inherited and that those so afflicted, lacking moral restraint, were more fecund than the population at large. Mentally defective women were the biological source of mental deficiency and as such they posed a threat to familial and sexual morality. If their morals were too weak to act as a restraining influence on their sexual activity and reproduction, then compulsory institutionalisation and segregation, provided by the 1913 Mental Deficiency Act, offered the answer. The Act was less stringent than the Royal Commission's recommendations: an anti-eugenicist lobby rallied its parliamentary troops. Josiah Wedgwood led a successful rearguard action to have a clause removed from the Act which would have prohibited marriage and criminalised procreation among the feeble-minded.[88] In practice it is hard to judge how closely local authorities followed the letter of the law, for war soon intervened, and in 1915 the Board of Control complained that feeble-minded women were not being transferred from workhouses to mental defective institutions.[89] These and other health strategies of Edwardian Britain continued to unravel in the war years.

NOTES

1. **Wohl A.** 1984 *Endangered lives: Public health in Victorian Britain.* Methuen, pp. 45, 47. First published in 1983.
2. **Benson J.** 1989 *The working class in Britain, 1850–1939.* Longman, pp. 60–1.
3. **Flinn M. W.** 1965 Poor Law Commission, 1834–47 *Report on the sanitary condition of the labouring population by E. Chadwick.* Edinburgh University Press, pp. 80–99.
4. PP 1903 vol. XXX Report of the Royal Commission on Physical Training (Scotland) vol. 1 Report and appendix vol. II Minutes of Evidence, p. 24.
5. **Rowntree B. S.** 1922 *Poverty: A study in town life.* Longman, pp. 221–26. First published 1901.
6. **Chamberlain M.** 1989 *Growing up in Lambeth.* Virago, p. 15.
7. **Wohl A.** *Endangered lives.* p. 299.
8. **Daunton M.** 1990 Housing. In Thompson F. M. L. (ed) *The Cambridge social history of Britain, 1750–1950 vol. 2 People and their environment.* Cambridge University Press, pp. 198–208.
9. **Lady Bell** 1985 *At the works: A study of a manufacturing town.* Virago, p. 87. First published 1907.
10. **Roberts E.** 1986 Working-class standards of living in Barrow and

Lancaster, 1890–1914. In Thane P., Sutcliffe A. (eds) *Essays in social history vol. 2*. Clarendon, pp. 251–9.

11. **Marks L.** 1990 'Dear Old Mother Levy's': The Jewish maternity home and Sick Rooms Help Society 1895–1939. *Social History of Medicine* **3**: 61–87.

12. **Oddy D.** 1990 Food, drink and nutrition. In Thompson F. L. M. (ed) *The Cambridge social history of Britain 1750–1950. vol. 2 People and their environment*. Cambridge University Press, pp. 253, 270–1, 275.

13. For example PP 1904 vol. XXXII Report of the Royal Commission on Physical Deterioration vol. 1 Report and Appendix col. 290; **Oren L.** 1974 The welfare of women in labouring families: England, 1860–1950. In Hartman M., Banner L. (eds) Clio's consciousness raised: New perspectives on the history of women. Harper Colophon Books, Harper and Row, New York, pp. 226–44; **Pahl J.** 1989 *Money and marriage*. Macmillan.

14. **Pember Reeves M.** 1979 *Round about a pound a week*. Virago, pp. 113–14. First published 1913.

15. **Ross E.** 1983 Survival networks: Women's neighbourhood sharing before World War I. *History Workshop Journal* **15**: 7.

16. Pember Reeves M. *Round about a pound a week*. p. 68.

17. Ibid. p. 131.

18. **Black C.** 1915 *Married women's work being the report of an enquiry undertaken by the Women's Industrial Council*. G. Bell & Sons, p. 127.

19. **Women's Cooperative Guild** 1911 *Working women and divorce: An account of evidence given on behalf of the Women's Cooperative Guild before the Royal Commission on Divorce*. David Nutt, pp. 5–39.

20. Ross E. Survival networks. *History Workshop Journal* **15**: 6.

21. Women's Cooperative Guild *Working women and divorce: An account of evidence given on behalf of the Women's Cooperative Guild before the Royal Commission on Divorce*. pp. 5–39.

22. **Knight P.** 1977 Women and abortion in Victorian and Edwardian England. *History Workshop Journal* **4**: 57–62; **McLaren A.** 1977 Women's work and regulation of family size *History Workshop Journal* **4**: 78.

23. **Jalland P.** 1986 *Women, marriage and politics, 1860–1914*. Clarendon, pp. 135–45.

24. **Checkland O., Lamb M.** 1982 *Health care as social history: The Glasgow case*. Aberdeen University Press, p. 120.

25. **Liddington J.** 1984 *The life and times of a respectable rebel: Selina Cooper, 1864–1946*. Virago, p. 212.

26. **Prochaska F.** 1989 A mother's country: Mothers' meetings and family welfare in Britain, 1850–1950. *History* **74**: 393–5.

27. **Lewis J.** 1990 Mothers and maternity policies in the twentieth century. In Garcia J., Kilpatrick R., Richards M. (eds) *The politics of maternity care: services for childbearing women in twentieth-century Britain*. Clarendon, p. 15.

28. **Martin A.** 1911 *The married working woman: A study*. National Union of Women's Suffrage Societies, p. 4.

29. **Women's Cooperative Guild** 1897 *Why working women need the vote.* WCG (nd), pp. 4–9; see also Liddington J. *The life and times of a respectable rebel: Selina Cooper, 1864–1946.* p. 212.

30. **Soloway R.** 1982 *Birth control and the population question in England, 1877–1930.* The University of North Carolina Press, Chapell Hill, pp. 133–54.

31. **Mort F.** 1987 *Dangerous sexualities: Medico-moral politics in England since 1830.* Routledge & Kegan Paul, pp. 117–38.

32. Ibid.

33. **Bland L.** 1982 'Guardians of the race' or 'Vampires upon the nation's health'? Female sexuality and its regulation in early twentieth century Britain. In Whitelegg E. et al. (eds) *The changing experience of women.* Martin Robertson, pp. 373–82.

34. **Dyhouse C.** 1981 *Girls growing up in late Victorian and Edwardian England.* Routledge & Kegan Paul, pp. 136–8.

35. **Dyhouse C.** 1978 Working-class mothers and infant mortality in England, 1895–1914. *Journal of Social History* **12**: 248.

36. **May Tennant** (1869–1946). Treasurer of the Women's Trade Union League; Assistant Commissioner on the Royal Commission on Labour (1891); in 1893 she had been appointed one of the first women Factory Inspectors.

37. **Black C.** 1915 *Married women's work. Being the report of an enquiry undertaken by the Women's Industrial Council.* G. Bell & Sons, pp. 220–1.

38. PP 1904 Interdepartmental committee on physical deterioration col. 255.

39. Black C. *Married women's work.* p. 221.

40. Dyhouse C. 1978 Working-class mothers. *Journal of Social History* **12**: 252–4.

41. **Black C.** 1907 *Sweated industry and the minimum wage.* Duckworth & Co., p. 133.

42. Black C. *Married women's work.* p. 8.

43. Black C. *Sweated industry and the minimum wage.* pp. 132–41.

44. **Springhall J.** 1986 *Coming of age; Adolescence in Britain, 1860–1960.* Gill & Macmillan, p. 73.

45. **Hendrick H.** 1990 *Images of youth: Age, class and the male youth problem, 1880–1920.* Clarendon, pp. 33–4.

46. **Hutchings B., Harrison A.** 1926 *A history of factory legislation.* P. S. King & Sons, pp. 259, 271–2; **Meyer C., Black C.** 1909 *Makers of our clothes: A case for Trade Boards.* Duckworth & Co., p. 1; **Tuckwell G.** 1908 *Sweating.* Society for Promoting Christian Knowledge, p. 5 and *passim*; **Tuckwell G. et al.** 1908 *Women in industry from seven points of view.* Duckworth & Co.

47. **Morris J.** 1986 *Women workers and the sweated trades: The origins of minimum wage legislation.* Gower, p. 227 and *passim*; **Vinson A.** 1982 *The Edwardians and poverty: Towards a minimum wage?* In Read D. (ed) *Edwardian England.* Croom Helm, pp. 81–2.

48. **Rickard J.** 1979 The anti-sweating movement in Britain and Victoria: The politics of empire and social reform. *Historical Studies* **18**: 583–97.

49. **Blackburn S.** 1991 Ideology and social policy: The origins of the Trade Boards Act. *Historical Journal* **34:** 59–60.

50. **Bythell D.** 1978 *The sweated trades: Outwork in nineteenth-century Britain.* Batsford, p. 246.

51. Public Record Office (PRO) LAB 11/166, Reid 16 April, year unknown but during First World War.

52. Until 1940 safety, health and welfare at work came under the Home Office. See below for workmen's compensation.

53. **Jones H.** 1988 Women health workers: The case of the first women Factory Inspectors in Britain. *Social History of Medicine* **1:** 165–81.

54. **White J.** 1980 *Rothschild Buildings: Life in an East End tenement block, 1887–1920.* Routledge & Kegan Paul, pp. 134–6.

55. PP 1903 vol. IX Report of the Royal Commision on Alien Immigration Cd 1741 pp. 5–6 col. 38.

56. **Holmes C.** 1971 *John Bull's Island: Immigration and British society, 1871–1971.* Macmillan, pp. 70–3. Figures are only a rough guide and are taken from the Jewish Year Book, quoted in Peach C., Robinson V., Maxted J., Chance J. 1988 Immigration and ethnicity. In **Halsey A. H.** (ed) *British social trends since 1900: A guide to the changing social structure of Britain.* Macmillan, p. 602.

57. Imperial War Museum PP/MCR/126. The memoirs of Dr C. J. G. Taylor.

58. **Black G. D.** 1987 *Health and medical care of the Jewish poor in the East End of London, 1880–1939.* University of Leicester PhD pp. 43, 222.

59. Marks L. 'Dear Old Mother Levy's': The Jewish maternity home and Sick Rooms Help Society 1895–1939. *Social History of Medicine* **3:** 61–87; Black G. D. *Health and medical care of the Jewish poor.* pp. 80–3, 92, 103–7. For some of the provisions made for Jewish and Irish immigrant unmarried mothers in London see **Marks L.** 1992 'The luckless waifs and strays of humanity': Irish and Jewish immigrant unwed mothers in London, 1870–1939. *Twentieth Century British History* **3:** 113–37.

60. **Püschel J.** 1980 *Die Geschichte des German Hospital in London 1845 bis 1948.* Vorlag Murken-Altrogge, Münster, pp. 116–17; **Specht M.** 1989 *The German hospital in London and the community it served 1845–1948.* Anglo-German Family History Society, pp. 43–4.

61. Black G. D. Health and medical care of the Jewish poor. pp. 251, 254, 256, 260, 308.

62. **Green D.** 1985 *Working-class patients and the medical establishment: Self-help in Britain from the mid-nineteenth century to 1948.* Gower.

63. **Abel-Smith B.** 1964 *The hospitals, 1800–1948: A study in social administration in England and Wales.* Heinemann, pp. 101, 201; **Crowther M.** 1981 *The workhouse system 1834–1929: The history of an English institution.* Batsford Academic, pp. 87–9, 190; **Meacham S.** 1977 *A life apart: The English working class 1890–1914.* Thames and Husdon, p. 10.

64. **Johnson P.** 1985 *Saving and spending: The working-class economy in Britain, 1870–1939.* Clarendon, pp. 13, 23, 39, 54, 73.

65. For a useful guide to the various arguments over the welfare reforms

of the period see **Hay J. R.** 1983 *The origins of Liberal welfare reforms, 1900–1914*. 2nd edn Macmillan; **Thane P.** 1982 *The foundations of the welfare state*. Longman, pp. 61–2, 84–5.

66. **Berridge V.** 1990 Health and medicine. In Thompson F. L. M. (ed) *The Cambridge social history of Britain, 1750–1950. vol. 3. Social agencies and institutions*. Cambridge University Press, pp. 217–18; **Dwork D.** 1987 *War is good for babies and other young children: A history of the infant and child welfare movement in England, 1898–1918*. Tavistock, pp. 223; **Harris B.** 1989 Medical inspection and the nutrition of schoolchildren in Britain, 1900–50. University of London PhD, p. 16; **Searle G.** 1976 *Eugenics and politics in Britain, 1900–14*. Leyden Noordhoff International Publishing, The Netherlands, p. 21.

67. Ibid. pp. 39–43; **Soloway R.** 1982 *Birth control and the population question in England, 1877–1930*. The University of North Carolina Press, Chapell Hill, p. 163.

68. **Bland L.** 1982 'Guardians of the race' or 'vampires upon the nation's health'?: Female sexuality and its regulation in early twentieth-century Britain. In **Whitelegg E.** et al. (eds) *The changing experience of women*. Martin Robertson, p. 375; **Jones G.** 1986 *Social hygiene in twentieth century Britain*. Croom Helm, p. 27; Searle G. *Eugenics and politics in Britain, 1900–14*. pp. 72–3, 86, 89, 104. For arguments over the extent to which those on the political Left supported eugenicist ideas, see **Freeden M.** 1979 Eugenics and progressive thought: A study of ideological affinity. *Historical Journal* **22**: 645–71; **Freeden M.** 1983 Eugenics and ideology. *Historical Journal* **26**: 959–62; **Jones G.** 1979 Eugenics and social policy between the wars. *Historical Journal* **25**: 717–28.

69. For the Mediterranean see **Premble J.** 1988 *The Mediterranean passion: Victorians and Edwardians in the South*. Oxford University Press, pp. 84–91.

70. PP 1904 vol. XXXII Report of the interdepartmental committee on physical deterioration. vol. 1 report and appendix para. 68.

71. **McLeary G.** 1933 *The early history of the infant welfare movement*. H. K. Lewis, pp. 39, 69–83.

72. PP 1904 vol. XXXII Physical Deterioration Committee para. 277.

73. **Davin A.** 1978 Imperialism and motherhood *History Workshop Journal* **5–6**: 13.

74. Dyhouse C. *Girls growing up in late Victorian and Edwardian England*. pp. 92–5.

75. **Lewis J.** 1980 *The politics of motherhood: Child and maternal welfare in England, 1900–39*. pp. 96–7.

76. Ibid. pp. 65, 27.

77. **Bryder L.** 1988 *Below the magic mountain: A social history of tuberculosis in twentieth-century Britain*. Clarendon, pp. 20–1.

78. **Dwork D.** 1987 *War is good for babies*. pp. 11, 14, 51, 165; Lewis J. 1980 *The politics of motherhood: Child and maternal welfare in England, 1900–1939*. Croom Helm; Lewis J. 1991 Models of equality for women: The case of state support for children in twentieth-century Britain. In Bock G., Thane P. (eds) *Maternity and gender: Women*

and the rise of the European welfare states, 1880s–1950s. Routledge, pp. 79–81.

79. PP 1904 vol. XXXII Physical Deterioration Committee paras 76, 224, 228, 240.
80. Lewis J. *The politics of motherhood*. p. 107.
81. **Harris B.** 1989 Medical inspection and the nutrition of schoolchildren in Britain, 1900–50. PhD University of London pp. 3, 35.
82. **Hennock E. P.** 1987 *British social reform and German precedents: The case of social insurance, 1880–1914*. Clarendon Press, pp. 3–4, 10, 166–99 and *passim*.
83. **Foley A.** 1973 *A Bolton childhood*. Manchester University Extra-Mural Department and North-West District WEA, pp. 75–7.
84. Quoted in **Brend W.** 1917 *Health and the state*. Constable and Co. Ltd, pp. 179–83.
85. Political and Economic Planning 1937 *Report on the British health services*. PEP, pp. 13–15, 211. The rates of benefit quoted are those which were initially in operation. Rates of benefit rose over the years.
86. Berridge V. Health and medicine. In Thompson F. L. M. (ed) *The Cambridge social history of Britain, 1750–1950*. p. 220.
87. PP 1908 vol. XXXIX Report of the Royal Commission on the care and control of the feeble-minded. Chair: Earl Radnor. p. 3.
88. **Porter D.** 1991 'Enemies of the race': Biologism, environmentalism and public health in Edwardian England. *Victorian Studies* 34: 162–3.
89. **Simmons H.** 1978 Explaining social policy: The English Mental Deficiency Act of 1913. *Journal of Social History* 11: 393–400.

Chapter 3

FIGHTING FIT? 1914–18

INTRODUCTION

It has long been thought that the First World War was an unmitigated disaster for the health and well-being of the nation. The slaughter of the troops, the food shortages and the trauma of the war affected not only combatants but also civilians to an unprecedented extent. Jay Winter has challenged this account, primarily, although not exclusively, on the grounds that improved nutrition increased the life expectancy of men aged over forty-nine and reduced the Infant Mortality Rate (IMR).[1] His thesis has not gone unchallenged.

The First World War was a cause of profound dislocation, personal and national; and although mortality rates for non-combatants may have improved during the war, as a result of rising standards of living and better diet, this does not mean that people's sense of well-being was enhanced. Mortality statistics (on which Winter relies) are not necessarily a good guide to the amount of ill-health in the country. There was widespread anguish first and foremost over the fate of men at the Front, but also over the supposed escalation in women's immorality, deteriorating housing conditions and vastly increased rents, and dangerous working conditions. Industrial unrest was eloquent testimony to serious public dissatisfaction. Good industrial conditions were the most immediate health concern of governments, yet many workers were employed in highly dangerous situations. Nationality or ethnicity, which normally acts as an important but not overwhelming influence on health, came to dominate all other influences on well-being for non-British nationals living in Britain. Gender differences were simultaneously lessened in some areas, such as paid work, and reinforced in other ones, such as attitudes towards sexual morality.

DOUBLE STANDARDS

The outbreak of war led to unemployment, high prices and general distress, particularly among the unskilled working class. As men enlisted, so chaos ensued at both the administrative and personal level. By mid-October 1914,

> Many of the women are now in a pitiful condition as well as their children. Many of them being in rags, and some of them without boots. The majority of their supporters were reservists, and of course they were called up on the 4th and 5th August. Practically speaking two months before they got any assistance whatever . . . Some of the women have pawned the very boots off their feet to get food . . . One of the cases reported to you yesterday had to borrow a skirt and shawl before she could come and report to me.[2]

In the East End of London, better-off suffragists made contributions to those women hardest hit by the upheaval of war; an employment bureau and even a communal restaurant were set up.[3]

On 6 August 1914 the Prince of Wales launched the National Relief Fund which aimed to relieve financial misery caused by the war. On the same day Queen Alexandra appealed for contributions to the Soldiers' and Sailors' Families Association (SSFA); on 11 August the two funds merged. The rates of separation allowances had not been raised since the Boer War and the tardiness with which payments were initially made led to hardship and bitter criticism of a system not designed to cope with many thousands of claimants. Women qualified for these benefits solely on the basis of their relationship with a man. It was *his* right to have his wife supported. The idea of a male breadwinner and dependent wife was at the heart of the system. The women could claim no automatic right to the payment, and indeed 16,000 women – about 2 per cent of claimants – had their allowance withdrawn, on grounds of their allegedly immoral behaviour. A team of SSFA women volunteers visited women receiving separation allowances to offer guidance on household management and to keep a watchful eye on the women's behaviour. Attempts were made to police the women receiving separation allowances, although the police force itself shrank back from undertaking the task when requested to do so by the War Office. Sylvia Pankhurst's East London Federation of Suffragettes and Charlotte Despard's Women's Freedom League demonstrated without avail against the state's surveillance of soldiers' wives.[4]

Before the war it had been widespread practice for working-class women and men to live together as wife and husband, without actually going through a marriage ceremony. Cohabitation caused much soul-searching over the rights and wrongs of public money (whether collected by private charity or the state) going to support the 'wives' of soldiers and sailors. It was argued that paying separation allowances to those women not married to the men with whom they had a home would be a blow to the self-respect of married women, it would legitimise immorality and it would encourage men to think that it did not matter whether they married or not as the women would be looked after.[5] This agonising contributed to the delay in paying separation allowances which were urgently needed by many women. In the event separation allowances were paid out to women who had made a home with a member of the Armed Forces, whether or not a marriage certificate could be produced.

The wildest rumours abounded about the extent of extra-marital sex and preceded any upturn in the illegitimacy rates, but once the rates began to creep up (albeit not as fast as was feared) they supposedly provided the evidence for those trumpeting their warnings from the high moral plains. Illegitimacy was not confined to unmarried mothers. If a married woman became pregnant by a man other than her husband (such as a soldier billeted with her) while her husband was away, the child was deemed to be illegitimate. During the war the illegitimacy rate rose by roughly 30 per cent, but as there were fewer births during the war, less women actually had illegitimate babies than before the war. The figures are no guide, anyway, to the amount of extra- marital activity. Before the war many working-class women did not marry before their first conception. The mobility of men in wartime made rushed weddings more difficult; even in wartime it was not possible for British marriages to take place by proxy.

There was a widespread assumption that a state of war led to heightened emotions, a lowering of moral standards and a loss of control. Both women and men condemned those women, but not men, suspected of immorality. The country was suddenly full of tempting Eves; double standards flourished:

> . . . there is a great danger of the men being damaged and made
> unfit for the hard and awful work in front of them unless parents
> and employers try to prevent the girls from getting excited, running
> wild in the evenings and forgetting their honour, their purity, their
> self-respect . . . It is terrible to think that the folly and sin of any of
> the women and girls should make these men *less* fit to die and send
> them away with a guilty conscience . . . .[6]

These fears were fuelled by claims that working-class women were spending their higher wartime wages on alcohol, which was inevitably linked with indecorous behaviour. Indeed, loud and unladylike behaviour in a public place was equated with low moral standards.

Concern over the immorality of working-class women moved their social betters to patrol those areas where it was feared large numbers of working-class women and girls might seduce soldiers, or vice versa. In areas where sailors and troops were stationed women patrols (forerunners of the women's police) tramped the streets in order to safeguard young girls from moral danger. In July 1915 the patrols were warned that their job was not to clear the streets of disorderly women or to stop improper conduct, but to play a preventative role, so that 'young and silly girls' would not drift into danger. In this work they were given the full co-operation of the naval authorities.[7]

In the pre-war years the debate over venereal disease (VD) had focused on its medical causes, and feminists had condemned the immoral behaviour of men who spread the disease. During the war, with the focus on women spreading VD among the Armed Forces, attention shifted towards women, either as prostitutes, or as women who slept with members of the Armed Forces to whom they were not married.[8]

During the course of the war VD came to be seen not only as a civilian problem affecting the quality of the race, the future of the nation and the protection of the innocent but also as a military problem. Under the Defence of the Realm Act (DORA) regulations the military authorities could prohibit anyone previously convicted of soliciting from residing in, or frequenting, the vicinity of stationed troops. This regulation proved unworkable, but in March 1918 further regulations under DORA made it an offence for any woman suffering from VD to have sexual intercourse with members of the Armed Forces or to solicit sex from them. Opposition to this regulation came from feminist organisations, as well as from the Trades Union Congress (TUC) and the press, and in the wake of the Armistice in November 1918 the regulation was revoked.[9]

In 1916 a Royal Commission on Venereal Diseases, set up in 1913, presented its report. It linked deaths at the Front, the declining birth-rate, the efficiency of the workforce and the scourge of VD.[10] The need to combat VD was seen as even more urgent than in peacetime. Its recommendation for the free diagnosis and treament of VD was incorporated into the 1916 Public Health (Venereal Diseases) Regulation Act. Feminists criticised the report for failing to recommend practical steps for the prevention of the disease, although it did lead to a network of clinics around the country offering a free and confidential service.[11] Attention continued to focus on the behaviour of women.

Women in the Auxiliary Forces were acutely conscious of critical eyes cast in their direction. The slightest whiff of scandal was snuffed out. Katharine Furse, the first woman in charge of the Voluntary Aid Detachment (VAD) in France, sent a young VAD back to England when she became engaged to an officer, even though there was no suggestion of impropriety. Furse later took charge of the Women's Royal Naval Service (WRNS). In her autobiography she explained that British women serving in France lived in fear of their behaviour being regarded as unsuitable. Pregnant women were always discharged, but those with VD were treated and allowed to remain in the service.[12]

Women in the Women's Auxiliary Army Corps (WAAC) were singled out for their allegedly depraved behaviour. When gossip about the conduct of WAACs was thought to be affecting recruitment, the Government appointed a five-strong, all-female committee of inquiry, with Mrs Deane Streatfield (a former Lady Factory Inspector) as chair and Violet Markham as Honorary Secretary. On an eight-day visit to France they found hard-working women who took their new responsibilities seriously; they did not find evidence to support the rumours of immoral conduct. The whole exercise was reduced to a farce when Markham, who was married but still used her maiden name in public and was therefore assumed to be single, was found on her first evening in France with an officer (her husband) in her bedroom. Markham, not a WAAC, had a charge of loose behaviour levelled against her![13]

Women who went abroad during the war in a medical or nursing capacity, with the First Aid Nursing Yeomanry (FANY), VAD and medical units, were inspired by a mixture of motives. Women such as Dr Elsie Inglis, an active suffragist, wanted to prove women's capabilities to men, as 'So much of our work is done where they cannot see it.' Inglis, with the help of the Scottish Federation of Women's Suffrage Societies, was the founder of the Scottish Women's Hospitals. On the outbreak of war she formed a women's medical unit whose services were offered to the War Office and rebuffed. The Allies welcomed the women, and hospitals (flying a flag in the suffrage colours of red, white and green with the Union Jack and red cross emblazoned on it) staffed by women opened in France, Serbia, Corsica, Salonika, Romania and Russia.[14] St Clair Stobart publicised her experiences in organising hospital work in Bulgaria, Belgium, France and Serbia in an attempt to show that women could be of service, not just in base hospitals but also in flying ones, and placed in positions of command. In 1916 she argued that women could perform many of the medical and nursing tasks undertaken by men and that, if they were allowed to do so, more men could be released for front-line fighting.[15]

Although one of the main arguments from the patient's point of view in favour of women doctors is that in many cases women doctors are more suitable for women patients than male doctors, women doctors actually won recognition for the work they undertook dealing with male patients. The wartime publicity surrounding women doctors and nurses enabled them to prove publicly their ability to undertake work which they had always performed in private. During the war it was claimed that, as a result of the female-staffed hospitals in England and France organised by Louisa Garrett Anderson and Flora Murray, women proved beyond doubt both to the medical profession and the outside world that women doctors and surgeons could equal men in every specialism, and not just in those areas dealing with women and children. Women nurses and doctors were extolled for their well-publicised caring for men, yet women's private (and usually unpaid), work of caring continued to go unrecognised.[16]

Self-fulfilment, a complete change of lifestyle and a sense of adventure were important to the women who served in a nursing and medical capacity abroad.[17] It could be hard to disentangle a complex web of motives. Katharine Furse reflected that going to France as a VAD was shot through with the pioneer spirit, excitement, glamour and a sense of adventure; it offered VADs the chance to put what they had learned into practice, and to help the troops. Whether in France or Britain, the VADs worked under such pressure that it was seldom possible for them to analyse their motives. Furse's work in France was later extended to Belgium by Rachel Crowdy. VAD work encompassed Rest Stations on the lines of communication, motor ambulance depots, hostels for relatives visiting the sick and wounded, hostels for VADs, sick bays for women in the auxiliary services, and veterinary services.[18] One FANY later wrote that the most important aspect of life in France was the sense of comradeship felt between all those who served.[19] New networks between women were established as the war united participants in a singleness of purpose; and they, like the men, were able to enjoy annual reunions to talk over what, for many, would have been the most extraordinary times of their life.

The publicity which a relatively small number of largely middle-class women received proved that middle-class women, like working-class ones, were capable of living under harsh conditions, that they could be tough and that, despite their sheltered upbringings, they could cope with the rigours of war service. The glamour associated with the FANYs was a far cry from the gritty reality of life in France. Looking after typhoid cases was no mean feat for this socially élite corps. The FANYs were the first group of British women in France to act in more than a nursing and medical capacity; they were the first women to drive ambulances up to the Front, a task which involved negotiating rough terrain, at times under gunfire. Such work had never before been assigned to women in war. At their peak there were never more than 450 FANYs in France, but their significance lay less in their numbers, than in the work they pioneered for middle-class women in wartime. It was middle-class women who needed to smash Victorian notions of women's frailty (such arguments had never been applied to working-class women anyway), and it was these women, supplying their own uniforms, paying £1 a year for the privilege of belonging to the corps rather than receiving payment, who knocked the final nail in the coffin of the medical profession's view of middle-class women as innately frail. They made their case not by arguments but by actions.[20] It is doubtful whether many of them would have identified with the feminist cause. Before the war a number of them had been anti-suffragists. In fact, Anne Summers sees the work of military nurses as a means of co-opting women for war service without threatening gender roles.[21] However, women's actions need to be judged not by the tactics and world views of a later generation but by the prevailing climate of opinion. Given the constraints on women at this time, these women did contribute to the feminist project, even if they were not always conscious of doing so. The women who received individual publicity tended to be identified with the suffragist cause.

While women by their actions were often challenging their assigned gender roles, wartime propaganda was attempting to reinforce them. The British nurse, innocent and romantic, was the quintessential English rose, embracing all the idealised virtues of a woman. She was set in sharp contrast to German nurses who were portrayed as evil and callous women. (Two important messages, one about women and the other about Germans, were thereby conveyed.) Edith Cavell, a nurse in charge of a hospital in Belgium, who was shot by the Germans for helping Allied soldiers escape, was the focus of propaganda about British nurses.[22] Two other incidents which would have conveyed a quite different message were ignored by the British press. First, it was the case that the French Allies also shot enemy nurses; and second, another British nurse, Grace Ashley-Smith, who was in Antwerp with the FANYs when it fell to the Germans, was not arrested by the German commandant, but allowed to escape to England. Such a story, portraying the humanity and flexibility of the Germans, was of no interest in a country full of anti-German sentiment.

'The noble sacrifices in the battlefield in the air and on the sea must not be made in vain, and every effort must be directed to securing the future of the race.'(Babies of the Empire Society)[23] As more and more men laid down their lives so the urgency increased to produce bouncing babies, who in their turn, at some future date, might offer the ultimate sacrifice. The 1914–15 Annual Report of the Local Government Board argued that the war, with its great wastage of life, accompanied by the continuing decline in the birth rate, underlined the importance of conserving infant life.[24] An article in the *British Medical Journal* maintained that greater attention should be paid to the problem of infant mortality in view of the double threat to the population. It was widely assumed that if the IMR was reduced more baby boys would be saved than baby girls because boys had a higher death-rate.[25] As we know from Chapter 2, concern over population replacement was nothing new, but the war acted as a spur to existing plans for a larger and healthier nation, and reinforced the traditional emphasis on a woman's role as wife and mother. The Babies of the Empire Society invoked every mother to discharge her duty to fit herself for the perfect fulfilment of the natural calls of motherhood.[26] This destiny for women was supported by a wide-range of opinion, from long-standing feminists to the bureaucrats of Whitehall. Millicent Fawcett, President of the National Union of Women's Suffrage Societies (linking reproduction with national service), Selina Cooper, a working-class feminist activist, the Women's Cooperative Guild (WCG), women trade unionists and the Labour Party leadership all enthusiastically embraced the campaign to reduce the death-rate among babies.[27] Action came from both the Government and voluntary bodies. On the outbreak of war a number of well-to-do women in London distributed pure milk to families who could prove their poverty.[28] The WCG sent deputations to Whitehall, put pressure on local authorities, organised lectures, meetings and relief work such as dinners, milk and home helps for pregnant and nursing mothers.[29] In 1915 the WCG published *Maternity*, a collection of letters from working-class women which highlighted the appalling lives of working-class mothers, and the need for change. In 1917 the National Baby Week Council (with all its top posts occupied by men) launched the highly popular Baby Week, a vehicle for the display of yet more patriotic fervour. The Babies of the Empire Society called for more nurseries, breast-feeding and better baby care.[30]

Central government demonstrated its commitment to new life, as every day it committed the living to death on the Western Front. From 1915 parents and medical attendants were obliged to notify the authorities of a birth, in order that a health visitor could visit the baby and try to persuade the mother to attend an infant welfare centre. By offering hefty subsidies to local authorities, the Local Government Board encouraged the establishment of more infant welfare centres and the extension of their work to antenatal care and to children between the ages of one and five. A number of local authorities, however, looked the gift-horse in the mouth. Some disapproved of the measures in principle, maintaining that they would undermine individual responsibility among the working class, who in any case, did not want health visitors entering their homes. Others were not interested in the scheme because they had to make a financial contribution. However, local authority parsimony would not have affected the babies as there is little evidence that infant welfare work had any immediate effect on babies' life chances.[31] Even so, there was little attempt to monitor the impact of infant welfare work. It was supposedly self-evident that educating working-class mothers in baby care would bring

41

down the infant death-rate. Thus the finger was still being pointed at working-class mothers.

As in the pre-war years, the debate over infant deaths was centred around married women who went out to work, and these traditional arguments took on an added urgency amid the relentless casualty lists. Did married women, by abandoning their domestic duties, lose a woman's innate moral capacity for childrearing, and did those married women who undertook arduous work outside the home reduce their physical capacity for childbearing?[32] It was at this juncture that women's two patriotic duties – to reproduce the race and to maintain the productive capacity of the country – came to a head-on collision.

Women struggled along with a host of perennial problems, such as pregnancy, childbirth, childrearing and housework. At the same time they were tempted into war work by the high wages on offer.[33] Transport difficulties, darkened streets and deteriorating housing all added to the stresses of life in wartime. Local authorities put sanitary improvements into abeyance. Food shortages worsened and women (especially poorer ones) spent much of their time queuing for scarce or rationed food.[34] Women who had moved to take up munition work might live in cramped conditions for which they paid high rent, with 'picture palaces' and church clubs their only form of entertainment.[35]

Lloyd George, Minister of Munitions from 1915 until the end of 1916 when he became Prime Minister, wrote of the entry of women into heavy industry, where previously only men had been employed, 'In most of these establishments rough and unseemly conditions had prevailed and had hitherto been put up with by the men workers, but it was recognised as impossible to ask women to submit to them.' If Lloyd George's claim is well-founded, working conditions should have improved most dramatically in those industries which had been most successful in attracting women workers. Yet, the largest increase in women workers came in transport and clerical work, not noted for their wartime improvements in working conditions; it was in fact manufacturing industry which experienced the greatest improvements in conditions.[36] Moreover, because of deputations to Whitehall and the annual reports of the Principal Lady Factory Inspector, the unsafe and unhealthy conditions in which many women worked were well known to governments before the war, but this knowledge had not, in itself, prompted them to deal with more than the very worst conditions.[37]

Contradictory evidence over standards of health and safety at work exists partly because conditions varied enormously from firm to firm, and partly because of the gulf between the propaganda about good conditions and the reality for many workers. Government propaganda romanticised women munition workers in films such as

'A Day in the Life of a Munition Worker' as attractive, skilled women who were coping with real physical strain. As if to emphasise the care the Government was taking of the women, one-third of 'A Day in the Life of a Munition Worker' was devoted to safety measures and medical examinations.[38] Working conditions for many women were a far cry from this documentary 'fiction'.

Fifty thousand workers were employed filling shells at any one time during the war; altogether about 100,000 were thus employed. The job required using Trinitrotoluene (TNT), and the Ministry of Munitions soon recognised it as being the most dangerous of all munition work. In 1916 Sir George Newman, chair of the Health of Munition Workers' Committee (HMWC), discovered high levels of illness among women TNT workers at Woolwich Arsenal. Over one-third suffered from a loss of appetite, nausea, constipation, depression, or some change in menstruation; while a quarter suffered from dermatitis. The Ministry kept very quiet about TNT poisoning, and from 1916 information on the effects of TNT was censored so as not to deter potential recruits from the work. During 1917 some efforts were made to reduce the dangers of TNT, and the death-rate from toxic jaundice fell, although it is not clear whether this fall was due to medical intervention. Factory doctors and the Ministry of Munitions aimed to keep workers who were not likely to die on the job filling shells; those employees displaying early signs of poisoning were removed from the work but, as there were such a wide range of possible symptoms, this was rather a hit-and-miss diagnosis. Working with TNT yellowed the skin and led to the nickname 'canary'. Despite the important war work these women were undertaking there was a stigma attached to yellow-faced women. Few of the women seem to have complained, probably because the wages were relatively high and they would have felt that they were helping in a very direct way the men at the Front whose death-rate made the dangers of any other work pale into insignificance.[39]

'Welfare' became part of wartime propaganda, illustrating the care that was being taken of women in industry. In 1917 Barbara McLaren wrote in praise of Lilian Barker, welfare superintendent at Woolwich Arsenal, that visitors were struck by the general sense of contentment and health, and even among workers in the danger zone, it was rare to see a sickly face.[40] (A far cry from the evidence unearthed by Ineson and Thom cited above.) Welfare manifested itself in two forms: facilities, such as canteens which were perfectly acceptable and indeed popular, and welfare supervision, which was heartily disliked and gave 'welfare' a bad name among workers for years to come.

Welfare supervision was aimed at women, girls and boys. During the war Robert Hyde founded the Boys' Welfare Society, which soon metamorphosed into the Industrial Welfare Society (now the Industrial Society). Welfare supervisors watched over physical welfare and helped to organise canteens and recreational facilities; they also took on the role of moral guardians. The dual role of welfare officers is well demonstrated by the concern of one officer in Coventry who fretted over the number of back alleys and passages, as well as small gardens, parks and heaths which were open all night and did 'not help towards the morality of the town. My works are so small that I don't suffer much. The bad women go to a bigger place where they cannot be found out.'[41] Working-class women as mothers and as workers were subjected to moral surveillance by women patrols and women welfare officers in the name of the future of the race and the nation. Governments' direct intervention in maintaining standards of health in order to boost productivity was more conventional and less controversial.

GOVERNMENT INTERVENTION, PRODUCTIVITY AND HEALTH

Until the summer of 1914 it was expected that in the event of war the British economy would function almost as normal: the war would be a short one and Britain would finance its Allies' forces rather than commit large armies to the Continent itself. From the outbreak of war in August 1914 it quickly became apparent that industrial production was an essential part of the war effort. Britain had both to manufacture munitions for its fighting forces and enough exports to pay for imports of munitions, raw materials and food in order to maintain the military and civilian populations. Only by doing this could the war be won. On the Home Front production was to be the guiding strategic tenet.[42]

The initial problem of unemployment soon changed, therefore, to one of labour shortage. Orders from the British Government and the Allies were placed in ever increasing quantities, and applications for flexibility in the Factory Acts poured in from all over the country.[43] In an effort to meet production demands, the requirements of the Factory Acts were immediately relaxed by the issuing of Orders. Orders for the hours of employment of women and young people (Emergency Orders) were made both for individual works (Special Orders) and for all works belonging to a particular class or industry (General Orders). The Orders allowed employment in shifts, overtime, Sunday work, employment prohibited by the Factory Act or Regulations and minor adjustments for mealtimes and periods of employment.[44] As well as changes in the types of goods being produced, other developments were occurring. Much old machinery was scrapped and new machinery introduced; many more of the new machines were electrically driven. The introduction of novel equipment, allied to the shortage of skilled workers, meant that maintenance standards fell and safety inevitably suffered.[45]

The worst violations of the law occurred in the early part of the war. During 1915 groundless pleas of a war emergency were used to justify law-breaking.[46] By 1916, however, Factory Inspectors felt that observance of the Orders was, on the whole, satisfactory. Excessive overtime and Sunday labour had been checked and 'as near as possible' abolished. As inspections progressed fewer factories worked irregular overtime or at night without sanction or regulation by an Order. In fact, the Chief Inspector of Factories thought that difficulties with enforcement were not as severe as might have been expected. However, there were notable exceptions, which it is worth recounting, as the infringements of, rather than compliance with, the law attracted attention. At Woolwich a firm was prosecuted and received the maximum fine for employing a boy of sixteen for illegal hours amounting to 108 a week. In the south-west boys worked twenty-five to twenty-nine hours consecutively except for intervals of four to five hours; at works on the outskirts of London a woman was employed for eighteen-to twenty-hour spells, and a Scottish firm employed girls, with short intervals for meals and rest, for continuous periods of thirty-five hours.[47] Severe penalties imposed by the courts were vital in securing compliance with the law. In the early years of the war, when the courts imposed only light fines or none at all, safety levels declined from pre-war standards.[48]

During the early part of the war, behaviour which was defined as criminal by the Statute Book was not considered so by the courts; criminal activity was portrayed in the courts and by the press as bolstering production and therefore patriotic. G.D.H. Cole, a member of the Fabian Society, wrote of a firm where a girl worked for thirty hours at a stretch and another girl for twenty-four and a half hours. The second girl had an accident and so the situation was brought to the notice of the Factory Inspector. A prosecution was started: at the first trial the case was dismissed and at the second one the counsel for the defence called the prosecution 'a piece of fatuous folly, only justified by extreme ignorance', and the Home Office, instead of prosecuting 'ought to have struck a special medal' for the girls. 'Now is not the time to talk about Factory Acts.' The employer was put on probation.[49]

Contemporaries often missed the point that the Home Office, unlike the courts, took a dim view of unsafe and unhealthy work practices. On 5 July 1915 William Anderson, Labour MP for Sheffield Attercliffe, stated in the House of Commons that a number of employers and magistrates were under the impression that protective legislation was no longer operative.[50] In 1917 the *Women's Trade Union Review* recounted Susan Lawrence, a prominent member of the labour movement, as saying that the Factory Act was 'in ruins' and dangerous privileges had been accorded to certain classes of employers. However, by 1918 the Chief Inspector could report that several important prosecutions had been undertaken by Inspectors, and while complaints had been made about the inadequate penalties inflicted in some courts, in others substantial fines were imposed for illegal employment and for failing to fence dangerous machinery.[51]

It was assumed that the law was less likely to be broken if a visit from a Factory Inspector was a possibility and so questions were repeatedly asked in Parliament about the numbers of Inspectors.[52] A decade after the end of the war it was admitted that heavy arrears in inspection had accumulated during the war.[53] More frequent inspection would not necessarily have maintained standards in all areas: repairs and limewashing were left almost in abeyance because of the problem of obtaining labour and materials.[54] The backlog of inspection was compounded by the changing emphasis in working conditions, from a narrower governmental concern with safety and health at work, to the broader question of welfare which accompanied the recognition of a need for higher standards.[55]

The Government's efforts to produce enough munitions to prosecute the war successfully were widely regarded as a failure. Criticisms had been mounting for months but came to a head in May 1915 over the alleged lack of shells on the Western Front. The political storm forced Asquith, the Prime Minister, to reorganise the Government and bring some Conservatives, albeit in relatively minor posts, into the Government. As part of this upheaval Lloyd George moved to the new Ministry of Munitions, established in June 1915 as a direct response to the political storm created over the alleged shortage of munitions, with the production of adequate supplies of munitions as its *raison d'être*. The Ministry took over the control of munitions factories and encouraged the introduction of the most up-to-date machinery, methods of production and management practices. In March 1915 the need to maximise production led the Ministry of Munitions to negotiate the compulsory arbitration of disputes, the suspension of trade union restrictions over output and the provision of extensive welfare facilities in its factories. The Ministry took up the cause of a healthy industrial environment in order to boost production and reduce labour turnover. It created a Health and Welfare Section 'to convince employers that it is both good business and good management as well as a duty, to regard with sympathetic consideration the health and comfort of their employees'. It was not long before the idea was seized upon that safety, health and welfare measures could be used to improve industrial efficiency and this in turn could increase productivity. From then on the Home Office, and the new Ministry, increasingly intervened in industry to boost production.

The Ministry of Munitions' best-remembered effort was the creation in 1915 of a Health of Munition Workers' Committee to 'consider and advise on questions of industrial fatigue, hours of labour, and other matters affecting the personal health and physical efficiency of workers in munitions factories and workshops'.[56] The Committee considered the relationship between industrial health and industrial efficiency and advised the Minister in a series of reports; the prior establishment of a Welfare Section at the Ministry of Munitions meant that the machinery for implementing the Committee's recommendations was in place. The Ministry's prime reason for providing welfare facilities in its factories was to boost productivity. The dangers of shell-filling in munition factories were largely ignored until it was seen to be affecting production levels, and throughout the war stress was laid on maintaining output, even at the expense of workers contracting toxic jaundice.[57] For all the HMWC reports, work in a munitions factory continued to be hazardous. Yet, concern was expressed that women in munitions factories should adopt a healthy lifestyle in order to maintain their efficiency at work. Advice was offered by welfare officers on clothes, diet, cleanliness and minor ailments.[58]

The Police Factories, etc. (Miscellaneous Provisions) Act 1916 was the Home Office's one legislative contribution to safety, health and welfare during the war. Its main provision gave the Home Secretary power to require by an Order proper arrangements for eating meals; the supply of drinking water, protective clothing, ambulance and first-aid facilities; the supply and use of seats in workrooms; washing facilities; cloakrooms and the supervision of workers. Compliance with these welfare provisions was erratic.

Poor working conditions were only regarded as a problem for governments when the correlation between good working conditions and the efficient use of scarce resources and maximum production came to the fore. Early in the war, when labour supply was seen as a more important issue, Factory Inspectors' energies were diverted to facilitating the large-scale substitution of women for men in industry. The close association between maximum productivity and good working conditions meant that when the former was no longer the guiding economic aim in the post-war world, good working conditions suffered accordingly. The clouds of war did allow a ray of sunshine to fall on some civilians who were making a direct contribution to the war effort, but for those whose involvement in the struggle was less direct, there was no such compensation.

THE EXPERIENCES OF ETHNIC MINORITIES

Throughout the war a hate campaign was waged against anyone suspected of being German. Atrocity stories fed on the exisiting stereotype of the evil Hun, and Germans in Britain endured brutal and vicious attacks.[59] Until the First World War there was a vibrant German community in Britain, and the full force of nationalist hatred was now directed against its members. In many ways the men of military age who were interned were the lucky ones. Those who were not interned: children, women, old men and the militarily unfit, suffered the brunt of hostility. 'German' embraced many who had lived in Britain for decades, if not all their lives, as well as British women who had married German *emigrés* and thereby forfeited their British citizenship.

A stop-go policy of internment of enemy alien males of military age (unless they were ministers of religion or medical doctors) operated. The first wave of internments began in late August 1914 and ended in October because of a shortage of prison places. Between November 1914 and May 1915 3,000 men were released, but the sinking of the *Lusitania* in May 1915 led to a second wave of internments. The Government set up tribunals at which 'hard cases' could appeal against their internment. The Anglo-Jewish leadership refused to attend the hearings and showed little concern for the fate of internees.[60] German-Jewish internees must have felt doubly abandoned. At the end of the war there were just under 25,000 enemy aliens still interned.

As in the Second World War, the worst physical conditions were to be found in transit camps. One internee recalled the humiliation of having to use buckets instead of toilets for the first few days.[61] Most civilians were interned on the Isle of Man. Once huts replaced tents, the physical conditions were adequate; the Americans who inspected the camps heard few grumbles. For the first couple of years complaints about the food were rare, although meals tended to deteriorate during 1917 after the introduction of rationing, and the diet of internees may have become less varied than that of the rest of the population.[62] Army doctors made regular visits to the camps, which had small hospitals attached; if an internee was seriously ill he was taken to an outside hospital. As in the outside world, those who could afford to pay for their medication did so. The experience of internment varied enormously, and most of the evidence historians now rely upon does not come from the internees themselves.[63]

All writers at the time and since are agreed that the major problem for internees was not the physical conditions of the camps, but the fact that they were interned at all. It was the loss of dignity and privacy, coupled with the monotony of the routine and the diet which were hardest to bear. One internee felt that the psychological effects were worse at the outset of imprisonment when an internee's fate seemed so hopeless and unjust.[64] The absence of work or solitude; the unknown duration of captivity; the irregular communication with the outside world, especially with women and children, and the popular hatred of foreigners led to what became known as 'barbed-wire syndrome', a form of depression, manifesting itself in irritability, loss of concentration, insomnia and a 'pessimistic outlook on life'.[65] Yet, release from internment was a mixed blessing, as life outside the internment camps brought its own problems.

The Aliens' Restriction Order of 5 August 1914 banned aliens from certain areas and restricted their movements. German social institutions were shut down, and a range of cultural oases evaporated overnight. Germans were boycotted by trading associations, trade unions, political parties and shopkeepers. Governesses, waiters, domestic servants, hairdressers and clerks were dismissed. No one wanted to employ a German, or even anyone suspected of being of German origin. Soon it became illegal to Anglicise a Germanic name. Children with German fathers were beaten up at school, and sporadic outbreaks of violence the length and breadth of the country, when gangs went on the rampage, left German shopkeepers without a livelihood or a safe roof over their heads. Goods for sale as well as personal household items were all liable to be stolen. During the anti-German riots following the sinking of the *Lusitania* one woman with a baby sought refuge on a roof all night in the pouring rain. The worst rioting occurred in August and October 1914, May 1915, June 1916 and July 1917.[66] Although the witch-hunt against Germans affected all levels of society, the poorest sections of the community suffered the severest hardship as better-off immigrants were more likely to have taken out British nationality.

Anti-German sentiment merged with anti-semitism against Jews of German origin. The initial economic disruption of the war hit Jewish trades hard, and immigrants initially found themselves excluded from the National Relief Fund. By early 1915, however, army contracts had revived trade and brought prosperity to a number of Jewish firms. Even so, Jews continued to run the gauntlet of sporadic street violence. Rationing tended to hit orthodox Jews harder than the rest of the population; coupons for bacon, hare and tinned meat were of no use to them and they had to make out a special case for their rations to be modified. Their requests led to charges of special pleading and fuelled existing prejudices.[67]

Many of the families of internees became destitute. With the male breadwinner removed, prices rising and the women unemployed, families ran short of food and clothes. The women inevitably suffered stresses and strains from poverty, from the hostility of those around them, from frustration at not being able to make a positive contribution to the war effort, as well as from anxiety over the fate of their interned relatives. There is evidence that their children's health deteriorated. The Quakers, the German government, via the Americans (there was a similar scheme for Britons living in Germany), and better-off naturalised Germans living in Britain all rallied round to help their nominal compatriots.[68]

THE ELDERLY

According to Jay Winter, the elderly also suffered disproportionately during the war, and this is reflected in their worsening death-rates, due to heart disease and respiratory infections. As a group, the elderly had no political muscle, and their complaints fell on deaf ears; unlike other vulnerable age groups (such as children) they suffered from a low profile. For some the labour demands of the war meant that employment opportunities were opened, but most old people, particularly middle-class ones, were having to eke out an existence on fixed incomes in an inflationary period when any savings they might have had were being severely eroded.[69] Distressed gentlefolk were hardly likely to galvanise the nation into charitable action. Yet, their material sufferings were matched by their emotional anguish as they fretted over grandsons who were paying a very high price for ultimate victory. Middle-class men died in disproportionately high numbers.

THE TROOPS

Pre-war concerns over the fitness of the population to fight in wartime proved to be justified. 'Fitness for military service' was ambiguously applied, and because of the need for men its standard tended to be low. Winter thinks that wealthier men, with their greater economic security, might have been more willing to leave their employment on the outbreak of war and hence they spent longer exposed to danger at the Front. Health and wealth contributed to the disproportionately high enlistment rate among salaried workers in the commercial and clerical classes, and to the disproportionately high death-rate of those higher up the social scale. Of those in uniform 40 per cent became casualties; one in eight was killed and over one in four was wounded. Those in the army suffered the highest casualty rates. A disproportionately large share of casualties came from among the officers.[70]

The sons of toil were more likely to fail the medical test for military service or fail to pass well enough for combat duty. As Jay Winter has pointed out, the poor health of many industrial workers probably saved their lives. For many men army rations would have been more nutritious than the plates of food their mothers and wives could have afforded for them; many were better clothed and shod in their uniforms; and army life away from the Front Line was no more overcrowded than their own homes. At home and at work most men would have been used to long, hard work under a strict regime and on low wages.[71]

Over 700,000 men died or were killed. By March 1919 approximately 190,000 widows' pensions and 10,000 orphans' pensions had been granted. Over 1,600,000 men were wounded or fell ill. In the 1920s and 1930s old soldiers shuffling around the streets were a common sight. Roughly 1.2 million men were entitled to disability pensions. Two-thirds of these men suffered from minor disabilities, such as the loss of a finger or toe. Forty thousand men were totally or almost totally disabled: without limbs or feet; blinded; paralysed; permanently bedridden; severely disfigured; mentally ill; or suffering from an incurable disease.[72]

Recurring nightmares, guilt at surviving when so many comrades fell, and failure to relate to their families at home meant that many of those who survived suffered for years in ways that do not necessarily show up in the official statistics. In the decade following the end of hostilities 114,600 ex-servicemen applied for pensions for shell-shock-related disorders alone. Indeed, the whole question of shell-shock raises interesting class and gender-related questions.[73]

Elaine Showalter has pointed out that in the course of the twentieth century it was only in the First World War that men have apparently suffered more mental illness than women. She also points to the fact that doctors noted that war neurosis took different forms in officers and men. Symptoms of hysteria (paralysis, blindness, deafness, mutism) were found among the men and neurasthenic symptoms (nightmares, insomnia, heart palpitations, dizziness and depression) among the officers. (Were military doctors unwilling to label men of their own class as susceptible to the 'female' complaint of hysteria?) Shell-shock was also four times higher among officers than men, a phenomenon which has been explained in terms of the pressures on officers to conform to British ideals of manly stoicism.[74]

Time did not necessarily heal. In the late 1930s the British Legion expressed concern over the growing number of ex-servicemen, suffering from chronic illnesses, who applied to the Legion for assistance. The Legion was convinced that many thousands of men who had seen active service had prematurely aged, as a result of their experiences during the war and the difficulties which they experienced once demobbed. The intangible effects of active service were obviously impossible to prove, yet it was particularly galling for men who had served their country in its hour of need to be forced to turn to the Public Assistance Committees (the Poor Law in all but name) in their hour of need.[75] Half a century later, Coroners' reports were still regularly mentioning war service, in particular the effects of gassing, as a contributory cause of death.[76]

THE BALANCE SHEET

It has usually been assumed that the war was bad not only for members of the Armed Forces, but also for civilian health. Jay Winter has attempted to show that civilian health, with the notable exception of the elderly, did not deteriorate during the war. (One conclusion following from this argument is that the virulence of the influenza pandemic of 1918–19 cannot be explained by the greater susceptibility of a nation after four long years of war; and anyway, the flu affected non-combatant nations just as much as the combatant ones.) Winter argued that between 1900 and 1930 there was a gradual decline in infant mortality, but the decline was most rapid during the war, mainly due to the decrease in deaths from infectious diseases, such as diarrhoea, bronchitis and measles.

Improvements cannot be put down to better obstetrics, medical care or housing. If the husband was a civilian his wages would have risen; if he was in the Forces his wife received a separation allowance, and with her husband away she would have had greater control over how the family budget was spent. (However, as we have already seen, not all wives received their allowance.) More married women were in paid work and this would have increased the overall family income. More money to spend meant more and better food, and this in turn affected the family's health. The most likely reason for improvements in health probably related to the mothers' better nutrition. Even during the worst periods of food shortages the distribution of food was more equitable than it had been before the war. Women's and men's health improved along with that of their babies, again because of an improved diet. The poorest and least skilled gained most as they moved out of the worst-paid jobs. Those in skilled work, clerical and service jobs did not gain so much. There was, therefore, an inprovement among the poorest sections of the working class towards the level of the skilled working class. Evidence from London shows that the health of schoolchildren, as judged by their cleanliness, teeth, nutrition and related illnesses, definitely improved.[77] This revisionist view, however, needs a certain degree of qualification.

Housing conditions and some people's working conditions actually militated against better health, and this is reflected in rising TB rates during the war. There is nothing to suggest that medical treatment or the health services contributed to improved life chances. While Winter has pointed to falling maternal mortality rates during the war as further evidence of improving standards of living and health, Irvine Loudon maintains that there is nothing significant about the falling maternal mortality rates during the war: maternal mortality also declined between 1907 and 1911 and between 1919 and 1923. The series of troughs and waves in maternal mortality rates can be explained, according to Loudon, largely by changes in death-rates, from puerperal sepsis.[78]

It is actually hard to judge whether earnings were rising faster than prices; standards of living seem to have risen for those in full-time (especially war-related) work, but those on fixed incomes (such as pensioners for whom there was a rising death-rate during the war) would have been hard hit. In the early days of the war there was widespread hardship which continued for certain groups, such as non-British nationals and the elderly, throughout the war.

Housing deteriorated, working conditions varied so enormously that it is imposssible to make generalisations about their effect on people's health; double standards and burdens intensified for women, although some people did have their horizons widened during the war, and middle-class women succeeded in scuppering the idea that they were uniquely frail. Overall mortality statistics would have masked great regional and other variations, and provide no guide to illnesses or general sense of well-being.

General improvements in death-rates tell us nothing about the agonies suffered during the war which might not have led to death, but which would have severely undermined an individual's sense of well-being. It is not possible to measure the psychological effects of war, either on civilians or on those serving in the Forces. A brief extension to one's life is unlikely to have been considered a gain set against the death of a brother, father or husband. Wartime experiences affected those men shell-shocked, injured or blinded for years to come:[79] the ghosts of the First World War stalked the land long after the guns on the Western Front had fallen silent.

NOTES

1. **Winter J.** 1986 *The Great War and the British people*. Macmillan.
2. **Jones H.** 1993 *A liberal feminist? The papers and correspondence of*

Violet Markham, 1896–1953. The Historians Press, R. Williamson JP to Sir George Riddell 13 October 1914.

3. **Pankhurst S.** 1987 *The home front: A mirror to life in England during the First World War*. The Creset Library, pp. 21, 22, 43 First published 1932.

4. **Pedersen S.** 1990 Gender, welfare and citizenship in Britain during the Great War *American Historical Review*. **95**: 983–1006.

5. Jones H. *A liberal feminist?* 16 September 1914 Charles Masterman to Violet Markham; Portsmouth Services sub-committee to E. H. Kelly 5 November 1914.

6. Ibid. Mothers Union 1915.

7. Imperial War Museum. Emp 42 4/11; Emp 42 4/13.

8. **Bland L.** 1985 'Cleansing the portals of life': The venereal disease campaign in the early twentieth century. In **Langan M., Schwarz B.** (eds) *Crises in the British state, 1880–1930*. Hutchinson, p. 206.

9. Ibid. pp. 203–4.

10. PP 1916 vol. XVI Royal Commission on Venereal Diseases Final Report.

11. Bland L., 'Cleansing the portals of life', p. 205; **Evans D.** 1992 Tackling the 'Hideous Scourge': The creation of the Venereal Disease Treatment Centres in early twentieth-century Britain. *Social History of Medicine* **5**: 432.

12. **Furse K.** 1940 *Hearts and pomegranates: The story of forty-five years, 1875–1920*. Peter Davies, p. 371.

13. **Markham V.** 1953 *Return passage: The autobiography of Violet R. Markham*. Oxford University Press, pp. 155–6. Violet Markham (1872–1959) sat on the Central Committee on Women's Employment during the war, and in 1917 she was Deputy Director of the Women's Section of the National Service Department. She is best known for her work in the 1930s on the Unemployment Assistance Board. In both wars she was involved in investigations into women's morals.

14. **Balfour F.** 1920 *Dr Elsie Inglis*. British Periodicals Limited, pp. 37–8; **McLaren B.** 1917 *Women of the war*. Hodder and Stoughton, pp. 11–23.

15. **St Clair Stobart M.** 1916 *The flaming sword of Serbia*. Hodder and Stoughton, p. 308; see also **St Clair Stobart M.** 1913 *War and women: From experiences in the Balkans and elsewhere*. George Bell & Co.

16. McLaren B. *Women of the war*. p. 3.

17. See for instance the title of **St Clair Stobart M.** 1935 *Miracles and adventures: An autobiography*. Rider and Co.; **Condell D., Liddiard J.** 1987 *Working for victory? Images of women in the First World War*. Routledge, p. 22.

18. Furse K. *Hearts and pomegranates*. pp. 347, 298, 325; Rachel Crowdy (1884–1964) trained as a nurse before the war and in 1911 she joined the VADs. From the end of 1914 she was in charge of VADs on the Continent. In 1919 she became a DBE.

19. Imperial War Museum 74/105/1 Beryl Butterworth Hutchinson.

20. On the FANYs, see **Popham H.** 1984 *FANY: The story of the Women's Transport Service, 1907–1984*. Lee Cooper, especially pp. 17–46.

21. **Summers A.** 1988 *Angels and citizens: British women as military nurses, 1854–1914.* Routledge & Kegan Paul, p. 278 and *passim.*
22. **Haste C.** 1977 *Keep the home fires burning: Propaganda in the First World War.* Allen Lane, pp. 89–90.
23. Imperial War Museum. Welfare 1/4 Babies of the Empire Society: For the health of mothers and babies.
24. PP 1916 vol. XII 44th Annual Report of the Local Government Board for 1914–15 p. 28.
25. Quoted in **Lewis J.** 1980 *The politics of motherhood: Child and maternal welfare in England, 1900–1939.* Croom Helm, pp. 28–9.
26. Imperial War Museum. Welfare 1/4 Babies of the Empire Society: For the health of mothers and babies.
27. **Pugh M.** 1992 *Women and the women's movement in Britain, 1914–59.* Macmillan, p. 17; **Braybon G.** 1981 *Women workers in the First World War: The British experience.* Croom Helm, p. 123.
28. Imperial War Museum. Welfare 5/5 Report and appeal of the National Milk Hostels Committee (n.d.).
29. Imperial War Museum. Welfare 1/10 **M. Llewelyn Davies** 9 June 1915.
30. Winter J. *The Great War and the British people.* p. 192; Pugh M. *Women and the women's movement in Britain, 1914–59.* p. 17.
31. Ibid. pp. 202, 204; Lewis J. *The politics of motherhood*, p. 34.
32. **Braybon G.** 1981 *Women workers in the First World War* pp. 117–19.
33. Ibid. p. 115.
34. **Braybon G., Summerfield P.** 1987 *Out of the cage: Women's experiences in two world wars.* Pandora, pp. 97–100.
35. Jones H. *A liberal feminist?*, November 1916 Adelaide Anderson to Violet Markham.
36. See **Dewey P.** 1984 Military recruiting and the British labour force during the First World War *Historical Journal* **27**: 199–223.
37. Public Record Office (PRO) LAB 14/196 Deputation to Prime Minister 1 May 1913 from Women's Trade Union League and National Organisation of Girls Clubs; Jones H. 1988 Women health workers: The case of the first women factory inspectors in Britain *Social History of Medicine* **1**: 165–81.
38. **Reeves N.** 1986 *Official British film propaganda during the First World War.* Croom Helm, p. 192.
39. **Ineson A., Thom D.** 1985 TNT poisoning and the employment of women workers in the First World War. In **Weindling P.** (ed) *The social history of occupational health.* Croom Helm, pp. 89–102.
40. **McLaren B.** *Women of the war.* pp. 10–11.
41. Jones H. *A liberal feminist?* Adelaide Anderson quoting a welfare officer 7 October 1916.
42. **French D.** 1982 *British economic and strategic planning, 1905–15.* George Allen & Unwin, pp. 1, 74 and *passim.*
43. PP 1914–16 vol. XXI Annual Report of the Chief Inspector of Factories (hereafter Annual Report) for 1914, p. 55; PRO HO 87/26 p. 453.
44. PRO LAB 14/36. No 6A of the Defence of the Realm Regulations.
45. **Bowers B.** 1978 Electricity. In **Williams T.** (ed) *A History of technology vol. 6 Pt 1.* Clarendon, p. 287; PRO LAB 14/333 p. 2; P.P. 1918 vol. X Annual Report for 1917.

46. *The Factory Times* 1 January 1915.
47. P.P. 1917–18 Annual Report for 1916, pp. 4, 6.
48. *The Factory Times* 4 June 1915.
49. **Andrews I.** 1921 *Economic effects of the war upon women and children.* Oxford University Press, pp. 126, 117.
50. H.C. Deb. vol. 73 col. 18 5 July 1915 William Anderson (Lab).
51. P.P. 1919 vol. XXII Annual Report for 1918 p. vii.
52. H.C. Deb. vol. 65 col. 1136–37 28 July 1914 Philip Morrell (Lib); H.C. Deb. vol. 80 col. 2284 16 March 1916 Philip Snowden (Lab); H.C. Deb. vol. 81 col. 46 21 March 1916 H. Cavendish-Bentinck (Con); H.C. Deb. vol. 112 col. 1303 21 February 1919 Frederick Roberts (Lab).
53. PRO LAB 14/333 Report on the Reorganisation of the Factory Department p. 2.
54. P.P. 1920 vol. XVI Annual Report for 1919 p. 47.
55. This broader definition had been used by women factory inspectors before the war.
56. *History of the Ministry of Munitions 1920 Vol. V. Pt III, Welfare: the control of working conditions.* HMSO, p. 1.
57. Ineson A., Thom D. TNT poisoning and the employment of women workers in the First World War. pp. 90, 96.
58. Imperial War Museum. Emp 45.18 Lilian Evans *To women war workers: Some homely advice in regard to the maintenance of their health and comfort* (n.d.).
59. Haste C. *Keep the home fires burning: Propaganda in the First World War.* p. 79; **Panayi P.** 1991 *The enemy in our midst: Germans in Britain during the First World War.* Berg, p. 223.
60. **Cesarani D.** 1990 An embattled minority: The Jews in Britain during the First World War. In **Kushner T., Lunn K.** (eds) *The politics of marginality: Race, the radical right and minorities in 20th-century Britain.* Frank Cass, p. 64.
61. **Cohen-Portheim P.** 1931 *Time stood still: My internment in England, 1914–18.* Duckworth, p. 36.
62. Panayi P. *The enemy in our midst.* p. 114.
63. However, see Cohen-Portheim P. *Time stood still* **Rocker R.** 1918 *Alexandra Palace internment camp in the First World War.* Typescript British Library.
64. For example see **Bird J.** 1986 *Control of enemy alien civilians in Great Britain 1914–18.* Garland Publishing, pp. 132, 138; Cohen-Portheim P. *Time stood still.* pp. 68, 70, 90, 126–7.
65. Panayi P. *The enemy in our midst.* pp. 126–7; **Yarrow S.** 1990 The impact of hostility on Germans in Britain, 1914–18. In Kushner T., Lunn K. (eds) *The politics of marginality: Race, the radical right and minorities in 20th-century Britain.* Frank Cass, pp. 106–7.
66. Panayi P. *The enemy in our midst.* pp. 50, 53, 60, 61, 223; University of London Library special collections. Caroline Playne folder 155.
67. Cesarani D. An embattled minority. pp. 61–76.
68. University of London Library special collections. Caroline Playne folders 10 and 155; Yarrow S. The impact of hostility on Germans in Britain, 1914–18. pp. 100–7.

69. **Winter J.** Some aspects of urban demography in wartime: Paris, London and Berlin, 1914–1919. I am grateful to Dr Jay Winter for allowing me to use his unpublished paper.
70. Winter J. *The Great War and the British people.* pp. 25, 49, 63–4, 72, 86.
71. **Winter J.** 1985 Army and society: The demographic context. In **Beckett I., Simpson K.** (eds) *A nation in arms: A social study of the British army in the First World War.* Manchester University Press, p. 196.
72. Winter J. *The Great War and the British people.* p. 273.
73. **Showalter E.** 1987 *The female malady: Women, madness and English culture, 1830–1980.* Virago, p. 190.
74. Ibid. pp. 194, 174–5.
75. PP 1937–38 vol. 10 Copy of reports made to the Prime Minister by the British Legion regarding the condition of ex-servicemen and of his reply. Cmd 5738, pp. 10, 21–2.
76. **Bourne J. M.** 1989 *Britain and the Great War, 1914–1918.* Edward Arnold, pp. 244–5.
77. Winter J. Army and society. pp. 202–6; Winter J. *The Great War and the British people.* pp. 103, 106, 132–5, 139, 211, 244–45; **Waites B.** 1987 *A class society at war: England, 1914–18.* Berg, pp. 114, 120, 168–70; **Wall R.** 1988 English and German families and the First World War, 1914–18. In Wall R., Winter J. (eds) *The upheaval of war: Family, work and welfare in Europe, 1914–1918.* Cambridge University Press, p. 51.
78. **Loudon I.** 1991 On maternal and infant mortality, 1900–60. *Social History of Medicine* 4: 42.
79. See for instance Winter J. Army and society: The demographic context. p. 201; **Briggs A.** 1987 *A social history of England.* Penguin, p. 299.

Chapter 4

POVERTY AND THE PUBLIC'S HEALTH: THE INTER-WAR YEARS

INTRODUCTION

The impact of the depression in the 1930s on standards of health has long been a source of bitter controversy. As a result of the enormous passion aroused over this issue, evidence about the nation's health in the 1920s has been overlooked or deployed in a debate primarily concerned with the 1930s. The argument has tended to focus on the impact of unemployment on men, or on their wives and children. The present debate is important and interesting, and parallels a fierce dispute at the time. Nevertheless, the debate needs to be slightly refocused.

First, the 1920s deserve more attention in their own right. During the 1920s a number of campaigns of long-term significance got underway: birth control, local authority housing and family allowances, for instance. Second, those who have written about ideas to improve the health of the British 'race' have tended to concentrate on the class bias inherent in eugenicist ideas: the poorer the family the more readily its members were identified as unfit, unintelligent and immoral. The discussion must be widened to take into account the debates revolving around race, ethnicity and anthropology, and the experiences of the Jewish and small black communities, previously confined to histories of 'race'. Third, the debate over the depression in the 1930s needs to be reorientated so that women are considered not only as the appendages of unemployed men, but also in their own right. The experience of unemployed women has been almost totally ignored. Indeed, any discussion of health in the inter-war years should have the role and experience of women at its centre. Women were the ones primarily responsible for promoting and maintaining health. Officials regarded this as a mother's role, and women who were not thought to be doing a good job of health care were subjected to official condemnation.

Yet, women's, and especially mothers', health suffered more than the male members of their families on account of differential feeding and income, childbearing, childrearing and domestic work and, for some women, the burden of combining these roles with paid work.

FEMALE PREOCCUPATIONS

Most treatment and nursing care was given by the mother, a female relative or neighbour.[1] (Both the costs and limitations of medicine kept the doctor at bay.) Women used a wide range of home remedies to cure and relieve illness. Children with measles and whooping cough stayed at home to be nursed, but those with notifiable diseases, such as scarlet fever or diphtheria, were taken into hospital.[2] Some surgery was still performed in the home: tonsillectomies, for instance, were quite often performed on a scrubbed kitchen table.[3]

Keeping the family clean and healthy was the responsibility of all the female members of the household. From a young age girls were expected to help with domestic work, such as cooking, cleaning and sewing, and to help look after sick relatives and neighbours. Such duties could take precedence over school attendance: girls provided busy mothers with an extra pair of hands while at the same time picking up domestic skills which they would need in later life as mothers themselves or as domestic servants. Older daughters helped to bring up the younger children. The larger the family, the greater the burden falling on the daughters.[4]

While in practice health promotion was carried out by various female relatives, 'official' condemnation for poor health was directed at working-class *mothers*. Mothers were culpable if they did not ensure cleanliness, along with healthy diets and lifestyles for their children.

Celia Petty has discussed the allegations that 'inefficient' mothers aggravated the effects of poverty. She has challenged the methods and the allegedly 'scientific' basis of the Medical Research Council's (MRC's) studies. A 1924 MRC Report on nutrition of miners and their families argued that poverty had no influence on ill-health, rather it resulted from the 'failure' of mothers. Improved hygiene and better cooking were cited as the answers to malnutrition. The Report dismissed claims that the 1921 coal stoppage had led to starvation. It opined that there were discrepancies in the efficiency with which wives spent their money, and an educational programme to teach them how to get the most out of their resources was required. The 'efficiency' of mothers related to slovenly standards of home care, carelessness and unwise shopping. The 1924 report concluded that there was no starvation in the coal fields because miners' children fell within the mean range of children in Britain and where they did not do so, the difference was not great. Petty argues that the incidence of malnutrition cannot be calculated from aggregate data as it conceals small numbers of severely undernourished children. Further, the children with whom the miners' children were compared were small for their age. Reworking the data contained in two MRC reports, Petty has shown that moderate and severe protein energy malnutrition existed. She has also challenged the MRC's methodology which led it to the conclusion that ill health was due to mothers' inefficiency. According to Petty, the data actually showed how well working-class women coped with their inadequate resources.[5]

Mothers were blamed not only for their families' ill health, but also for their own poor health. In 1935 the *Report on Maternal Morbidity and Mortality in Scotland*, written by Charlotte Douglas and Peter McKinlay for the Department of Health for Scotland, claimed that 57 per cent of antenatal deaths in their study were directly the 'fault' of the woman because she did not follow advice; in nearly half the postnatal deaths the patient or relatives were 'at fault'.[6] Mothers were criticised for their own ill health because of their alleged ignorance and unwillingness to attend antenatal and postnatal clinics. Critics failed to understand the reasons behind women's non-attendance at clinics. One sympathetic Medical Officer of Health (MOH) explained that home responsibilities took up all a mother's time and energies, leaving no time for her to take care of herself and, anyway, discomfort and inconvenience were so familiar and seemingly inevitable that mothers did not think to seek help.

Local MOHs were, on the whole, more in touch with the constraints on mothers' abilities to promote good health than were central government officials. In 1931 one MOH warned that rising infant and maternal mortality rates were probably caused by social conditions, such as unemployment and low wages: not enough money was available for food, clothing and housing.[7] Such observations might have been more numerous but for the fact that when MOHs pointed to a link between the state of the local economy and mortality rates they came into head-on collision with senior colleagues at the Ministry of Health, so jeopardising their careers.[8]

Contemporary studies and qualitative evidence all point to the overall poor health of married women. In 1933 the Women's Health Inquiry Committee conducted an investigation into the health of 1,250 working-class women. The inquiry brought to light an enormous amount of illness among married women. In part, women's illnesses were hidden because their health usually only received attention in connection with childbearing. Many women took their ill health for granted because they had never had the opportunity of forming high standards of good health; good health for many meant intervals between illnesses or the absence of any incapacitating ailment. Many women had to put up with their illnesses because the alternatives were impractical. Women would abandon hospital treatment because of the expense of travelling to and from the hospital and the time they wasted waiting to be seen. The inquiry's main recommendations included the following: higher wages; better social service provision for children; family allowances to be paid to the mother; subsidised housing; improved maternal health services; the extension of National Health Insurance (NHI) to include wives and dependent children; women's clubs for recreation; agricultural subsidies for certain foodstuffs; better education in the care of the home and the health and hygiene of the family, and housing subsidies.[9]

As women and girls shouldered the burden of family health care, cooking and cleaning in difficult conditions and dragging washing, coal and children up and down flights of stairs, they were the ones hardest hit by damp and dangerous housing. Poorer women were also more likely to be pregnant and to have large families. A 1931 report on maternal mortality in Liverpool described the housing conditions of all the dead mothers – an implicit recognition that bad housing affected the survival chances of pregnant women. (Almost all the dead mothers' housing was 'slum' or 'very poor'.)[10] For middle-class families living in large and draughty Victorian houses, which were expensive to heat and awkward to maintain, the pressures increased on a wife who before the war would have been supported by domestic servants.[11] Women's groups and magazines saw housing very much as a woman's issue and gave it high priority. They endeavoured to improve women's living and working conditions in the home, although they did not challenge the domestic sexual division of labour.[12]

Following the First World War two linked problems, a housing shortage and rents which were too high for many to afford, led to widespread overcrowding in sub-standard homes. In 1925 a temporary MOH for Bethnal Green wrote: 'The indelible picture of dying Tuberculosis patients in small and very overcrowded rooms, sleeping in the same bed with their children and so of necessity infecting these also, will haunt my mind for the rest of my life.'[13] Only houses built after the First World War had running hot water and bathrooms. Older houses were also more likely to be infested with bedbugs, fleas and cockroaches.

Not until the local authority slum clearance campaigns, following the 1930 Greenwood Act (implemented in 1933), was there any proper linkage between health policy and housing policy. Even then success was patchy. It was difficult to quantify the extent of overcrowding since families went to great lengths to ensure that the local authority was kept in the dark about the number of occupants in a house, fearing that either they would be prosecuted or they would have their children removed.

Slum clearance was only a partial success. Rising living standards meant renewed pressure on women to keep their homes up to the new standards. New blocks of flats were soon spotted as a menace to people's well-being and were opposed by women in the Labour Party and the Women's Co-operative Guild (WCG). Often people were moved to new estates where they missed their old familiar environment and felt isolated. There were problems with lifts; too few amenities, such as safe play areas for children, shops, cinemas, clinics and buses; and the rents were normally much higher than they had been used to paying. Indeed, a well-publicised piece of research by G.C.M. M'Gonigle, the MOH for Stockton-on-Tees, into the health of people moved from a slum clearance area to a new estate found that their health worsened. He blamed the deterioration on the relatively high rents which left even less money for food than in the past. Yet, it was the provision of over three million new and decent homes and the reconditioning and destruction of unfit houses which Kingsley Wood, Minister of Health from 1935 to 1938, believed to be the greatest contribution to the improved health of his generation. His claim may well have been true for those moving to the new suburban private estates, where homes were light, easy to clean, with well-equipped kitchens and gas or electricity.[14]

Feeding and clothing families remained women's main preoccupation in the home. Elizabeth Roberts has argued that in working-class households it was the woman who held the family purse strings. Whereas she sees this as a source of power for women, in reality it was a constant source of worry and stress as various strategies to make ends meet had to be devised. Women undertook paid work, children were sent out to work, goods were bought on credit and belongings pawned.[15]

Mothers, and to a lesser extent daughters, would go without food in order that the men of the family could have enough to eat. There is some evidence that differential feeding was connected to the higher death-rate of girls than boys.[16] Mothers were the first to feel the pinch. 'In working-class homes it is the mother who makes the sacrifice. It is she who goes short. She sees to it that, within the power of the wages, the man who goes to work gets the best that those wages can buy, low as they are. She sees to it that the children do not suffer . . .'[17] In 1933 Sir Edward Hilton Young, Minister of Health from 1931 to 1935, warned that when local authorities were looking for malnutrition in a family it was the mothers who would show the bad effects of unemployment and deprivation.[18] One sinister reason for this being the case was that depriving oneself of food in order that the man of the family had enough to eat was possibly a means of reducing domestic violence.

In many homes violent attacks by husbands on their wives were an accepted fact of life, although the extent of violence is impossible to quantify, and few historians have ventured into this quagmire. A non-violent husband was an important criterion for a 'good husband'. (If he also brought home a steady income and was not much interested in sex, he was a dream come true.) Violence often followed an argument over money or a drinking bout. Drinking could drain a family's meagre resources and lead to violence, yet a belief (shared by some women) in the food value of beer was used by some men to justify spending money in the pub.[19]

Even when no actual physical violence took place, the threat of it hung heavily over wives and children. Practical problems, not least the financial one, as well the social stigma for a woman who left her husband meant that women endured years of violence. Women might help other women who had been attacked, but neighbours tended not to 'interfere' or report incidents to the police. Only very rarely would an attack come to light in court.

Attacks on women in the home remained well hidden from the public and political world. In the 1920s and 1930s most organised feminist groups worked on the assumption that the family and motherhood were positive features of society; any problems were essentially financial at root, and (consciously or unconsciously) they were not interested in exposing the nastier side of married life, which so brutally conflicted with the ideal they were promoting.[20] Domestic problems were to be tackled by raising a mother's income. It was a woman's status as a mother within a family which would entitle her to state financial support.

The most significant proposal for improving a mother's income was for a payment to be made to her for each child, a family allowance, financed by the state. Supporters of family allowances often saw them as going hand-in-hand with better maternity care, free milk and state nurseries. Different arguments were put to different groups in order to gain broad-based support. For instance, eugenicists were courted with the argument that family allowances would cut the birth-rate among the lowest sections of society by enabling them to move out of slums to more spacious accommodation. The Family Endowment Society, launched by Eleanor Rathbone in 1917, argued that family allowances would indirectly lead to equal pay for men and women as the former would no longer be able to argue that they needed a bigger wage to keep a family. The strongest argument for family allowances, however, was that they would help to alleviate poverty, especially among women, and so reduce the widespread chronic ill health among poorer women. Sick mothers produced sickly children who grew up to be inefficient workers given to frequent absenteeism. Hence there were strong economic arguments for family allowances.

Opponents of family allowances argued that equal pay and opportunities in the labour market were far more important for women than family allowances, and that by focusing on women as mothers the idea of separate spheres for men and women was reinforced: tying purse and apron strings together was no strategy for gaining freedom.

Winifred Holtby, a journalist and novelist, condemned the saccharine sentimentality which surrounded motherhood and infancy, when the lack of any real respect for motherhood was demonstrated by poor housing and inadequate maternity services.[21] Governments failed to respond either to demands for more economic assistance for married women or to requests for birth control. In order to improve women's health, governments concentrated on behavioural changes and hospitalisation at childbirth. Jane Lewis has shown how state provisions for mothers and infants were only part of the demands made by women themselves. Women's organisations unsuccessfully campaigned for adequate financial independence for women, medical treatment and easy access to advice about birth control and free contraceptives. Knowledge about contraception was imperative at a time when there was widespread ignorance among both children and adults about their bodies; despite the close living quarters of many working-class families, young people remained remarkably ill-informed about sex and reproduction. Even pregnant women could be ignorant about how a baby was born.[22] Sex education formed no part of the school curriculum, and the National Council for Combating VD aimed to frighten rather than enlighten.[23] In fact, some of its propaganda was downright misleading.

The lack of information about birth control or free contraceptives hit women far harder than men. Women were worn down by too many pregnancies, childbirth was extremely dangerous, and to be unmarried and pregnant carried a colossal stigma. Between 1923 and 1933 the Maternal Mortality Rate (MMR) rose by 22 per cent,[24] and not until the late 1930s did it begin to fall.

There are three possible explanations for the high MMR. First, maternity services varied enormously from one local authority to another. G.D.H and M.I. Cole, two prominent Fabian socialists, argued at the time that many local authorities, especially in small towns and rural areas, provided little or no service. This inevitably meant that there were glaring disparities in the care and attention which rich and poor mothers received.[25] It was not until the 1936 Midwives' Act that all local authorities were obliged to provide enough full-time, salaried and qualified midwives. Obstetric care was also of a low standard. In 1930 Rochdale had the highest MMR in the country. Andrew Topping, Rochdale's MOH, introduced major improvements in the quality of obstetric care, and Rochdale's MMR rate fell from one of the highest to one of the lowest in the country. In other parts of the country the MMR rate was not so amenable to medical intervention.

In 1933 a scheme to improve medical services in Rhondda made no impact on the MMR. This failure led to a change in tactics and provides the second explanation for the high MMR rates. In 1935 food was distributed to women at clinics and the MMR fell dramatically. This experiment strongly suggests that when women did not have enough money to spend on food for themselves, they suffered from malnutrition and this was the chief cause of maternal mortality.[26] Certainly, as improvements in the economy began to show in the late 1930s, the MMR began to fall.

One major problem with laying the blame for the loss of so many wives and mothers entirely on social and economic circumstances is that maternal mortality remained high for middle-class women as well as working-class ones. Irvine Loudon offers a third explanation for the high MMR. He argues that the dramatic reduction in maternal mortality after 1935 was due to the introduction of sulphonamides to treat puerperal fever. The high MMR had, therefore, been due to puerperal fever.[27]

It seems likely that it was a combination of rising standards of living and the introduction of sulphonamides which led to improvements in the MMR. The Ministry of Health's response to the high MMR had been to expand facilities for hospitalisation at childbirth, a strategy developed mainly in response to pressure from obstetricians, keen to establish their specialism.[28] The policy of hospitalising women at childbirth could in fact spread infections and it distracted attention from women's basic financial needs. Relatively little attention was given to antenatal and postnatal care.

In the late 1920s 15 per cent of women went into hospital to have a baby, by the late 1930s it was 25 per cent. Midwives helped at the birth, although it was not until 1936 that local authorities were required to provide a trained midwife. This meant that in the late 1930s some (mainly rural) areas still had untrained midwives. Common household items were adapted for deliveries at home.[29] At some antenatal clinics women who were recognised as being poorly nourished were urged to enter hospital early, and poor women who had their babies at home were encouraged by the midwife to stay in bed as long as possible, for once mothers got up husbands normally gave up any housework they had been undertaking. Hospital stays were long-drawn-out affairs, for women were kept in bed for ten to fourteen days,[30] and when they finally did get up they were weak, not only from the birth, but also from the long stay in bed.

The pre-war policy of educating mothers in hygiene and baby care continued with the growing band of health visitors who were employed to visit and advise all mothers after the birth of a baby. In practice, visiting targeted the poorest women who viewed the health visitor with a mixture of respect and suspicion. The health visitors were in an awkward position as they were trying to change mothers' attitudes and behaviour in a very personal context; inevitably their influence varied.[31] Their work had little effect on either unmarried mothers who suffered the highest maternal death-rates or their babies who had the worst infant death-rates.

To be unmarried and pregnant was one of life's greatest calamities. Unmarried pregnant women found themselves shunned, isolated and labelled 'delinquent'. The women often tried to conceal their pregnancy for as long as possible because of the stigma and their lack of money; they were, therefore, less likely to attend antenatal clinics than married women, and more likely to work almost up to the birth of the baby. An unmarried mother might have the door slammed in her face by relatives, private landlords and even local authorities, who preferred to offer their council housing to 'respectable' families.[32]

The first attempt to co-ordinate formal provisions for unmarried pregnant women came in 1918 with the founding of the National Council for the Unmarried Mother and her Child which acted as a centre of information and advice, but it did not run Mother and Baby Homes where women went as a last resort. The atmosphere in the Homes varied, but the regime would normally have been a punitive one. Women who went into Public Assistance Institutions (the old workhouse) might be admitted under the 1890 Lunacy Act and deprived normal 'privileges' such as going outside for a walk. If a mother did go out she had to take the baby with her, making it hard to look for work.[33]

As the stigma associated with unmarried motherhood very gradually declined, more women were exposed to the risks of becoming pregnant outside marriage. Evidence about the extent of pre- and extra-marital sex is anecdotal and contradictory, but on balance it suggests that it became more common as the century progressed.[34] One report found 39 per cent of women who had married between 1914 and 1924 had enjoyed pre-marital sex, and roughly one in three women conceived their first child before marriage.[35]

Every year numerous women sought an abortion, putting their lives and their freedom (the penalty for a criminal abortion was much higher than that for rape) at risk. The reasons for these desperate attempts to terminate a pregnancy were complex. First, economic factors could lead a woman (sometimes helped by her husband) to seek an abortion: poverty and an unemployed husband could mean that the wife was the sole breadwinner. Too little money coming into the home might well mean that the woman suffered from poor nourishment. Bad housing, overcrowding or new houses with high rents all acted as a deterrent to having another child. A relatively well-off couple might feel that another mouth to feed would lower their standard of living. Second, women feared for their health, especially if a previous pregnancy had been a difficult one. Third, for an unmarried woman to have a baby brought condemnation, ostracism and a multitude of practical problems, from which the only escape was marriage or an abortion.[36] The extent to which women resorted to an abortion is hard to gauge. Elizabeth Roberts suggests that abortion was relatively uncommon, but Jane Lewis maintains it was a widespread practice.[37]

Procuring an abortion was relatively easy. Advertisements for abortions could be found by leafing through a newspaper, where they were usually discreetly described as potions or pills 'to restore regularity' or to 'remove obstructions'.[38] Some chemists sold prepared medicines for 'female irregularities', otherwise drugs could be bought individually and mixed at home.[39] The definition of an abortion remained vague, and indeed many women did not regard 'bringing on a period' as an abortion.[40] Abortionists were usually lower middle-class or working-class older married women.[41]

In the late 1930s abortion became a matter of public anxiety, largely because it was a common cause of maternal death. In 1934, for instance, 13 per cent of maternal deaths resulted from an abortion. Official concern was also linked to fears about the falling birth-rate. In 1934 the Women's Co-operative Guild spoke out for legalised abortion; the following year a British Medical Association (BMA) Committee on abortion recommended legalisation in cases of rape or danger to the physical or mental health of the mother, and in 1936 the Abortion Law Reform Association was founded by a small group of middle-class women who campaigned to make available to poor women what money could already buy.[42]

The crude birth-rate shows that more people were limiting the size of their families, and this was achieved both by practising birth control and terminating pregnancies. Contraceptives could be obtained from birth control clinics, rubber shops and barbers; they could also be bought by mail-order. In the 1920s and 1930s the main methods of birth control were abstinence, *coitus interruptus*, condoms, or the cap.[43]

The birth-rate, which had long been falling among the middle class, was also declining among the working class. J.A. and O. Banks argued that a desire for smaller families and knowledge about how this was achieved filtered down from the middle class to the working class. However, both Diana Gittins and Elizabeth Roberts have challenged this view, arguing that the working class spread information among themselves. Roberts believes information was obtained from peer groups, friends, relatives and workmates, although the last of these groups was least likely to discuss contraception.[44] Gittins, however, argues that the workplace was the main arena for working-class women to pick up information about family limitation. As employment patterns changed and more working-class girls and women found work in factories, they learnt about contraception from older married workmates. In the 1930s formal contraceptive advice was still virtually non-existent for most working-class women.[45]

Birth control was a divisive issue for women's organisations. Women could be split as much over tactics as the principle involved in pressing for birth control advice to be made widely available. Some women, such as Marion Phillips, herself a doctor and women's organiser in the Labour Party, favoured a softly-softly approach for fear of splitting the party (which relied heavily on Roman Catholic support). Other women, most notably Dora Russell, another active member of the Party, wanted to attack the issue head on, and she argued publicly that better maternity care and contraception should go hand-in-hand. Her campaign slogan 'It is four times as dangerous to bear a child as to work in a mine, and mining is men's most dangerous trade', underlined the need for contraception in order to improve women's health.[46]

From the end of the First World War Marie Stopes campaigned for birth control information to be made easily available. In March 1918 she published *Married Love* which was devoted largely to discussing how women could enjoy sex. A few months later *Wise Parenthood* appeared, providing a practical, although somewhat idiosyncratic, guide to various contraceptive methods. Both books sold like hot cakes. They helped to move the subject of contraception from a very private world to the public domain.[47] In 1921 Stopes opened the first birth control clinic in London. Consultations were free and contraceptives were sold at cost price, except to women who could not afford to pay for them, and they received them free. Stopes helped to make the subject of contraception respectable, but it was a slow and tortuous process. Clinics opened around the country at a snail's pace, frequently in the teeth of intense and violent opposition. Often they were run on a shoe-string with staff giving their services free. Providing a 'cover' for a birth control clinic, such as combining it with weighing babies and handing out clothes could be important, especially in areas where the Roman Catholic Church put the fear of God into women, and attacked the clinics.[48] In 1930 the Government agreed that local authorities could provide birth control information to married women in poor health whose condition would be made worse by a further pregnancy – a measure which could always be justified on the grounds that it was protecting the quality of the race, as sickly women were likely to produce sickly children. Stopes's motives remain controversial: some see her primarily as a eugenicist,[49] while others have emphasised her concern to relieve the suffering of poor women by making reliable contraceptives accessible to them. Stopes has not only been criticised for advocating birth control on eugenicist grounds, but also for appearing out of touch with the practicalities of working-class life.[50]

More extensive birth control was opposed because of fears that the population was in terminal decline. Pleasure without procreation was thought to be immoral for women, and to encourage their infidelity; it also threatened the man's domination in the home. The medical profession was often ignorant on the subject. Unsubstantiated claims were made about the harmful side-effects of contraception, such as sterility and mental illness, and the positive gains for women's health of fewer unwelcome pregnancies were downplayed.[51]

Smaller families were attractive for a number of reasons: a higher standard of living was only possible if there were fewer mouths to feed; children could only be showered with love and affection if there was enough time to devote to each child, and this was much easier to achieve in smaller families. The lower middle class and upper working class were increasingly concerned about their children's education. In the 1930s 14 per cent of all eleven-year-olds went to secondary school and only 7 per cent had a free place. Even a free place often proved a great financial strain.[52] Moreover, expectations were rising, and families sought more than the basic struggle for existence: they also wanted some relaxation, and the opportunity to enjoy it.

HEALTH AND LEISURE

From the end of the First World War, with shorter hours of work in industry, there was more leisure time, especially for men and to a lesser extent for women too. After industrial negotiations in 1919 reduced the working week to forty-eight hours it was rare for workers to be employed beyond the legal limit of fifty-four hours a week. Although there was a voluntary trend towards shorter hours of work, serious infringements of the law still occurred.[53] A large proportion of offences related to the illegal employment of young people.

Leisure was now seen as a right to which everyone was entitled. Women and men found an escape in dance-halls and the cinema. Football continued in popularity, but in the early 1930s attendance figures fell in those areas worst hit by the depression: not everyone had the opportunity to forget their troubles even for one afternoon a week.[54] Participatory sports flourished.

In the immediate post-war years physical exercise for women was still controversial. The pervasive nineteenth-century argument that physical exercise made women sterile, aggressive, asexual, and gave them bad nerves, heart trouble and filthy minds was still advanced,[55] but such views soon fell out of fashion. There was no radical break with the past, however, as women's healthy physical activities were linked with contemporary notions of femininity and beauty.

Voluntary organisations, rather than the state, organised most sporting and recreational activities. The Boy Scout and Girl Guide movements, begun before the First World War, the Youth Hostel Association formed in 1930, and the Ramblers Association all promoted fresh air, exercise and outdoor pursuits for both sexes. Camping and hiking were part and parcel of the 1930s fitness craze and a particularly popular holiday activity. In the 1930s the Women's League of Health and Beauty transformed 'keep fit' exercises for women into a national craze. The League, which boasted 100,000 members by 1939, aimed to make women better wives and mothers. For its members, the League was a source of great fun and friendship. In 1937 the Government reinforced these popular activities by passing the Physical Training and Recreation Act. The aim of the Act was to establish local recreational facilities, such as sports grounds, around the country. Until the late 1930s, however, the development of sport was held back by a lack of playing fields in many areas, and the inability of poor parents to afford sports clothes and equipment for their children.[56]

More leisure time was accompanied by a growth in the number of families enjoying an annual holiday. Throughout the 1920s and 1930s more and more workers began to enjoy holidays with pay until suddenly in the late 1930s a whole host of employers offered their employees paid holidays in an effort to avoid state intervention. The employers' tactic failed and in 1938 the Holidays with Pay Act was passed. By the late 1930s one in three of the population enjoyed a week away from home every year. In 1938 the Industrial Welfare Society (IWS) commented 'holidays are now part of the standard of living aimed at by nearly everyone'.[57] Families who could not afford an annual holiday, or even day trips, felt bitterly disappointed.[58]

IN AND OUT OF WORK

For the majority of workers, who were not employed in large firms or firms based in the south of England, standards of health and safety remained Victorian, and close to those laid down in the 1901 Factory and Workshop Act. In the potteries, for example, illness clouded people's lives and sent them to an early grave. The most dangerous jobs were taken by those most desperate for the money or living in an area where there was no other form of employment.[59]

Standards of cleanliness in factories were notoriously low. Many floors were dirty, and in some engineering and joinery works the floors were hardly ever cleaned unless it became necessary for production purposes. Floors were so badly constructed or maintained that they were extremely difficult to keep clean.[60] Noise, bad light and lack of space continued to plague British industry.[61]

During the depression some people's working conditions worsened. In the early 1930s it was claimed that conditions in Lancashire cotton mills were worse than within living memory. Workers breathed an atmosphere of cotton dust and dirt, and this had a serious effect on health, especially for those working in preparatory processes where raw cotton was broken up, cleaned and carded. The local MOH reported a prevalence of respiratory diseases such as bronchitis and catarrhal conditions, and rheumatism. Noise and the risk of accidents were intensified by the speeding-up of processes, the use of low-quality materials, technical economies and the badgering of workers. In the 1930s the new industries tended to recruit women rather than men to work on tedious, repetitive, machine-paced and unskilled assembly line jobs where they had little control over their work.[62]

No major legislative changes were introduced until the 1937 Factory Act was passed which embraced many more workers than previously and raised standards of safety, health and welfare. Most governmental activities in the 1920s and 1930s (in contrast to the pre-war years) tended to emphasise general safety, health and welfare, rather than particular industrial diseases. The main emphasis was on light, ventilation, noise, cleanliness, accidents (particularly those associated with young people and new processes), machinery and methods, and welfare facilities, such as canteens.

During the inter-war years it became increasingly common for large, well-organised and successful firms to offer their workers welfare services in which health and medical provisions played an important part. Employees might enjoy medical care, youth clubs, recreational facilities and canteens, along with pensions and holidays with pay. Management, particularly in the growing number of large firms which found it hard to communicate on a personal level with the workforce, used welfare to promote good industrial relations and a disciplined workforce. A variety of new, employer-orientated organisations, such as the IWS, National Institute of Industrial Psychology, and Institute of Labour Management, promoted industrial medicine as a part of industrial welfare. The most direct application of industrial medicine lay with the appointment of works' doctors, but by the outbreak of the Second World War there were still only about sixty of them.

It has been claimed that in the 1920s the unemployed would have been significantly worse off than those in work because the cost of living and wages for those in work were relatively high.[63] In contrast, the depression of the 1930s was often blamed for the poor health of those in work as well as the unemployed. Low incomes were related to unemployment. Those on low wages and in irregular employment might be better off on benefits.[64]

Poor working conditions, short-time working, short periods of unemployment, shadow and unemployment all lowered resistance to physical and mental illness. The least fit workers were more likely to lose their jobs and their poor health made them more vulnerable to the stresses and strains associated with unemployment. Moreover, the ill-effects of work might not show up until a period of unemployment. Unemployment, as Noel Whiteside has pointed out, both caused ill health and revealed it.[65]

The specific effects of unemployment on standards of health are hard to disentangle from all the other influences on poor people's health. Despite the hazards of work and the poverty associated with low wages, the unemployed appear to have carried an extra burden. Although poverty could be as great for those on the margins of the labour market, the longer someone was out of work the harder it became to maintain social contacts and the previous standard of living. In 1938 the Pilgrim Trust did not think that poverty was confined to the unemployed, but unemployment made the poverty more acute. In Manchester and Salford unemployed men became a race apart, as they found it hard to scrape together the money to go to the pub, a football match or the cinema.[66]

Most writers point to the effects of unemployment on people's sense of well-being and their mental state. The Pilgrim Trust suggested that the unemployed became more demoralised by their slum housing than those in work. H.L. Beales and R.S. Lambert in *Memoirs of the Unemployed* (1934) concentrated on the psychological effects of unemployment, and E. Wight Bakke in *The Unemployed Man* (1933) wrote about the effects of unemployment insurance on the unemployed. He concluded that the scheme alleviated the worst physical effects of unemployment but it could not relieve 'mental and moral fatigue and discouragement'.[67] Indeed, the way the system was administered was humiliating, and this in itself was a strain. The family Means Test took away self-respect and forced members of a family to be beholden to each other, whether they wanted to be or not.

The diets of the unemployed were worse than those in work, which suggests that the physical health of the unemployed was also worse. The unemployed certainly complained of feeling unwell more frequently than those in work; this may have been due to a deterioration in health or to the fact that they had more time to dwell on their illnesses and, because they were depressed, to be worse affected by physical ill health.[68]

Unemployed women were often in poor health, although their plight has gone largely unrecognised as contemporaries and historians have tended to focus on the ill-effects of unemployment on the unemployed man and his family. A study of unemployment published in 1938 by the Pilgrim Trust is a rare exception. It found that the impact of unemployment on men and women was in certain respects similar. In Blackburn unemployed women with young children missed their workmates; the long-term unemployed suffered physical and mental strain, and they lost confidence in their own ability to hold down a job in the future. One difference between the unemployed men and women was that the latter still had plenty to do, looking after children and husbands.[69]

Violet Markham, the only woman member of the Unemployment Assistance Board (UAB), undertook a study of the ill-effects of unemployment on older women. Her account is impressionistic and shot through with her own prejudices, but she does provide evidence for a hidden problem, while at the same time demonstrating that members of the UAB were aware of the poor health of the unemployed. Markham described how the women who had seen better days were often anchored with their bits of furniture salvaged from the wreck of past prosperity in a room, the rent of which was disproportionately high in relation to their income. The health of the older women interviewed was very poor. A large number of UAB applicants suffered from rheumatism, bronchitis, nerves, bad eyes, bad teeth and a host of minor ailments. Some had had serious operations from which, owing to the absence of aftercare, they had never made a complete recovery. It was the exception, not the rule, to hear a woman say that her health was good. The strain of looking after sick or elderly relatives and previously arduous working conditions, combined with low wages all contributed to poor health. Anxiety about the future preyed on their minds and as the weeks and months passed by, the futile task of registering at the Labour Exchange and seeking illusory jobs took the heart out of them. Many had lost all social contacts and were incredibly lonely. Nervous strain was common, due to unemployment, unsatisfactory home conditions and insufficient food.[70]

Mothers' diets were thought to be particularly hard hit by the depression. Organisers of a special clinic for delicate children in the East End of London feared that the children's health was being maintained at the expense of the diet and health of the mothers, for whom there was a definite deterioration in health.[71]

In the 1930s the impact of nutrition on health became a hotly debated issue. One side, which claimed to be non-political and scientific and whose findings were seized upon by the bulk of government supporters, claimed that individual failing, rather than lack of food, accounted for poor nutrition. In 1936 one Conservative MP taunted the Opposition by asserting that much ill health resulted from over-eating or a bad choice of food. He maintained that 'Hunger to a certain extent is a very good thing.' He went on to criticise school milk and school dinners: 'Because of the State provision, less is provided by bad or careless parents at home.'[72]

As the 1930s progressed, an impressive bank of evidence was collected to support the argument that poor nutrition, due to a lack of money, was a serious problem. G.C.M. M'Gonigle and J. Kirby in *Poverty and Public Health* (1936) focused on the effect that poor diets were having on the incidence of rickets and tooth decay. M'Gonigle argued that there was a very high incidence of partially unrecorded physical defects due to sub-nutrition which in turn was caused by poverty.[73] The importance of nutrition and the difficulty of obtaining an adequate diet on a low income was also taken up by J. Boyd-Orr in *Food, Health and Income* (1936), which claimed that over 50 per cent of the population's diets were inadequate for good health. Throughout the 1930s the BMA remained at the centre of the row over nutrition as its standard was used in a series of local studies to establish the prevalence of malnutrition. A number of other writers, relying on more anecdotal evidence, recognised the link between poverty and ill health. Ellen Wilkinson in *The Town that was Murdered* (1939) made the connection between housing, health and poverty.

The central government view, which blamed ill health largely on bad habits, ignorance and fecklessness, was increasingly challenged in the inter-war years. Critics of the Government blamed ill health on structural factors, such as low incomes, bad housing and unemployment. In Parliament, the Government was attacked for the poor nutrition of substantial sections of the population, in particular women and children: greater purchasing power through cheaper food and higher wages was needed, not more education about nutrition.[74] The debate has recently been taken up again and is focused around two questions. First, how reliable were the official statistics used during the 1930s to support various governments' claims that health was improving? Second, how should the health reports be interpreted?

Charles Webster has convincingly demonstrated that a number of the optimistic reports of local MOHs which the Government used, notably in a debate in the House of Commons in 1933, were politically inspired. The Chief Medical Officer of Health, Sir George Newman, picked out MOHs' positive comments about the health of schoolchildren, and made a point of offering the most optimistic interpretation of local reports.[75] Further, Webster is critical of the way in which the Ministry of Health produced impressive statistics based on cursory examinations of children. Doctors in poor areas were so used to seeing children with rotten teeth, bad eyesight and poor physique that they used a lower yardstick for judging children's health than doctors in more prosperous areas. Moreover, historians can hardly have much faith in the official utterances of Sir George Newman when we now know that in private he wanted the extent of women's ill health to be kept hidden from public scrutiny in order to avoid embarrassment for his department.[76]

Second, there are differing interpretations of various statistics and reports. Babies between the ages of one month and one year are especially vulnerable to infectious diseases and illnesses which can be linked to environmental causes. Hence the post-neonatal (one month to one year) death-rate is often seen as the most sensitive indicator of standards of living and health. Jay Winter goes along with the Ministry of Health's statistics from the 1930s which show a fall in the death-rate of babies. Winter does not claim that the country was full of bonny babies, but he does believe that many were saved from the jaws of death by unemployment insurance and council housing.[77] From the end of the First World War to the beginning of the Second World War mortality figures certainly show an overall improvement. The dark cloud which infectious diseases such as measles, whooping cough, TB, diphtheria and scarlet fever cast over people's lives was lifting.[78] The number of mothers who died in childbirth declined from 4.33 per thousand in 1920 to 2.24 per thousand in 1940 (although most of that improvement occurred in the late 1930s). The IMR declined from 74.9 per thousand in 1921–25 to 56.8 per thousand in 1940.[79]

Charles Webster attacks this broadly optimistic approach mainly on the grounds that improvements in the IMR slowed down in the 1930s, and Britain's IMR declined more slowly than in comparable countries.[80] Further, Webster argues that aggregate data showing no adverse affects of the depression are misleading as they mask pockets of ill health in the depressed areas. For Scottish babies aged one month to one year to have had as good a chance of celebrating their first birthday as babies in the most prosperous areas of the country, or in the healthiest countries their death-rate would have to have been reduced by 75 per cent.[81] Keith Laybourn has shown that death rates in most industrial areas were at least a quarter and sometimes half again the average for the whole of England and Wales. Some prosperous areas had death-rates which were one-fifth below the national average.[82] Differences in IMR closely followed variations in the prosperity of different wards within a city: poor babies had poor life chances. In one city in 1938 the IMR ranged from 16 per thousand to 109 per thousand.[83] Death-rates were disparate long before the depression, but it does seem as if the disparity was widening. According to Webster, class differences in mortality rates were increasing in the inter-war years.[84]

Evidence from the depressed areas indicates that high levels of unemployment retarded improvements, rather than reversed the trend towards better health. Inequalities were rooted in economic disadvantage, therefore, the depression did directly affect standards of health.[85] If it had not been for the impact of the economy on the depressed areas, standards of health could have been much higher. The health services did not compensate for social and economic deprivation.

FORMAL HEALTH SERVICES

In 1919 a Ministry of Health had been created. It embraced a number of health services previously under the Local Government Board and Health Insurance Commission. The Ministry gained responsibility for the health of mothers and children from the Board of Education, and for infant life protection (under the 1908 Children Act) from the Home Office. Health and safety at work remained under the Home Office. The Ministry of Health dealt with a whole range of local authority health services, at one removed.

During the 1920s and 1930s local authorities ran a wide range of facilities, including maternity and infant welfare clinics; VD clinics, TB clinics and sanatoria. They were responsible for environmental health, such as clean food and milk, refuse removal, clean air, river and water pollution, and provisions for the blind. The 1929 Local Government Act abolished the Boards of Guardians and transferred their responsibilities to local authorities, so increasing the power of MOHs as they assumed control over general hospitals. (The limitations of the NHI system have already been mentioned in Chapter 2.) It is hard to generalise about hospital provision, although in crude terms the south of the country and cities were better off than the north and rural areas in terms of numbers of beds and staff. High-quality care was probably to be found in large hospitals in cities where specialist staff were employed.[86]

As in the early years of the century, a wide variation existed in local authority provision; often law enforcement was lax or authorities chose not to exercise their powers at all. Clean air, clean rivers, clean food, cheap milk for schoolchildren and free school meals depended on the attitudes and wealth of each local authority.

The widely held belief that good health was a matter of individual responsibility, habit and behaviour meant that road safety, the health of mothers and children, and healthy and safe working conditions depended on adapting the population to health hazards, rather than removing their cause. The message underpinning safety campaigns was that personal carelessness was the cause of accidents, whether at work, in the home or on the street. The main thrust of the health education campaigns was to emphasise healthy behaviour and the overwhelming importance of cleanliness. Low incomes and social and economic factors which contributed to ill health were largely ignored.

During the 1930s the competitive success of Europe's totalitarian states (demonstrated most dramatically at the 1936 Olympic Games) caused widespread unease. Despite a desire to demonstrate that British democracy did not breed wimps, suggestions that exercise should be compulsory for British youth were firmly rejected in Whitehall where fascist methods were deemed inappropriate for Britain.[87]

The Ministry of Health's and Board of Education's first large-scale educational campaign was launched in the autumn of 1937 by the Prime Minister, Neville Chamberlain. The aim of the campaign was to improve the take-up rate of health services, and to this end leaflets were distributed, posters displayed, films screened and local lectures and exhibitions arranged.[88]

Not everyone accepted that health education was an appropriate strategy for raising standards of health. In Parliament the Government's emphasis on health education and fitness campaigns was questioned. Instead, calls were made for better working conditions, improved nutrition, decent housing, good clothing and a reduction in the MMR.[89]

Sir George Newman, in contrast, laid far less stress on inequalities in standards of health than on an overall improvement in mortality statistics and an expansion of health services. He compared standards of health in the twentieth century with those in the Victorian era, and emphasised improvements in health provision. When the Ministry of Health was set up Newman had warned that its impact would be slow, yet year after year he wrote of its progress. In 1931 even he admitted that there was a range of problems with public health provision, but his attitude towards local authority cuts remained complacent.[90]

In the 1930s the Ministry of Health claimed that there were improvements in standards of health due to improved housing, better working conditions, rising living standards, advances in medical science, improved water supplies, sanitary services, better recreational facilities, open spaces and swimming pools, changes in personal habits and the ever-increasing and improving state health services.[91]

During the 1920s and 1930s the Ministry of Health bombarded the country with a constant stream of self-congratulatory reports. The impression given was of increasing priority for health policy and ever-better services. However, variation in provisions, take-up rates, use of permissive powers and implementation of the law undermines any notion that the Ministry of Health raised the status of health policy or acted as an effective co-ordinating body. The Ministry's greatest efforts went into child and maternal health, which were hardly a success story, although there were tremendous improvements in the IMR. By 1939 under 3 per cent of schoolchildren were eating free school dinners. Enormous local variation meant that those who needed the health services most were more than likely receiving the worst service. The Ministry of Health did not help those families with too little to eat.[92]

To criticise the Ministry requires some kind of assessment of what it might reasonably have been expected to achieve. It would be fair to say that there could have been less manipulation of health reports for public consumption and a greater willingness to accept the authenticity of varying opinions on the impact of poverty on sections of the nation's health, instead of putting forward fallacious 'scientific' evidence in support of various governments' policies. Such an approach might have led to health services more responsive to people's felt and expressed needs, and more in tune with the health problems created by poverty and poor housing. More effort could have been made to remove health hazards rather than adapt individuals to them. It was not, therefore, that public health policy failed solely because it lacked co-ordination, or adequate financing. It was not only a matter of too little, too late, but also of a fundamental flaw in the ideology behind the policy – an ideology of individual and personal responsibility, strong in its emphasis on behavioural modifications, hygiene, fitness and the individual's contribution to the future of the race.

HEALTH, RACE AND ETHNICITY

The pre-war arguments of eugenicists that the race was degenerating continued into the 1920s and 1930s. During the 1920s, however, the medical profession and Eugenics Society all expressed reservations about a policy of sterilisation of the unfit. The medical profession as a whole was split over the desirability of voluntary sterilisation, and even the Eugenics Society was nervous of the legal implications, of the backlash an all-out voluntary sterilisation campaign would provoke, and of the 'freedom' mental defectives would have to spread VD or behave in an anti-social manner if they were let loose in the community.[93] The publication in 1929 of an inter-departmental committee on mental deficiency report (the Wood Report) gave advocates of sterilisation a second wind. Eugenicists played what they hoped was their trump card in arguing that sterilisation was desirable on economic grounds; the country simply could not afford to maintain the socially inadequate. From the late 1920s arguments in favour of sterilisation seemed to gain popularity, and in 1934 the departmental committee on sterilisation, chaired by L.G. Brock of the Board of Trade, recommended voluntary sterilisation. The proposal was never taken up by governments as, according to John Macnicol, those strongly opposed to sterilisation effectively lobbied the Ministry of Health, and anyway the Ministry, which comprised those largely of an environmentalist rather than eugenicist persuasion, was disinclined to believe alarmist predictions about the declining population. Indeed, Macnicol has shown that the eugenicists' influence on policy outcomes was virtually nil, primarily because of the opposition of the labour movement.[94] While eugenicist views may well have had little direct impact on government policies, nevertheless, assumptions about the health of the British race continued to display unpleasant racist overtones.

Throughout the 1920s and 1930s the Irish were the largest ethnic minority in Britain, but it was Jews and Germans who suffered after the passing of the 1919 Aliens' Act. Under the Act many thousands who had lived in Britain for years were deported, often in traumatic circumstances. In the 1920s and early 1930s the small number of black seamen and the children of their relationships with white women were the target of (largely hostile) debates and reaction over their presence in Britain. However, from the mid-1930s, Jewish refugees displaced black people as the focus of unwelcome attention.[95]

During the First World War, black seamen from the Caribbean, West Africa and the Middle East had been engaged on British ships; at the end of the war they found themselves out of work in British ports. They were popularly linked with crime, prostitution and the 'problem' of mixed race (or 'half-caste' as they were known at the time) children. Competition for scarce jobs and black men going out with white women led to vicious attacks and racist abuse. In April and June 1919 race riots flared up in the port cities of Cardiff, Bristol and Liverpool. Black people's homes were ransacked, white girlfriends of black men were abused, black men were beaten up, and in Cardiff three died. Once the riots died down, the quality of life for many of these ex-seamen remained poor as they struggled along in isolation. Paul Rich has argued that the 'coloured alien seamen' issue was not especially significant in terms of the numbers involved, but it did demonstrate ideas about race and empire.[96]

Deeply ingrained prejudices, revolving around the supposed social-sexual threat posed by non-whites, manifested themselves in a near obsession in the popular press, and among academics and social workers, with the children of mixed-race relationships. In 1929 the *Daily Herald* screamed that 'hundreds of half-caste children with vicious tendencies' were 'growing up in Cardiff as the result of black men mating with white women', and dockland cafés run by coloured men of a 'debased and degenerate type' were a rendezvous for 'immoral purposes'.[97]

Links between anthropology and eugenics led to the study of mixed-race children in dockland areas, including Liverpool, where in 1929 the Association for the Welfare of half-caste children (in 1937 renamed the Liverpool Association for the welfare of coloured people) was set up. In 1930 the Association sponsored an investigation into the 'colour problem' in port cities. The investigation's report, written by one Muriel Fletcher, repeated a number of racist myths about sexual relations between blacks and whites, the intelligence of black children and family relationships in black communities. Fletcher portrayed mixed-race children as a social and moral problem; she claimed that such children were no less healthy than other children, but that their intelligence and aptitude were below average. Although the report was roundly criticised in local circles, it was welcomed by John Harris of the Anti-Slavery Society who linked mixed-race marriages with disease, immorality and slums. In 1935 a Report for the British Social Hygiene Council linked immorality, dirt and 'coloured' men, but mixed-race children were now seen more as the victims of their natures, the environment and prejudice against them than as the vicious children of the 1929 *Daily Herald* article.[98] By the mid-1930s the 'problem' of mixed-race children was overshadowed by the 'problem' of Jewish refugees from Nazism.

As with black people, Jews had been subjected to sporadic racist attacks, both physical and verbal, but in the mid-1930s these attacks became more organised in areas such as the East End of London, Leeds and Manchester. There were physical assaults on individual Jews, and attacks on shops and synagogues. Hostility to Jews came not only from gangs of thugs, but from 'respectable' sections of society, which at times even included verbal attacks on new-wave refugees from long-established and prominent British Jews.

The refugees' initial response to their arrival in Britain was one of relief, but they soon faced deep-rooted prejudice from Jews and non-Jews on a number of fronts, making it difficult for them to find housing, work and even insurance cover. Hostility to Jewish refugees was based on two grounds. First, it was claimed that Jews displayed undesirable characteristics, such as aggressiveness, pushiness, arrogance, and a tendency to conspire together to bring about a world economic crisis or to exploit others. (Some claimed that these characteristics were genetic, and could be identified by Jewish physical features). Second, it was argued by the medical profession, and others, that Jewish refugees aggravated the job shortage. The BMA set up a committee to advise the Home Secretary on the entry of Jewish doctors, which in 1938 preened itself on having strictly curbed the number of refugee doctors allowed into the country. Each applicant was carefully scrutinised and forced to undertake two years clinical study before practising.[99]

Even those Jews who were not newly arrived experienced prejudice from the medical profession. Some medical schools were disinclined to accept Jewish students, although there is evidence of medical schools making allowances for religious differences.[100] A few newly qualified Jewish doctors found work at the London Jewish hospital.[101]

Greater compassion for the victims of fascism was generated for those far removed from Britain's shores. In 1936 the outbreak of war in Spain prompted a broad cross-section of British society (from Communists to Conservatives, but with the Women's Co-operative Guild and women's sections of the Labour Party to the fore) to collect milk, clothes, medical aid and food for Republican victims of fascism. Enormous support was aroused for 4,000 refugee Basque children who arrived in England, even though gossip circulated about the bad behaviour and manners of the children which was to be echoed a couple of years later when urban British children were evacuated. By the summer of 1937 the London-based Spanish Medical Aid Committee had sent 126 nurses, doctors and relief workers to Spain. Others went to Spain with organisations such as the Quakers and Independent Labour Party. They went for a mixture of political and compassionate reasons, and paid a high price in deaths, injuries and illness. (There were no British doctors or nurses working on Franco's side.)[102]

The medical lessons learned in Spain were soon to be applied to Britain's war effort. During the Spanish Civil War advances were made in the treatment of wounds and fractures. Dr Janet Vaughan spent some time in Spain where blood transfusion services were developing. Back in Britain she and her colleagues worked on the collection, storage and administration of donated blood. Their ideas were incorporated into the civil defence schemes of a number of London boroughs. At first it was difficult for health workers who had been in Spain to arouse governmental interest in the lessons they had learned, but when war broke out, their expertise was in sudden demand.[103]

In 1939, as the country braced itself for war, men, women and children were better fitted to withstand the deprivations and strains of war than their parents and grandparents had been a generation earlier. Mortality statistics made hopeful reading. Life had become less arduous as standards of housing and working conditions rose; childhood tragedies had lessened; childbirth was safer; there were fewer mouths to feed in each family, and more leisure time. Between 1921 and 1937 the percentage of the Gross

National Product dedicated to the health services rose from 1.1 per cent to 1.8 per cent.[104]

However, local authority services, hospitals and birth control clinics were unevenly and thinly spread. Glaring disparities remained within and between families, classes, regions and ethnic groups. There were still severe stigmas attached to those suffering the misfortune of unemployment, unmarried motherhood or refugee status. The selectivity and differential treatment of government services was supposedly blown to smithereens by the people's war, when universal services developed. The following chapter looks at whether this was a myth or reality.

NOTES

1. **Chamberlain M.** 1981 *Old wives' tales: Their history, remedy and spells*. Virago, pp. 132–4; **Faley J.** 1990 *Up oor close: Memories of domestic life in Glasgow tenements, 1910–45*. White Cockade, pp. 150, 156–7.
2. Ibid. p. 136; Ibid. p. 153.
3. Stalybridge Oral History archive 111 Alice Ollerenshaw b. 1925.
4. **Clarke J., Critcher C., Johnson R.** 1979 *Working-class culture: Studies in history and theory*. Hutchinson, pp. 126–9; **East End History Project** 1985 *Them were the days . . . or were they? Life in Sunderland's East End in the 1930s*. Community Art project, Sunderland, pp. 12–13; **Jewish women in London group** 1989 *Generations of memories: Voices of Jewish women*. The Women's Press, pp. 54–6; Stalybridge Public Library, Oral History Archive 093. Elizabeth King born c. First World War.
5. **Petty C.** 1985 The Medical Research Council's inter-war dietary surveys. *Society for the Social History of Medicine Bulletin* **37:** 76–8.
6. **Douglas C., McKinlay P.** 1935 *Report on maternal morbidity and mortality in Scotland*. Department of Health for Scotland, HMSO, pp. 15, 23–4.
7. Annual Report for 1931 on the health of Bethnal Green, p. 35.
8. **Webster C.** 1982 Healthy or hungry thirties? *History Workshop Journal* **13:** 112.
9. **Spring Rice M.** 1981 *Working-class wives: Their health and conditions*. Virago, pp. 43, 20–1, 29, 72, 207–8.
10. Medical Officer of Health for Liverpool Annual Report for 1931, pp. 100–3.
11. **Beddoe D.** 1989 *Back to home and duty: Women between the wars, 1918–39*. Pandora, p. 92.
12. Ibid. p. 90; **Manchester women's history group** 1986 Ideology in bricks and mortar – Women's housing in Manchester between the wars. *North West Labour History* **12:** 35.
13. Annual Report for 1925 on the Health of Bethnal Green, p. 18.

14. Beddoe D. *Back to home and duty.* p. 97; **Davidoff L.** 1990 The family in Britain. In **Thompson F. L. M.** *The Cambridge social history of Britain, 1750–1950 vol. 2 People and their environment.* Cambridge University Press, p. 123; Manchester women's history group, Ideology in bricks and mortar. *North West Labour History* **12:** 32; **M'Gonigle G. C. M., Kirby J.** 1936 *Poverty and public health.* Victor Gollancz, pp. 108–29; Annual report for 1925 on the health of Bethnal Green, p. 18.
15. **Roberts E.** 1986 Women's strategies, 1890–1940. In **Lewis J.** (ed) *Labour and love: Women's experiences of home and family, 1850–1940.* Basil Blackwell, pp. 225–44.
16. Richard Wall's evidence quoted in Davidoff L. *The family in Britain.* p. 124.
17. HC Deb. 1936 vol. 314 col. 1300 James Griffiths 8 July.
18. HC Deb. 1933 vol. 280 col. 657 Hilton Young 7 July.
19. **Davies A.** 1992 *Leisure, gender and poverty: Working-class culture in Salford and Manchester, 1900–39.* Open University Press, p. 65.
20. **Ayers P., Lambertz J.** 1986 Marriage relations, money and domestic violence in working-class Liverpool, 1919–39. In Lewis J. (ed) *Labour and love: Women's experience of home and family, 1850–1940.* Basil Blackwell, pp. 208–9; **Clark H., Ineson A., Moreton G., Sim J.** 1989 Oral history and reminiscence in Lothian *Oral History* **17:** 39; East End History Project *Them were the days . . . or were they?* p. 14; **Lambertz J.** 1990 Feminists and the politics of wife-beating. In **Smith H.** (ed) *British feminism in the twentieth century.* Edward Elgar, pp. 25–6, 32, 36–7; **Sarsby J.** 1988 *Missuses and mouldrunners: An oral history of women pottery-workers at work and at home.* Open University Press, pp. 102–5.
21. **Holtby W.** 1934 *Women.* Bodley Head, pp. 166–8.
22. **Roberts E.** 1984 *A woman's place: An oral history of working-class women, 1890–1940.* Basil Blackwell, p. 110.
23. **Humphries S., Mack J., Perks R.** 1988 *A century of childhood. Sidgwick and Jackson, p. 158.*
24. *Webster C. Healthy or hungry thirties? History Workshop Journal* **13:** 117.
25. **Cole G. D. H., Cole M. I.** 1937 *The condition of Britain.* Victor Gollancz, pp. 92–9.
26. **Mitchell M.** 1985 The effects of unemployment on the social conditions of women and children in the 1930s. *History Workshop Journal* **19:** 115.
27. **Loudon I.** 1988 Maternal mortality: 1880–1950. Some regional and international comparisons. *Social History of Medicine* **1:** 199.
28. **Lewis J.** 1980 *The politics of motherhood: Child and maternal welfare in England 1900–1939.* Croom Helm, p. 120.
29. Ibid.; **Richardson R., Chamberlain M.** 1983 Life and death *Oral History* **11:** 39.
30. Stalybridge Public Library Oral history archive. Tape no. 1009 Rose Foley, trained as a midwife 1933.
31. **Peretz E.** 1989 The professionalisation of childcare *Oral History* **17:** 22.
32. **Brookes B.** 1986 Women and reproduction, 1860–1939. In Lewis J.

(ed) *Labour and love: Women's experiences of home and family, 1850–1940*. Basil Blackwell, p. 151.

33. **Ferguson S., Fitzgerald H.** 1954 *Studies in the social services*. HMSO and Longman, pp. 81–4.
34. **Humphries S.** 1988 *A secret world of sex Forbidden fruit: The British experience 1900–1950*. Sidgwick and Jackson. Gives the impression that extra-marital sex was more widespread than Roberts E. *A woman's place: An oral history of working-class women, 1890–1940*.
35. **Weeks J.** 1981 *Sex, politics and society: The regulation of sexuality before 1800*. Longman, p. 209.
36. **Ministry of Health and Home Office** 1939 *Report of the inter-departmental committee on abortion*. HMSO, pp. 37–9.
37. Roberts E. *A woman's place*. p. 100; Lewis J. *The politics of motherhood*. p. 199.
38. **Brookes B.** 1983 The illegal operation: Abortion 1918–39. In London feminist history group *The sexual dynamics of history: Men's power, women's resistance*. Pluto Press, p. 167.
39. Chamberlain M. *Old wives' tales: Their history, remedy and spells*. p. 122.
40. Brookes B. The illegal operation. p. 165.
41. Chamberlain M. *Old wives' tales*. p. 120.
42. **Oakley A.** 1986 *The captured womb: A history of the medical care of pregnant women*. Basil Blackwell, p. 91; Brookes B. The illegal operation. p. 173.
43. Lewis J. *The politics of motherhood*. p. 203.
44. Roberts E. *A woman's place*. p. 95.
45. **Gittins D.** 1975 Married life and birth control between the wars *Oral History* **3**: 55–6; Spring Rice M. *Working-class wives*. p. 44.
46. **Thane P.** 1990 The women of the British Labour Party and feminism, 1906–45. In Smith H. (ed) *British feminism in the twentieth century*. Edward Elgar, pp. 137–8.
47. **Stopes M.** 1918 *Married Love*. Putnam & Co.; **Stopes M.** 1918 *Wise parenthood*. Putnam & Co.
48. National Sound Archive BBC2 'Yesterday's Witness' 14 July 1982 BIRS 6084.
49. **Beddoe D.** 1989 *Back to home and duty: Women between the wars, 1918–39*. Pandora, p. 107.
50. See for example her preference for the cap over the condom. Stopes M. *Wise parenthood* (23rd edn) pp. 67–8.
51. **Leathard A.** 1980 *The fight for family planning: The development of family planning services in Britain, 1921–74*. Macmillan, pp. 1–2.
52. Gittins D. Married life and birth control between the wars *Oral History* **3**: 63.
53. PP 1924 vol. IX Annual Report of the Chief Inspector of Factories for 1923, p. 40.
54. **Davies A.** 1992 *Leisure, gender and poverty: Working-class culture in Salford and Manchester, 1900–39*. Open University Press, p. 44. Lack of money meant cutting back on the cinema as well.
55. **Fletcher S.** 1984 *Women first: The female tradition in English physical education 1880–1980*. Athlone Press, pp. 74–5.

56. **Welshman J.** 1988 The school medical service in England and Wales, 1907–1939. D Phil Oxford, pp. 211, 216, 234; **Matthews J. J.** 1990 They had such a lot a fun: The Women's League of Health and Beauty. *History Workshop Journal* **30:** 23–5, 28, 47.
57. **Walvin J.** 1978 *Leisure and society, 1830–1950.* Longman, pp. 134–43.
58. Davies A. *Leisure, gender and poverty.* p. 43.
59. Sarsby J. *Missuses and mouldrunners: women pottery workers at work and at home.* Open University Press, pp. 66, 106.
60. PP 1922 vol. VII Annual Report of the Chief Inspector of Factories for 1921, p. 55.
61. **Levinson M.** 1946 *The trouble with yesterday.* Rich and Cowan, pp. 185–6; **Dobbs S.** 1928 *The clothing workers of Great Britain.* George Routledge and Sons, p. 199.
62. **Glucksmann M.** 1990 *Women assemble: Women workers and the new industries in inter-war Britain.* Routledge, pp. 3–4.
63. See for instance, **Nicholas K.** 1986 *The social effects of unemployment on Teeside.* Manchester University Press, p. 52.
64. **Constantine S.** 1980 *Unemployment in Britain between the wars.* Longman, pp. 29–30.
65. **Whiteside N.** 1987 Counting the cost: Sickness and disability among working people in an era of industrial recession, 1920–39. *Economic History Review* 2nd series **40:** 240, 245.
66. Davies A. *Leisure, gender and poverty.* p. 43.
67. **Wight Bakke E.** 1933 *The unemployed man: A social study.* Nisbet and Co., p. 251.
68. **Boyd-Orr J.** 1936 *Food, health and income.* Macmillan; **Wilkinson E.** 1939 *The town that was murdered: The life story of Jarrow.* Victor Gollancz; **Beales H. L., Lambert R. S.** 1934 *Memoirs of the unemployed.* Victor Gollancz; Wight Bakke E. *The unemployed man. p. 251;* **The Pilgrim Trust** 1938 *Men without work.* Cambridge University Press, p. 263; Constantine S. *Unemployment in Britain between the wars.* pp. 27, 31, 34, 36, 39–40; Davies A. *Leisure, gender and poverty.* p. 43.
69. The Pilgrim Trust *Men without work.* pp. 232–41.
70. **Jones H.** 1993 *A liberal feminist? The papers and correspondence of Violet Markham, 1896–1953.* The Historians' Press 31 May 1937 UAB memorandum on training for older women in London.
71. Annual Report for 1932 on the health of Bethnal Green, pp. 52–3; see also references cited in Constantine S. *Unemployment in Britain between the wars.* p. 31.
72. HC Deb 1936 vol. 317 col. 157 Sir F. Fremantle 4 November.
73. M'Gonigle G., Kirby J. *Poverty and public health.* pp. 63–76.
74. HC Deb 1936 vol. 317 col. 453 Duncan-Sandys 6 November.
75. Webster C. Healthy or hungry thirties? *History Workshop Journal* **13:** 115, 119, 123 and *passim*; see too Celia Petty's comments mentioned earlier.
76. Ibid. 118, 123; **Webster C.** 1983 The health of the school child during the Depression. In **Parry N., McNair D.** (eds) *The fitness of the nation: Physical and health education in the nineteenth and twentieth centuries.* History of Education Society, Leicester, p. 80.

77. **Winter J.** 1983 Unemployment, nutrition and infant mortality in Britain, 1920–50. In **Winter J.** (ed) *The working class in modern British history: Essays in honour of Henry Pelling.* Cambridge University Press, p. 252. See also **Winter J.** 1977 The impact of the First World War on civilian health in Britain *Economic History Review* **30:** 487–503; **Winter J.** 1979 Infant mortality, maternal mortality and public health in Britain in the 1930s *Journal of European Economic History* **8:** 439–62.

78. For figures see **Stevenson J.** 1984 *British society 1914–45.* Penguin, p. 204.

79. **Butler J., Vaile M.** 1984 *Health and health services: An introduction to health care in Britain.* Routledge & Kegan Paul, p. 34.

80. Webster C. Healthy or hungry thirties? *History Workshop Journal* **13:** 115, 123 and *passim.*

81. Ibid. 124.

82. **Laybourn K.** 1990 *Britain on the breadline: A social and political history of Britain between the wars.* Alan Sutton, p. 61.

83. Annual Report for 1938 on the health of Plymouth, p. 6.

84. Webster C. Healthy or hungry thirties? *History Workshop Journal* **13:** 116.

85. **Nicholas K.** 1986 *The social effects of unemployment on Teeside.* Manchester University Press, p. 103 and *passim*; Webster C. Healthy or hungry thirties? *History Workshop Journal* **13:** 125; Mitchell M. The effects of unemployment on the social condition of women and children in the 1930s. *History Workshop Journal* **19:** 107.

86. **Powell M.** 1992 Hospital provision before the National Health Service: A geographical study of the 1945 hospital survey. *Social History of Medicine* **5:** 503.

87. **Grant M.** 1990 The national health campaigns of 1937–8. In **Fraser D.** (ed) *Cities, class and communication: Essays in honour of Asa Briggs.* Harvester Wheatsheaf, pp. 217–33.

88. PP 1937–38 vol. XI Annual Report of the Ministry of Health for 1937–38, p. 2.

89. HC Deb 1936 vol. 317 col. 401 Arthur Greenwood 6 November; HC Deb vol. 320 col. 638 11 February 1937 **J. R. Clynes;** HC Deb vol. 320 col. 664 11 February 1937 Willie Brooke.

90. PP 1931–32 vol. X 13th Annual Report of the Ministry of Health 1931–32, p. 45.

91. PP 1936–37 vol. X 18th Annual Report of the Ministry of Health for 1936–37, pp. viii–ix.

92. **Webster C.** 1985 Health, welfare and unemployment during the depression *Past and Present* **109:** 214, 218–9; Webster C. 1983 The health of the school child during the Depression. In Parry N., McNair D. (eds) *The fitness of the nation: Physical and health education in the nineteenth and twentieth centuries.* History of Education Society, Leicester, p. 77.

93. **Jones G.** 1986 *Social hygiene in twentieth-century Britain.* Croom Helm, pp. 88–91.

94. **Macnicol J.** 1980 *The movement for family allowances, 1918–45: A study in social policy development.* Heinemann, pp. 90–1; **Macnicol J.**

1989 Eugenics and the campaign for voluntary sterilisation in Britain between the wars *Journal of the Social History of Medicine* **2:** 147–69.

95. **Holmes C.** 1988 *John Bull's island: Immigration and British society, 1871–1971.* Macmillan, pp. 119, 156 and *passim*; **Cesarani D.** 1987 Anti-alienism in England after the First World War *Immigrants and Minorities* **6:** 5–15.

96. Holmes C. *John Bull's island.* p. 159; **Law I., Henfrey J.** 1981 *History of race and racism in Liverpool, 1660–1950.* Merseyside Community Relations Council, p. 30; **Rich P.** 1990 *Race and empire in British politics.* Cambridge University Press, pp. 120–1; **Walvin J.** 1973 *Black and white: The negro and English society, 1555–1945.* Allen Lane, pp. 206–7.

97. Quoted in Rich P. *Race and empire in British politics.* p. 131; Holmes C. *John Bull's island.* p. 159.

98. Law I., Henfrey J. *A history of race and racism in Liverpool.* p. 31; Rich P. *Race and empire in British politics.* pp. 133–9; **Fletcher M. E.** 1930 Report on an investigation into the colour problem in Liverpool and other ports. Liverpool Association for the welfare of half-caste children.

99. **Hirschfeld G.** 1984 *Exile in Great Britain: Refugees from Hitler's Germany.* Berg, p. 12; **Holmes C.** 1979 *Anti-semitism in British society, 1876–1939.* Edward Arnold, p. 206; Holmes C. *John Bull's Island.* pp. 126, 144; **Lebzelter G.** 1978 *Political anti-semitism in England, 1918–39.* Macmillan, pp. 30–45; **Lipman V.** 1990 *A history of the Jews in Britain since 1858.* Leicester University Press, pp. 197, 215. For further evidence of anti-semitism in the medical world see **Honigsbaum F.** 1979 *The division in British medicine: A history of the separation of general practice from hospital care, 1911–68.* St Martin's Press, New York, pp. 169, 275–8.

100. National Sound Archive C525/78/1–2 Isaac (Ian) Gordon, born 1906.

101. National Sound Archive C525/77 Israel Prieskel, born 1907.

102. **Fyrth J.** 1986 *The signal was Spain: The Aid Spain movement in Britain, 1936–39.* Lawrence and Wishart, pp. 22–3, 80, 137–8, 158–80, 204, 218–40, 243–4, 256, 260–1, 276.

103. Ibid. pp. 140–56; **Fyrth J., Alexander S.** 1991 *Women's voices from the Spanish Civil War.* Lawrence and Wishart, pp. 68–70.

104. These estimates are taken from **Webster C.** 1990 Conflict and consensus: Explaining the British health services. *Twentieth-century British history* **1:** 142.

Chapter 5
THE PEOPLE'S HEALTH: 1939–45

WARFARE AND WELFARE

According to popular memory and most historical studies, the Second World War created a common bond of citizenship as the old electric fence of class antagonism was switched off for its duration. Everyone believed in fair shares and equality of sacrifice for duchesses, doctors and dustmen alike. The war brought people together from all walks of life and created a sympathy for the less well-off; moreover, it acted as a catalyst for social change, forging a new middle ground in British politics and laying the foundation stones for the post-war welfare state.[1]

In *Problems of Social Policy* Richard Titmuss provided the seminal exposition and explanation for these monumental events. The guiding principles throughout the war were that national resources should be pooled and risks shared. The Government shouldered new obligations and set new standards. Common sense, science and common humanity all worked together. In 1939 reports about the poverty of evacuated children aroused the conscience of the nation. The evidence of poverty which evacuation brought to light coupled with the blitz which united the nation, stimulated inquiry and proposals for social reform. Military disaster and the fear of invasion changed the mood and values of the country. Dunkirk prompted national self-criticism and introspection. Over the next five years pressures for higher standards of welfare and greater social justice gained ground. A desire for universal social provisions and greater economic equality underpinned social policies.[2]

Many scholars have followed Titmuss's lead and trumpeted the positive effects of the war. Jay Winter, for example, has catalogued a raft of specific changes. Overtime, piecework and separation allowances for wives of servicemen helped to raise family incomes. A more progressive tax system contributed to a redistribution of income away from the middle class towards the working class. The years 1943–1945 saw a rise in incomes, as food was rationed, free milk provided under the National Milk Scheme, strict limitations placed on the production and distribution of alcohol, and rents controlled. All these measures helped to stabilise the working-class family economy. The need for women in paid work to assist the war effort meant that factory crèches, nurseries and child and maternal welfare centres mushroomed at an unprecedented rate. In 1943, for the first time, a majority of women attended antenatal care centres early in pregnancy. The provision of maternity services became more evenly distributed around the country than in the past.[3]

A closer look at the health experience of differing sections of society and the policies pursued by governments towards them suggests that this cheerful picture obscures a bleaker reality. Evacuation and fears of invasion often intensified prejudices towards vulnerable groups, such as the elderly, unmarried mothers and ethnic minorities (enemy aliens, black British, black members of the Empire and British Jews). Evacuation frequently provoked horror rather than sympathy for the urban working class and a condemnation of working-class mothers. Working-class women, the elderly, unmarried mothers and ethnic minorities suffered hardships and traumatic experiences not directly related to the exigencies of war. Moreover, in the early years of the war, the effects of the depression were still being felt, and production demands meant greater dangers and stresses at work. Gradually, the treatment of vulnerable groups was modified, working conditions improved and, despite the stresses of war, there does seem to have been an overall improvement in standards of health.

Longstanding assumptions about the Second World War have meant that the health of the nation has been analysed by historians tracing the contribution of wartime experience to the creation of the post-war National Health Service. This has tended to obscure a range of health experiences during the war quite unrelated to future health-care planning. Moreover, it was not until relatively late in the war that serious thought was given to the future of the health services; in the early days of war governmental interest in health services flowed less from a concern with people's health *per se* than with maintaining law and order.

PLANNING TO PROTECT CIVILIAN HEALTH

In the 1930s there was a widespread assumption, articulated in 1933 by Stanley Baldwin, leader of the Conservative Party, that 'the bomber will always get through'. Later, evidence to support this view was drawn from the Spanish Civil War. Those with vivid memories of the flying bombs at the end of the First World War were terrified that the next war would wreak even greater damage.[4] Fears about the inevitability of mass death, destruction and despair were fed by popular literature. One novel described an attack on London leading to a mass exodus into the countryside where men killed each other to survive and only the army could maintain any kind of order.[5]

It was this expectation of a breakdown in law and order which coloured the planners' paperwork. According to Sir Samuel Hoare, the Home Secretary from 1937 to 1939, the main purpose of Air Raid Precautions (ARP) was to prevent panic.[6] A committee established in 1937 to review ARP, hospitals and fire brigade schemes assumed that the main aim of these services was to maintain morale. A committee of leading London psychiatrists formed in 1938 calculated that psychiatric casualties would outnumber physical ones by three to one, and an elaborate mental health-care system was suggested. The Government considered, but then rejected, the idea that the army and police should be on stand-by to control thousands of nervous citizens. In fact, the Government only ever toyed with suggestions for coping with the psychological effects of war; no concrete plans were laid and, indeed, it was assumed that, if the system was not to be swamped, it would only be possible to treat the worst psychiatric cases.[7]

The dramatic aspect of the impact of war remained to the front of planners' minds. The Ministry of Health estimated that up to 2,800,000 beds would be needed for air-raid casualties. Outbreaks of typhoid fever, typhus and tetanus were all expected. The Home Office assumed that there would have to be mass burials, and corpses burnt in lime. Although discussions had been underway since the 1920s, much of the detailed planning was carried out in a rush in the last year of peace and was not completed until after the outbreak of war. It was not until July 1938 that the principles on which evacuation would operate were drawn up. The plans were never completed.

As it was not thought possible to evacuate all who might wish to go, certain groups were designated priority groups: schoolchildren removed as school units under the charge of their teachers; younger children accompanied by their mothers; pregnant women, and disabled adults. The numbers in each category could not be estimated because the scheme was voluntary. Evacuees were to be billeted in private homes. Ironically, Whitehall did not regard Plymouth, a dockyard and naval city, as a prime target for German bombers and, in the very early stages of the war, people were actually evacuated to Plymouth. Only after central government bungling was Plymouth organised to withstand the blitz of around 250,000 incendiaries, one for every adult and child of the pre-war population.

As a result of the type of war envisaged, no comprehensive health service was created. The plan was to collect casualties; give first-aid, blood transfusions and emergency surgery; cleanse the gassed, and dispose of the dead. In June 1938 the Ministry of Health was given responsibility for organising a national service for air-raid victims.[8]

All hospital facilities were to be co-ordinated on a regional basis. The vast majority of hospitals were to treat, or administer first aid to, casualties in their area, while those outside the danger zones were to carry on their routine work, but admit casualties and other patients transferred from the towns. Each hospital authority or governing body continued to be responsible for the maintenance of its service while the Government could determine the type of work for each hospital, including the reception and transfer of both casualties and other patients.[9] The voluntary hospitals were brought into the scheme and received generous financial support from the Government. Hospitals which already had a particular specialism were used for their strengths, so, for instance, rheumatic servicemen were sent to the Royal Devonshire Hospital.

A national hospital service for air raid casualties was organised in four ways: moving some patients out of existing hospitals; crowding beds together and putting more beds into existing hospitals; providing new equipment in some hospitals; and building annexes to hospitals. By the outbreak of war 150 hospitals had been selected for upgrading, which included installing operating theatres, X-ray rooms and laboratories, but only half the work had been completed. The organisational task was immense, and was made worse by the need for hospitals to be protected against air raids. By the end of 1939, 650 hospitals were building shelters, bricking-up operating theatres, sandbagging, and improving fire-fighting equipment. A centrally directed transport service had to be organised for moving patients between hospitals. A data base of information on hospital admissions, casualties, deaths, discharges and vacant beds was arranged, although it was not completed until after the outbreak of war.[10]

In the expectation that the Germans would use poison gas everyone was issued with a gas mask. Children had Mickey Mouse masks, and babies were placed inside a gas tent, similar to an oxygen tent. At first the masks could be frightening to wear and difficult to breathe through. As gas attacks never materialised, bomb shelters proved to be of greater use than the gas masks. Shelters were either communal or built in back gardens. Some people chose to stay in their own homes and shelter under the stairs rather than trek out to cold, dark and damp shelters. At first people were prevented from using the London Underground, but tube shelters later offered shelter to many Londoners, especially those in the East End. In some shelters people ran canteens and organised church services. Although infectious diseases could spread like wildfire in the communal shelters, on the whole they provided a safe haven from clouds of dust, flying glass and falling debris. Shelters were, however, no protection against a direct hit. (A notorious disaster at Bethnal Green in 1943, when 172 people were crushed to death, was not, however, the result of a direct hit. When the air-raid siren sounded, rockets were fired up. The black-out meant that people could not see what was happening; they panicked and began running down the steps into the Underground, so crushing those beneath them.)[11]

COPING WITH THE STRAIN

Pre-war alarm about lengthy civilian casualty lists comprising demoralised and disorderly citizens proved largely unfounded. The direct effects of war were not as devastating as had been feared. There is no evidence of an increase in serious mental illness, there were no epidemics and no victims of gas attacks. In 1940 and 1941 about 43,000 civilians were killed in Britain from air raids and 17,000 during the course of the remainder of the war. Statistics for injuries resulting from air raids are not accurate, but it has been estimated that about 86,000 were seriously injured. Just under 270,000 died in the Armed Forces.[12]

The bombing and evacuation produced a range of contradictory effects. The disruptive effects of war could be either stressful, or exciting and stimulating. In John Borman's autobiographical film, 'Hope and Glory', bombing raids were portrayed as an exciting escapade. More typical was the response of one woman who felt 'so dazed, so tired, so numb, I can hardly think'.[13] A woman living in the south-east commented that although the constant danger could not be ignored, it blunted the sensibilities.[14] A London woman wrote that her family's self-preservation was her sole preoccupation, and that through sheer desperation scenes of devastation were ignored.[15] This is a typical coping mechanism in disaster situations, but it is likely to have repercussions in the longer term.

The failure to co-ordinate services on a bombed site meant that people, anxious and confused, could spend days hunting for the appropriate personnel to help them. A woman whose London flat was blown to smithereens while she was away described her feelings as,

> Thankfulness for the lives of one's next of kin and one's friends came first, next came the wish to find out as quickly as possible the extent of one's loss and lastly an angry determination developed to save from the hands of looters and fools those things which the Act of God and

the King's enemies had left untouched. It is when this last stage is reached that the trouble begins.[16]

Civilians could claim compensation for injuries sustained in a raid, but under the 1939 Personal Injuries Act women incapacitated by a bomb were paid seven shillings a week less than a man. It took a sustained campaign before the Government conceded that from April 1943 men and women were to be paid compensation at the same rates.[17]

Although there was a wide range of responses to a direct attack, Tom Harrison, co-founder in 1936 of Mass Observation, identified a number of stages which many people passed through after an attack: shock and stupefaction (first few minutes); return to a sense of reality, with a concern for others and the extent of the damage (one to two hours); uncontrollable flood of communication by relating personal experiences and anecdotes; sense of intense pride and personal worth (couple of days); and thereafter most returned to 'normal'. What we now know about post-traumatic shock syndrome (the early stages of which may take the course Harrison describes) must lead us to question the reality behind this return to 'normal'.[18] Bombing devastated lives. One woman later recalled a landmine hitting the house, killing her husband and his sister, and badly injuring her son who was in and out of hospital for years undergoing plastic surgery. She had been trapped from the waist down and was unable to walk properly for some time, and long after she suffered from back pain.[19]

The incessant disruption of sleep led to chronic tiredness. A Board of Education report, compiled after the war, found that when bombing was accompanied by evacuation and the break-up of families it led to emotional distress. How far this in turn may have produced physical symptoms was not known.[20] A minority of Londoners did become ill with fright; Tom Harrison has suggested that the number remained relatively small because those who felt they would not be able to stand up to the stress had already left the city.[21]

The indirect effects of the blitz also took their toll. The black-out was the earliest and most enduring side-effect of war. In 1940 Mass Observation commented 'Bag-snatching, cat-snatching, woman-following and sudden death from cars are the urban jungle battles on the home front.'[22] Road accidents soared. As the war dragged on the black-out became even more depressing and harder to bear.

When war was declared the first mass evacuation was already underway, but when the expected shower of bombs did not fall, many made a hasty return to the cities, where they remained until the blitz began. The effects of evacuation have usually been portrayed as wholly beneficial, not only for the health of those evacuated, but also for the social fabric of society. Evacuation supposedly brought home to the middle class and rural dwellers the appallingly low standard of living of the urban working class. These revelations helped to break down class barriers and forge a consensus in society over the need for a welfare state.[23] This happy picture is not borne out by the bulk of contemporary reactions to the sight, sound and smell of children from the cities. John Macnicol has drawn attention to the pejorative and judgemental language used about evacuees and their mothers in the House of Commons, in the press, in reports to government departments and in popular folklore.[24]

Panic spread about the export from the cities of infectious diseases, particularly those associated with dirty habits such as head lice. Evacuation took place at the end of the school holidays before the School Medical Service had a chance to examine the children. Complaints about bed-wetting were legion: the Cambridge evacuation survey commented that, 'For some it would appear that . . . the evacuation produced a Niagara all over English and Scottish country beds.'[25] The outcry linked physical health and cleanliness with bad manners. It was hardly surprising, of course, that many children would have arrived in a dirty state after long hours on a train with inadequate facilities for young children, and that some children would have wet their beds when staying away from home for the first time in a strange and seemingly hostile environment.[26] The experiences of evacuated children and their hosts varied enormously. While some hosts were very kind, occasionally evacuated children were treated unkindly by their hosts, who might use the children as unpaid domestic servants, or give them too little to eat. The potential for physical child abuse is obvious but it would be hard to elicit evidence about this aspect of evacuation. One mother took her children home after they had told her that they ate standing up and shown her evidence of thrashings.[27]

Racial prejudice was experienced by some Jewish evacuees when host families refused to accept them or showed a lack of understanding and sympathy for Jewish observances. Throughout the war Jews were used as a scapegoat for food shortages and the black market. There was relatively little violence against Jews, but personal insults and ostracism were common.[28] Black children and their mothers could also find it hard to find billets.[29] There was, too, a rural-urban divide, and some children found hostility in the countryside whatever their class background.

Cleanliness being next to godliness, the dirty state in which many children arrived at evacuation centres was seen as a poor reflection on their mothers' moral fibre. It reinforced assumptions already current about the inadequacy of many working-class mothers. The journalist and historian R.C.K. Ensor wrote to *The Spectator* that many of the mothers 'were the lowest grade of slum women-slatternly malodorous tatterdemalions trailing children to match'.[30]

Moralising about the behaviour of others was given a new lease of life. This can be seen not only in the condemnation of the mothers of evacuees, but also in the scaremongering about soaring VD rates and the rumours that were rife about the immorality of women in the Forces, especially in the Auxiliary Territorial Service (ATS), the most working-class of the women's services. There was no parallel panic over men's behaviour, even though the VD rates for men in the Forces were twice that of women. The Government blamed women for the spread of VD and for weakening the military might of Britain, 'As early as 1940, Government Departments were concerned that there were no satisfactory means of bringing under treatment a number of girls and women who were responsible for much inefficiency of Servicemen through their infection with venereal disease.'[31] From 1942 anyone suspected of infecting two or more VD patients could be forced to undergo an examination and treatment. In the same year a publicity campaign was launched on the causes of and cures for VD. Local authority treatment centres increased from 188 at the outbreak of war to 229 by its close.[32]

Rumours about the immorality and high illegitimacy rates among women in the Forces alarmed the Government, which feared that this gossip would damage the war effort: women would be deterred from joining up and the morale of the men abroad would be undermined (worrying about the good time their wives and girlfriends were having at home). A government committee, chaired by Violet Markham, was set up to investigate the state of affairs in the women's services. The committee found no justification for the vague and sweeping charges of immorality; allegations of drunkenness and immorality in the camps were based on one or two cases, multiplied in the course of gossip. Illegitimate pregnancies were actually less common in the Services than in other walks of life, but as Markham wryly observed, 'Virtue has no gossip value.'[33]

Illegitimacy rates soared, supposedly providing hard evidence of an increase in sexual activity outside wedlock. This brought condemnation for women but not for men. (There was a sub-text to the charges of immorality levelled at women, which was that they should not be so 'unfeminine' as to work in munitions factories or to wear paramilitary uniforms.)[34] Between 1940 and 1945 more than 300,000 illegitimate babies were born in England, Wales and Scotland – over 100,000 more than in the six years preceeding the war. In fact, the illegitimacy rate is an unreliable guide to sexual mores or habits. The proportion of all babies conceived out of wedlock (this includes the figure for those women who subsequently married as well as those who did not do so) was well below the pre-war level (except in 1945). The apparent increase in pre-marital sex was caused by fewer women marrying when they discovered they were pregnant.[35] Extra-marital sex was not a wartime phenomenon.

The wonder is that the illegitimacy rate was not higher, given the increased difficulty in wartime of obtaining contraceptives. During the war the Family Planning Association's (FPA's) activities declined, it was refused permission to make contraceptive advice available to women in the Forces and a shortage of rubber affected the supply of both condoms and caps. The FPA even used discarded decorated rubber sheeting which had been ordered for the bathroom floors of a Paris hotel to make caps. They 'almost became heirlooms. No two were alike. Marbled patterns of all colours appeared and the rubber lasted so well'.[36]

Despite difficulties in obtaining contraceptives it seems that almost everyone was trying to limit the size of their families, even if the methods used were unreliable and dangerous. Attitudes remained highly judgemental towards women who went to desperate lengths to end an unwanted pregnancy. A trainee nurse recalls that on her first day on the wards she tried to comfort a woman who looked very grey and was in great pain. She was told not to spend much time with the woman because she had been brought in following a criminally induced abortion.[37]

Ignorance about birth control was still widespread, and unwanted pregnancies affected both married and unmarried women. In the first group were those women who had had affairs with men while their husbands were away.[38] (There could be a strong sense of loneliness among a number of young wives whose husbands were in the Forces.) The group of women who probably suffered most, however, were unmarried pregnant women who did not subsequently marry the child's father.

At the outbreak of war, services for unmarried pregnant women were inadequate, and they became steadily worse as the war progressed. There were too few places in the Homes and Hostels for unmarried pregnant women, which were run on a variety of principles. Some Homes still locked women up, emphasising their sin and the need for repentance; there could also be crude religious pressure to win women over to a particular denomination. Other Homes had a more enlightened outlook and told women about their legal position and services available to them. Some Mother and Baby Homes closed down and there were fewer hospital beds. In one Poor Law Institution (PLI) unmarried pregnant women were expected to undertake the cooking as a means of paying for their confinement.[39]

Social services for unmarried mothers were at this time quite inadequate. A local authority would not usually help an unmarried pregnant woman if she came from another authority. So, when most mothers and babies were being encouraged to leave the cities, unmarried pregnant women were often under pressure to return to their homes, whether or not they were in a danger zone. The local nature of social services meant that they were ill-suited to a situation in which many people were living away from home. Local authorities regarded unmarried mothers as a menace and showed little regard for their welfare. Public opinion was uninformed or hostile, and this applied to landlords, neighbours and often relatives. Even so, there is some evidence to suggest that women showed greater sympathy than in the past towards those women who found themselves unhappily pregnant. There was, after all, great pressure for women to have sex with men when they might soon be killed on active service.[40]

Traditionally, much has been made of the wartime welfare and child-care facilities for working women. Penny Summerfield, in contrast, has shown the shortcomings of such provisions for women and the continuing dual burden of domestic and war work. Shopping problems for women in paid work caused much anxiety.[41] Although more day-time nurseries were provided than in the past, they were woefully inadequate. The demands of the war economy, which required as many women as possible in full-time work, jostled with notions about mothers' responsibilities for young children. A woman's role was still regarded as that of wife and mother. William Beveridge (chairman of the Committee on Social Insurance and Allied Services and the single most influential figure in post-war planning for social welfare) believed that maternity was the principal object of marriage and that 'housewives as mothers have vital work to do in ensuring the adequate continuance of the British race and of British ideals in the world'.[42] The Ministry of Health claimed that nurseries spread infection and it was far better for young children to be looked after at home. In fact, there is no evidence that wartime nurseries endangered children's health, rather the reverse was true. One reason for the improved health of children attending nurseries may have been that a child's quota of rationed food was not affected by meals eaten at nursery school. (Likewise, if mothers were in paid work they could often eat unrationed food in the works' canteen.)[43] Children attending nursery schools may, therefore, have enjoyed a healthier diet. Moreover, if the mother went out to work the family probably enjoyed a higher standard of living.

From January 1940 when rationing was introduced the smell of sizzling bacon, lashings of butter on hot toast and a snow-storm of sugar in a cup of tea became the stuff of dreams. A weekly ration comprised 4 oz (almost immediately raised to 8 oz) of bacon or ham, 4 oz of butter, and 12 oz of sugar. From March 1940 meat was rationed. Over the next two years rationing was extended to a range of goods including clothes and fuel. (Beer and tobacco were never rationed and bread was not rationed until after the war.) Rationing was generally welcomed as the fairest means of distributing scarce products. Women still suffered from poorer eating habits than men, filling up on puddings, cakes and biscuits whereas men ate more meat. Considering the pressures women were under during the war, it is not surprising that numerous women suffered from anaemia and nervous disorders.[44]

Inevitably, the nation's health was affected by long-term influences. For instance, the malnutrition identified by some MOHs during the depression of the 1930s still affected some poor families, and especially women. Areas of high unemployment in the 1930s, such as Glasgow, Liverpool and Merthyr Tydfil, continued to experience lower standards of health than the rest of the country. A number of Royal Ordnance Factories were located in the 'special' or 'depressed' areas, and it was thought that workers recruited from these areas were less productive because 'malnutrition was common amongst both young and old'.[45] Large families still found it difficult to afford adequate meat, fish, vegetables and fruit.

Surveys by the Ministry of Food into expenditure on, and consumption of, rationed and unrationed foods, repeatedly found that a number of large families, and particularly the mothers, had diets inferior in quality and variety to smaller families. Surveys of health carried out in the latter part of the war found distinct inequalities in standards of health. Better-off and professional families enjoyed a higher standard of health than poorer and industrial workers' families. Differences also existed between those living in rural and urban areas. City-dwellers were more likely to be afflicted with diseases of the skin and cellular tissues, as well as with VD. Those living at close quarters suffered more frequently from diseases of the mouth and teeth than those with more space. Regional inequalities also existed independently of the urban-rural divide. There was less illness and injury among those living south of the line running from East Anglia to Wales. Women also suffered more illness than men, which may have been due to their poorer diets and the strain of doing both paid war work and unpaid housework.[46]

In 1940 and 1941 civilian health deteriorated and working conditions in industry were particularly hazardous. There is some evidence from sickness benefit statistics of increased short-term illnesses, which may have been due to a combination of factors: the least healthy sections of society and more older people were drawn into work; a higher proportion of married women undertook paid work while continuing their domestic duties, and the general stresses and strains of a nation at war took their toll.[47]

A Mass Observation investigation carried out in 1942 found that there was little difference in numbers between those who felt better and those who felt worse since the beginning of the war, although women said that they felt better twice as often as men. People's sense of well-being was affected primarily by their own health and the weather, followed by war news.[48]

From 1942 the health of the nation improved. Mortality rates show particular improvements between 1941 and 1944 for infants, young children and mothers in childbirth. In Scotland, however, it was the better-off groups whose stillbirth rates improved most, belying ideas of a war-time reduction in inequalities. Other causes of death did not decline so dramatically, but nevertheless there were improvements, except in TB rates.[49]

For many people there were definite signs of improved health in the later stages of the war, and this was closely linked to rising standards of living. (Overall standards of health were rising, but inequalities in standards of health remained significant.) From 1941 the Government controlled prices effectively, there was full employment and essential foodstuffs were available to most, but not all, people. There were government schemes to supplement the diet of particular groups, such as pregnant women, who were entitled to extra clothes and food rations, free orange juice and a free pint of milk; young children; the families of servicemen; the war-injured, and the elderly. At the same time the standard of bread was improved, and cheap meals were provided through school meals, works' canteens and British Restaurants. Although more milk was consumed there was an increase in bovine TB among schoolchildren because of the poor quality of the milk. For most of the war it was impossible to buy citrus fruits or bananas. In 1944 one woman exclaimed with delight 'Oranges and lemons! Quite a lot of them. Now we know that the Mediterranean really is open again.'[50] One boy ate his first orange at the end of the war and, not knowing that the peel should not be eaten, was promptly sick.[51]

The contribution of better nutrition to rising standards of health is not clear. A British Medical Association Report on wartime nutrition, the Chief Medical Officer at the Board of Education's wartime review and Richard Titmuss, official historian of wartime social policy, all cited nutrition as one important factor among many which led to improved health.

In contrast to the self-satisfied reports emanating from the Ministry of Health in the 1930s, the improved statistics of the 1940s were regarded as a signal for still greater efforts. In 1944 Henry Willink, the Minister of Health from 1943 to 1945, chose to emphasise how much ill health still existed and how much still remained to be done, while Aneurin Bevan, Minister of Health from 1945 to 1951, saw war time improvements as evidence that much more progress could be made in peace time.[52]

The health-care provision for civilians could not have contributed to the rising standards of health. There were shortages of doctors, nurses and dentists, affecting school medical services, maternity

99

and child welfare clinics and a range of public health provisions. Complaints were voiced by women about the poor quality of maternity care.[53] A woman recalled the nightmare of having a baby in 1942 in a hospital which had been largely commandeered for wounded soldiers. There were hardly any nurses and the food was dreadful. There were no clothes or nappies for the babies and some were even wrapped in old bits of khaki. Although the mothers were kept in hospital for two weeks, they could not be looked after properly.[54] During the war the number of GPs plummeted by one-third. There were delays in patients receiving treatment, and in June 1943 a War Cabinet special inquiry warned that the standard of medical service available to the civilian population was 'dangerously low'.[55]

The Emergency Hospital Service (EHS) had been designed for the victims of war, whether air-raid casualties or members of the Armed Forces. During the course of the war, the scope of patients treated widened, but a clear hierarchy remained. Many civilian sick were initially discharged from hospitals, whether or not there was someone to look after them at home, causing hardship and suffering. In Bradford, and possibly other areas, 'higher grade mental patients' were moved out of hospitals and billeted with local families.[56] Over the following few months a better balance between the needs of all patients was sought. As Titmuss has shown, what began as an improvised casualty scheme for air raid victims had, by the summer of 1940, been transformed into a national hospital service for growing sections of the population. Civilian and civil defence victims of air raids were included from the outset, along with members of the Armed Forces, members of the police, merchant seamen, prisoners of war, internees and unaccompanied evacuated children. Improvements brought about by the EHS could not be restricted to particular groups of patients, and changes had a knock-on effect. Even so, large numbers of patients remained outside the scheme. Too few resources in terms of personnel and equipment meant that some patients' hospital treatment suffered at the expense of others.[57] Tensions existed between PLI and EHS nurses. Nurses found it depressing to work with inadequate supplies.[58] One nurse recalled a large hospital in York in 1944 where there was a shortage of doctors, nurses and domestic staff. Nurses undertook domestic duties and even porters' work. In the operating theatres threadbare gloves and blunt razor blades were used.[59] As well as difficulties and delays for those receiving hospital treatment, the School Medical Service along with maternity and child welfare clinics also suffered shortages. Those hardest hit were often the elderly and chronically sick.

At a time when the threat of invasion and the Dunkirk spirit was supposedly uniting the nation as everyone pulled together to defeat the common enemy, very different treatment was being meted out to people according to their perceived relationship to the war effort.

Only later, after the threat of invasion had passed, when England no longer stood alone, the United States had entered the war and the Beveridge Report had been published, did a more humane attitude emerge. Two groups in particular suffered especial hardship in our Finest Hour; refugees from Nazism and the elderly.

The experience of enemy aliens in the early part of the war was quite distinct from the rest of society. Enemy aliens, as with older people (and indeed many of the enemy aliens were themselves elderly), suffered greatest hardship in the first eighteen months of the war; their worst experiences were relatively short-lived. On the outbreak of war there were 74,000 enemy aliens living in Britain. The majority were Germans and most of them were interned, along with 4,000 of the 17,000 Italians living in the country. There was a popular belief that the fall of France had been the result of fifth columnists. In the summer of 1940, when the country was under threat of invasion, there was a fear that an unknown number of those with German or Italian backgrounds might be spies or sympathetic to the enemy. (In fact, many of the enemy aliens were refugees from Nazi persecution.) On 10 June 1940, when Italy entered the war against Britain, there was anti-Italian rioting and internment of Italian men. Even after the violence had subsided, hostility towards Italians remained.

Internment of enemy aliens began in September 1939, intensified in the spring of 1940, and then relaxed over the next year, although some people remained in internment camps until the end of the war. Camps were established around the country. The best-known camp was on the Isle of Man; the most notorious camps were the transit and temporary ones. For many refugees it was a great shock to be rounded up and imprisoned; it had never occurred to them that the British might imprison them when they faced a common enemy.[60] At one camp food was in such short supply that the prisoners assumed that Britain had already been invaded. Internees saved food parcels in case worse shortages lay ahead. As newspapers and wireless sets were banned it was virtually impossible to know what was going on in the outside world. Many did not know the fate of their relatives, and when news came through that the *Arandora Star*, a ship carrying German prisoners of war, German and Italian internees and British troops bound for Canada, had been torpedoed there were nervous breakdowns and suicides. In another camp there were too few beds and chairs when the prisoners first arrived. In one transit camp the prisoners arrived after a day's travel to find that they had only boards to sleep on; some blankets had to be returned because they were infested; internees had to eat standing up; there were eighteen water taps for 2,000 people to wash; and a fight broke out over the lavatories which consisted of sixty buckets in the yard. Lack of medicines, toilet paper, soap and bedlinen were typical complaints. In some camps refugee doctors organised a camp hospital, but prisoners with infectious diseases were crammed in with the fit, and depression seems to have been a common complaint. Tensions existed between those Germans who were Nazi sympathisers and those who were German refugees. One Austrian Jew wrote that the people he was interned with showed enormous hostility to a group of Italians when they arrived and refused to work with them. The seriously ill were usually transferred to prison or military hospitals, where they were not allowed to communicate with their relatives, however serious their illness. One man, in Wrexham Emergency Military Hospital in July 1940, wrote that the hospital was well-equipped but he was treated unkindly. The prisoners had to stay in bed, wearing army pyjamas, and there was a guard of young soldiers who kept the patients awake at night. Such conditions lasted for a couple of months.

When information filtered out about conditions in the internment camps there was a public outcry. François Lafitte produced a Penguin Special, *The Internment of Aliens*, which detailed many horror stories.[61] It was sympathetically received, although by the time it was published in late November 1940 the invasion panic had subsided and there was a new Home Secretary, Herbert Morrison, who took a more lenient line. Conditions in the camps now improved. Although anxiety and depression continued to plague the camps, the internees were able to organise activities for themselves, ranging from Austrian cafés to educational classes and music.[62] An Austrian Jew interned with a number of Italian ice-cream makers and pastry cooks recalled enjoying 'magnificent' cuisine.[63]

Even though troops from many parts of the empire fought for Britain during the war, the presence of black people in Britain continued to meet a mixed response. Black workers employed in munition and chemical factories felt that they were allotted the dirtiest and most unpleasant jobs. A group of roughly 300 technicians specially brought over from the West Indies experienced discrimination not only at work but also when they tried to find housing.[64] Racial prejudice could at times outweigh manpower demands. A group of men brought over from Honduras to Scotland as forestry workers lived in cold, isolated and poorly equipped camps. A doctor paid them only occasional visits and those who fell ill were dissatisfied with the treatment they received. Hostility was displayed both towards them and the Scottish families who befriended them. In 1941 the unit was disbanded.[65]

Black American servicemen also experienced hostility. It was feared that if white English women went out with black Americans it would lead to violence on the part of white Americans against the black soldiers. If the British appeared to be treating black servicemen in an overtly prejudiced fashion, it was feared that those countries of the empire loyally supporting Britain would take offence. In an effort to frighten English women away from black troops, rumours were put around that they were riddled with VD.[66] Even Queen Mary tried to set in motion attempts to dissuade English women from being seen with black servicemen.[67]

At first glance it might seem that the elderly were treated more generously in wartime. After all, by the 1940 Old Age and Widows' Pension Act pensions could be topped up through the Assistance Board (previously the Unemployment Assistance Board, helping the unemployed). However, wartime inflation hit those on fixed incomes, such as pensioners, especially hard, and Assistance Board provisions may well have been a means of avoiding an all-round increase in pensions. During the first year of the war many of the old and sick suffered hardship, not just from inflation, but also because, as one middle-class woman who had difficulty finding a home or hotel that her parents could move into commented sadly, there was no place for old people in wartime.[68]

On the outbreak of war many patients were discharged from hospitals in order to empty the beds for the expected flood of air-raid victims. It may be assumed that a high proportion of older patients were among those discharged. At the time it was claimed that this caused enormous suffering and unnecessary deaths. Those hardest hit were the chronically sick, the bedridden, the paralysed, the aged, people suffering from advanced cancer or from TB who were discharged from hospital to homes where they were an intolerable burden on the family, or even to homes from which all the relatives had already been evacuated.[69] The Nuffield Foundation believed that many old people were dying in squalor and loneliness because there were no hospital beds for them. Ironically, as the expected air attacks were not taking place, many hospitals had empty beds.[70] When the bombing did begin the situation of many old people deteriorated still further. Old people who were using air-raid shelters were regarded as a menace by the Government because it was thought that they might increase the health risks of shelters, lower morale and be a serious hindrance to others. So, in order to get the elderly out of the shelters many were now evacuated to hospitals, along with those old people who had taken refuge in Rest Centres (temporary accommodation for those who had been bombed-out). Many old people were alarmed at being despatched to hospital. Numerous hospitals were former workhouses, and therefore carried a terrible stigma. Many elderly people dreaded ending their days in such an institution. They feared that they were going to be given treatment, that they would be separated from their spouses and that the hospitals were more obvious air-raid targets than the Rest Centres or shelters. This movement of the elderly into hospitals ended at the close of 1940 when it was decided that the beds were needed for air-raid casualties. It was thought best to leave the elderly sick in the cities; for if invasion occurred they could hardly pose a threat to civil order by flocking out of the cities.[71] Henry Willink, who was appointed Special Commissioner to co-ordinate services for London's homeless, later wrote that as bombing and evacuation led to loss of homes and the break-up of families, so many thousands of old people were left in tragic isolation.

Gradually a more sensitive attitude towards the elderly developed, although the Government's main concern was that they should not block facilities which might be required by others. Older people were encouraged to find billets in the country, even though this was always difficult for anyone who was not a child, and hostels were set up for older people who had been bombed-out. Among those old people living in the country, and therefore relatively safe from bombs, life could still be hard if they were left to undertake outdoor chores in all weathers.[72]

There was a definite hierarchical order so far as assistance to the elderly was concerned. Help tended to be given to those old people who might affect the morale of those contributing to the war effort, for instance, by disruptive behaviour in air-raid shelters or by writing to the press.[73] In the early part of the war conditions for people living in Public Assistance Institutions (PAIs) (the old workhouse now operating as old people's homes) were austere and regimented. From 1943 unease at the conditions in PAIs was voiced publicly. A report in 1943 by the Nuffield Foundation roundly criticised not only PAIs, but also private old people's homes, where cases of cruel exploitation and neglect were discovered. The Government made sympathetic noises, but action was slow. From December 1944 the home help scheme was extended to old people in an effort to keep them in their own homes and out of overstretched institutions.

Lack of help in the home was seen as threatening morale in all classes: poorer people could not afford help and the middle class could not find it. A Women's Voluntary Service (WVS) report made explicit the link between the war effort and domestic help. The report warned that prompt action was required if the nation's health, and the war effort, were not to be gravely affected. Much compassionate leave had to be granted to Service men and women, and there was considerable absenteeism among women workers. Meals-on-wheels were launched by various voluntary organisations, although provision was soon dominated by the WVS. At a time when the state was expanding its social welfare activity, so too were voluntary organisations. The expansion of voluntary work in the war was funded in part by donations from the United States and the Dominions. Between 1940 and 1946 much of this money was channelled throught the Lord Mayor's National Air-Raid Distress Fund, which attempted to provide immediate help with food, clothing and other basic necessities for the victims of air raids.[74]

While those who were not regarded as central to the war effort received poor health care and suffered especial hardship, at least in the early part of the war, the health of those workers who were seen as directly contributing to war-related productivity tended to be given a higher priority. This was not, however, a simple cut-and-dried situation. All-out efforts to meet productivity targets were hampered by assumptions about the appropriate role for women in society, and prejudice against foreigners and non-whites.

WORKING FOR VICTORY

Good health was especially important in wartime because it could affect productivity levels. The lessons of the First World War may have been lost on many employers in the early stages of the war, but the war nevertheless gave a spur to advocates of a healthy and safe work environment, and to industrial medicine.

The war intensified the hazards of industry. People who had not previously worked in factories were more likely to have accidents. Longer hours and nightwork caused tiredness, which in turn made people more susceptible to illness. Travelling difficulties lengthened the time spent away from home and added to the strain of long hours of work.[75] For safety reasons plants handling explosives had to be isolated and individual buildings dispersed. Employees had long journeys to work and long walks between buildings. Young women who left home to work in munition factories might suffer from homesickness as well as from terrific noise, monotonous work (often on very small components) and the disorientation brought about by shift-work.[76] These stresses actually undermined productivity because workers felt the need to take time off to relax. As in the First World War, many women entered industries where toxic substances were used. Better precautions were taken than in the previous war, but even so, many contracted dermatitis and suffered from the toxic effects of TNT.[77]

In May 1940 Ernest Bevin was appointed Minister of Labour and National Service. He immediately obtained the transfer of the Factory Department from the Home Office and made safety, health and welfare at work a priority. Improving physical health at the workplace proved an attractive strategy because it offered an apparently concrete and self-contained goal. In the official history of labour in the munitions industries it was suggested that physical amenities in industry were dealt with promptly because the need for improvements was so obvious and they were more straightforward than industrial relations.[78]

The Factories (Medical and Welfare Services) Order of July 1940 encouraged the budding pre-war industrial medical supervision. The Order enabled the Chief Inspector of Factories to demand munitions or crown factories to provide medical supervision, nursing and first-aid services, and welfare supervision. The Government encouraged all aspects of health and safety at work during the war by making welfare orders, establishing an Industrial Health Advisory Council, working with various bodies in organising conferences, and supporting both the training of personnel and campaigns to reduce the accident rate. The Labour Party, Trades Union Congress (TUC) and medical profession all contributed to the mounting activity.

From 1940 the Central Council for Physical Recreation (CCPR) received a grant from the Ministry of Labour which helped to provide physical recreation facilities for use after work by those engaged on work of national importance. Later, when it was thought that suitable physical training could reduce accidents and absenteeism, the Ministry of Labour approved classes in work-time.

The Central Council for Health Education (CCHE), which had previously worked through local authorities, now took its message direct to industry. In this way it was possible to target large numbers of people while monitoring the effectiveness of the CCHE's work. Posters, films and leaflets were distributed on subjects such as food handling, rehabilitation of injured workers, spitting and TB. Information was also aimed at particular groups of workers, such as those on night-shift who were advised on sleeping, eating, leisure and family life, and the importance of good ventilation (this last point was aimed at management).

With long hours of work and irregular mealtimes the provision of hot meals at the workplace was increasingly common. People often blamed their illnesses on the poor food they were eating.[79] (Even so, people were better fed at the end of the war than they had been at its outset.) At the outbreak of war there were about 1,500 factory canteens, as well as cafés around dock sites. From 1939 the Home Office, with the co-operation of the British Employers' Confederation, encouraged firms to provide adequate facilities, and in November 1940 the Factories' (Canteens') Order empowered the Chief Inspector of Factories to require a canteen to be provided at any factory employing over 250 workers engaged in munition or other government work. Under the wartime building programme people were often living in remote camps or in billets where there were feeding difficulties. In January 1941 an Order was made under which canteens could be required at construction sites; in February a similar Order was made for dock sites.[80]

An increase in nightwork and overtime, and the complete or

partial blacking-out of factory premises even in daytime meant more time was spent working in artificial light, which aggravated the ill-effects of bad lighting on the vision, morale and output of workers. In order to overcome these problems the Factories' (Standards of Lighting) Regulations were made in 1941, which imposed a minimum standard of general illumination in factories where long hours were regularly worked; this tended to include factories in which the work was essential and involved a substantial use of artificial light.

When manpower shortages began to hit production targets 'rehabilitation . . . became a watch word, the most fashionable word in medicine'.[81] Before the war few facilities for rehabilitation existed, although from the mid-1930s there had been a growing interest in the subject. As rehabilitation was closely linked with manpower, it was the Minister of Labour, not the Minister of Health, who in 1941 launched a short-term scheme to train partially disabled people for war work and to provide various types of training and allowances. Significantly, the scheme met with a dusty response from the War Cabinet's Home Policy Committee on the grounds that it 'would virtually lead to a free state medical service for all persons during and after the war' and this would have the unfortunate effect of undermining the National Health Insurance scheme and the voluntary hospitals.[82] Whitehall's support for rehabilitation schemes was based solely on wartime production requirements. One Treasury official wrote 'I'm not clear facilities should be provided expressly for training disabled men unless their services are required for war purposes.'[83] Nevertheless, following the 1942 Interdepartmental Committee on the Rehabilitation and Resettlement of Persons Injured by Accidents, chaired by George Tomlinson, a permanent scheme was established. Various government rehabilitation schemes sprung up during the war, although they only treated those expected to take up employment after rehabilitation. The main problem for those admitted to the schemes was the poor co-ordination between the medical and industrial rehabilitation.

The adverse effects of absenteeism on productivity levels produced a spate of enquiries. Women's absenteeism rates were found to be twice as high as men's rates, and married women's rates were 'significantly' higher. A 1945 Medical Research Council (MRC) report assumed that high absenteeism rates were due to the strain of war, a gradual lowering of physical fitness of those accepted for employment, and a huge increase in the numbers of older women and women with family responsibilities in paid employment. Moving from a peacetime job to a war-related one was also stressful. The three main causes of illness were respiratory, nervous disorders and fatigue, and digestive problems. The MRC report went on to show that the sickness rates of manufacturing workers were more than twice those of clerical workers. To some extent the differences were seen as a reflection of variations in types of work and in working conditions. It was recognised that factors outside the place of work, such as transport, housing and nursery provision could also affect production rates, but the only advice given in the report was to 'make sure that you observe the commonsense rules of hygiene. Cleanliness, well-balanced and, if possible, regular meals, enough sleep, and as much fresh air as you can get . . .'[84]

The treatment meted out to different groups of patients and the priority given to the most 'useful' members of society raises serious doubts about the existence of a sense of equality of sacrifice and of common citizenship. Rather, the war seems to have reinforced hierarchical attitudes among officials. This should be borne in mind when discussing the driving forces behind the creation of the National Health Service (NHS).

LOOKING TO THE FUTURE

The orthodox view of the creation of the NHS was provided by Richard Titmuss, who argued that the welfare measures of the war and immediate post-war years were the direct result of wartime circumstances. The Dunkirk spirit of 1940 and the air raids led to a sense of social solidarity; evacuation made many aware for the first time of the extent of poverty and ill health among the urban working class. Moreover, the Government was aware of the importance of sustaining both morale and an efficient workforce. For Titmuss, the wartime hospital service had provided a blueprint for the future, though he himself emphasised the shortcomings of wartime health-care services for civilians. Most historians have subsequently accepted Titmuss's thesis and explained the creation of the NHS in terms of wartime experience and consensus.[85]

Even those historians who underline the disagreements between the medical profession and Whitehall tend to agree with their colleagues that the NHS was born of a consensus peculiar to the war.[86] However, a challenge to the once ubiquitous view of social and political consensus as the prime cause of the welfare state has recently been mounted by Kevin Jefferys,[87] who has argued that there was controversy on party political lines both before and after the publication of the 1944 White Paper on the Future of the Health Services. According to Jeffreys, Labour and Conservative MPs endorsed the White Paper for very different reasons. The Labour Party attacked the secret agreements reached after the publication of the White Paper between Henry Willink, the Conservative Minister of Health from 1943 to 1945, and the BMA. When the parties endorsed a national health service in the 1945 general election they were envisaging two quite different services.[88]

As early as September 1939 civil servants were elaborating plans for the creation of a national hospital system after the war. Yet, in February 1941 the Minister of Health was still frosty towards any wartime schemes which might lead to a virtually free state medical service for everyone either during the war or in the longer term. Civil servants at the Ministry of Health and Ministry of Labour joined a private chorus singing the praises of the national health insurance scheme and the voluntary hospitals; one civil servant claiming that the voluntary hospitals had brought out 'much of the best in this country both by way of large contributions from the wealthy and small contributions from the thrifty'.[89] A serious reassessment of the health-care services was not embarked upon until some time later.

In June 1941 the Beveridge Committee on Social Insurance and Allied Services was set up to review the whole question of unemployment and health insurance as well as workmen's compensation. By the summer of 1941 the Ministry of Health and Department of Health for Scotland still had no definite views on the future shape of the health services, although in October 1941 the Ministry of Health pledged the Government to a national hospital service after the war, with local authorities having considerable influence over the running of the voluntary hospitals.

When the Beveridge Report appeared in November 1942 it recommended a comprehensive social security system, based on subsistence rate benefits 'from the cradle to the grave'. A basic assumption of the report was that there would be child benefit, full employment and a national health service for prevention and cure of disease and disability.[90] It was the implication of these assumptions which made the report so far-reaching.[91] Beveridge's assumptions went further than the Government's mention a year earlier of a hospital service, and gave a sharp jolt to the Ministry of Health's ruminations. Almost immediately Conservative MPs secretly reported that in order to protect private medical practice they wanted national health insurance restricted to those with incomes under £420 a year. The next month, however, the Government, following the popular reception of the Beveridge Report, publicly accepted it in principle. There was no question at this or at any other time during the war, that the voluntary hospitals would be 'nationalised'.

Meanwhile, the Ministry of Health had been working on its own document with Ernest Brown, the Minister of Health from 1941 to 1943. In November 1943 Brown was replaced by a Conservative, Henry Willink, partly because Brown had not got on well with the doctors and partly because Churchill may well have wanted a Conservative in a major home department.

In February 1944 the Cabinet approved a White Paper on the future of health services and the following month it was debated in the House of Commons. As the White Paper was vague on all the contentious issues it allowed maximum agreement at the time of its publication while storing up controversy for the future. Labour ministers had ensured that the White Paper included the establishment of health centres, which would lead to a salaried health service, and Labour generally accepted the document although it would have liked it to have gone further. One major omission from the White Paper was a pledge to incorporate an occupational health service into the new health service. All Ernest Bevin's efforts to improve industrial health were undertaken on the assumption that the Ministry of Labour's wartime responsibility for industrial health would continue into the peace, and the Ministry of Health had neither the resources nor the inclination to take on the Ministry of Labour over the issue of an occupational health service.

Both the Ministry of Labour and the Ministry of Health were conscious of external pressure for an occupational health service, although neither Bevin nor successive ministers at the Ministry of Health, first Ernest Brown and then Henry Willink, spent much time on the problem. Throughout the war years a separation between industrial and personal health services was resolutely maintained, even though Bevin was well aware of the interrelationship between industrial health and overall health. The two departments discussed the wording of the relevant sections of the 1944 White Paper so that they at least would not disagree in public, and consequently the wording was purposely left vague. Brown had told Bevin that,

Tactically my aim in the White Paper will be to keep to the main principles and general idea of a comprehensive service – which is a considerable hurdle to jump, with the profession's present attitude – and not to risk prejudicing the main chances by inviting criticism on too many detailed issues all at one bite. I shall have to put something in the White Paper to explode the criticism . . . that no service can be comprehensive if a separate factory service remains . . .[92]

Willink, following Brown, had to walk the same tight-rope, and when the White Paper was published in 1944 it did not envisage a comprehensive health service, for the medical supervision of industry 'is part of the complex machinery of industrial organisation and welfare, and it belongs to that sphere more than to the sphere of the personal doctor and the care of personal health'.[93] For such views the White Paper, as feared, was roundly criticised in the press. *The Economist*, for instance, thought it illogical for the state to provide a health service for people at home and to ignore them while they were at work.[94]

The Conservatives, like Labour, were broadly in favour of the White Paper (far more so than they had been of the Beveridge Report), but there were rumblings of discontent which suggests that even in its cautious generalisations the Government had gone too far for many of its supporters. A number of Conservative MPs feared that the voluntary hospitals might be underfunded in the future and that a salaried medical service would destroy the special doctor-patient relationship. Few attacked the White Paper's underlying principles.[95] The publication presaged a long and contentious series of negotiations between Willink and the BMA. Discussions with Lord Moran, President of the Royal College of Physicians, were especially protracted, for as Churchill's personal doctor he was frequently out of the country with the Prime Minister, and in any case Willink found him a difficult man with whom to reach agreement. Willink was involved in discussions which led to proposals even more acceptable to doctors and unacceptable to the Labour movement. It was agreed that the administrative role of local government would be weakened, new financial provisions would be made for the voluntary hospitals and doctors in health centres would not be the salaried employees of local government. By the time the Coalition broke up, the Government was close to accepting a national health service in principle, but on Willink's own later admission it was different from the one created by the post-war Labour Government. In particular, Willink did not believe that the Conservatives would have accepted the nationalisation of the voluntary hospitals, yet if two hospital systems had continued it would have been impossible to finance the voluntary hospitals or to have had a national hospital plan for the whole country. In retrospect Willink praised Bevan for the 'wise and important' change which introduced one unified hospital system.[96] At their Annual Conference in March 1945 the Conservatives welcomed, after brief criticism, a comprehensive service, available to all. In contrast, the Labour Conference bitterly attacked the concessions it was rumoured the medical profession had prised out of Willink. If the Conservatives had won the 1945 general election they would have introduced a national health service, but it would have been very different from either the one outlined in the Coalition's White Paper or the service that was introduced by Labour after the war.

Similarly, in 1945 when family allowances were introduced they were welcomed by various groups, but for different reasons; their introduction does not reflect a consensus in wartime society. The Family Endowment Society had based its campaign around family poverty, encouraging the birth-rate and raising the economic status of women and children. Such arguments cut no ice with the Government which saw the introduction of family allowances as a means of avoiding the question of a minimum wage and of maintaining work incentives and labour mobility.[97] Any benefits which might accrue to the health of women and children from the introduction of family allowances were incidental.

Throughout the war years conflict surrounded a range of fundamental issues, all of which affected people's health. There was disagreement over the extent to which wartime production requirements should take priority over long-standing assumptions about the place of women and of ethnic minorities in British society. Attitudes did change during the course of the war towards groups such as the elderly and towards the type of health service which should be provided after the war. However, there was never a consensus in society over these issues. The population's health improved overall, but the strong relationship between inequalities in standards of living and inequalities in standards of health remained intact. There was, however, an expectation that the projected national health service would sever this relationship. Hopes for a brighter and healthier future were never higher than at the end of the war.

NOTES

1. **Addison P.** 1977 *The road to 1945*. Quartet, p. 14. First published 1975.
2. **Titmuss R.** 1950 *Problems of social policy*. HMSO, pp. 506–17.
3. **Winter J.** 1983 Unemployment, nutrition and infant mortality in Britain, 1920–1950. In Winter J. (ed) *The working class in modern British history: Essays in honour of Henry Pelling*. Cambridge University Press, pp. 249–51.
4. Imperial War Museum tape, The Home front: Life in Britain, 1939–45. Section 1.
5. Quoted in **Ceadel M.** 1980 Popular fiction and the next war, 1918–39. In **Gloversmith F.** (ed) *Class, culture and social change: A new view of the 1930s*. Harvester Press, pp. 161–84.
6. H.C. Deb vol. 329 col. 42 15 November 1937 Sir Samuel Hoare.
7. Titmuss R. *Problems of social policy*. pp. 19–21.
8. Ibid. pp. 24–35.
9. Ibid. p. 60.
10. Ibid. pp. 73, 78.
11. Imperial War Museum tape section 6.
12. **Calder A.** 1969 *The people's war: Britain 1939–1945*. Panther, p. 261.
13. Imperial War Museum 84/46/1 Mrs G. Cox London war diary, 1939–45 2 October 1940.
14. Imperial War Museum Mrs E. M. Mascall unpublished diary 'All change' p. 170.
15. Imperial War Museum Mrs I. Byers unpublished diary p. 41.
16. **Jones H.** 1993 *A liberal feminist? The papers and correspondence of*

Violet Markham 1896–1954. The Historians Press, Rachel Crowdy to Violet Markham 14 September 1944.

17. **Braybon G., Summerfield P.** 1987 *Out of the cage: Women's experiences in two world wars*. Pandora, p. 182.
18. **Harrison T.** 1978 *Living through the Blitz*. Penguin, pp. 86–7.
19. **Townsend C., Townsend E.** 1989 *War wives: A Second World War anthology*. Grafton, pp. 2–3.
20. **Macnicol J.** 1986 The effect of evacuation of school children on official attitudes to state intervention. In **Smith H.** (ed) *War and social change: British society in the Second World War*. Manchester University Press, p. 5.
21. **Harrison T.** *Living through the Blitz*. p. 96.
22. **Harrison T., Madge C.** 1940 *War begins at home*. Chatto and Windus, pp. 216–17.
23. Titmuss R. *Problems of social policy*. pp. 506–7 and *passim*; **Gosden P.** 1976 *Education in the Second World War: A study in policy and administration*. Methuen, p. 18, pp. 3–4 and *passim*; **Minns R.** 1980 *Bombers and mash: The domestic front, 1939–45*. Virago, pp. 17–21.
24. **Macnicol J.** The effect of evacuation of schoolchildren on official attitudes to state intervention. p. 15.
25. **Isaacs S. S.** (ed) 1941 *The Cambridge evacuation survey: A wartime study in social welfare and education*. Methuen & Co., p. 47.
26. Similar complaints were not made about children evacuated to Canada. **Bilson G.** 1988 *The guest children: The story of the British child evacuees sent to Canada during World War II*. Fifth House, Saskatoon, p. 106.
27. Imperial War Museum tape section 3.
28. **Kushner T.** 1989 *The persistence of prejudice: Antisemitism in British society during the Second World War*. Manchester University Press, pp. 76–7.
29. **Ayers P.** 1988 *Women at war: Liverpool women, 1939–45*. Liver Press, p. 5.
30. Quoted in **Crosby T. L.** 1986 *The impact of civilian evacuation in the Second World War*. Croom Helm, p. 34.
31. **Ferguson S., Fitzgerald H.** 1954 *Studies in the social services*. HMSO and Longmans, Green & Co., p. 15.
32. Ibid.
33. PP 1941–42 vol. IV Report of the committee on amenities and welfare conditions in the three women's services. Chair: Violet Markham. Cmd 6384, pp. 49–51.
34. Braybon G., Summerfield P. *Out of the cage: Women's experiences in two world wars*. p. 218.
35. Ferguson S., Fitzgerald H. *Studies in the social services*. pp. 78, 90–2.
36. Quoted in **Leathard A.** 1980 *The fight for family planning: The development of family planning services in Britain, 1921–74*. Macmillan, p. 71.
37. Imperial War Museum 81/45/1 Mrs P. M. Clewett 1939 p. 7.
38. Ferguson S., Fitzgerald H. *Studies in the social services*. p. 99.
39. Imperial War Museum Miss Kay Phipps diary 22 September 1944.

40. Braybon G., Summerfield P. *Out of the cage: Women's experiences in two world wars*. pp. 217–18.
41. **Mass Observation** 1942 *An enquiry into British war production: Part 1 People in production*. The Advertising Service Guild, p. 228; Summerfield P. 1984 *Women workers in the Second World War*. Croom Helm, p. 99.
42. **Beveridge W.** November 1942 *Social Insurance and Allied Services*. Cmd 6404 HMSO.
43. **Riley D.** 1983 *War in the nursery: Theories of the child and mother*. Virago, p. 111.
44. **Summerfield P.** 1984 *Women workers in the Second World War*. Croom Helm, p. 125.
45. **Inman P.** 1957 *Labour in the munitions industries*. HMSO and Longman, p. 281.
46. **Ministry of Information** 1946 *The social survey of sickness October 1943 – December 1945*. HMSO.
47. Titmuss R. *Problems of social policy*. pp. 527–8.
48. Mass Observation *An enquiry into British war production: Part 1 People in production*. The Advertising Services Guild, pp. 253, 256.
49. **Mcfarlane N.** 1989 Hospitals, housing and tuberculosis in Glasgow, 1911–51. *Social History of Medicine* **2:** 74.
50. Imperial War Museum Helena Harrison war diary February 1944.
51. Imperial War Museum tape section 10.
52. PP 1943–44 vol. 3 Summary Report of the Ministry of Health for year ending 31 March 1944, p. 3; PP 1945–46 vol. 12 Summary Report of the Ministry of Health for year ending 31 March 1945, p. 3.
53. **Women's Cooperative Guild** 1943 *Head Office monthly bulletin* **4**(5): 4.
54. **Croall J.** 1988 *Don't you know there's a war on? The people's voice, 1939–45*. Hutchinson, p. 9.
55. Titmuss R. *Problems of social policy*. p. 531.
56. Bradford Heritage Recording Unit H0003 man born 1913, working in hospital as clerk.
57. Titmuss R. *Problems of social policy*. pp. 183, 193–4, 201, 467, 485–6.
58. Imperial War Museum Miss Kay Phipps 12 November 1941, 22 September 1944.
59. **Longmate N.** (ed) 1981 *The home front: An anthology of personal experience 1938–45*. Chatto and Windus, pp. 207–8.
60. Croall J. *Don't you know there's a war on? The people's voice, 1939–45*. p. 133.
61. The above section draws on cases detailed by **Lafitte F.** 1940 *The internment of aliens*. Penguin, pp. 95–254.
62. **Kochan M.** 1983 *Britain's internees in the Second World War*. Macmillan, pp. 51–76 and *passim*.
63. Croall J. *Don't you know there's a war on? The people's voice, 1939–45*. p. 134.
64. **Law I., Henfrey J.** 1981 *A history of race and racism in Liverpool, 1660–1950*. Merseyside Community Relations Council, p. 32; **Sherwood M.** 1984 *Many struggles: West Indian workers and Service personnel in Britain, 1939–45*. Karia Press, p. 82 and *passim*.

65. **Ford A.** 1985 *Telling the truth: The life and times of the British Honduran Forestry Unit in Scotland, 1941–44.* Karia Press, pp. 57–75.
66. **Smith G.** 1987 *When Jim Crow met John Bull: Black American soldiers in World War II Britain.* Tauris and Co. Ltd., pp. 42, 195–96.
67. Jones H. *A liberal feminist? The papers and correspondence of Violet Markham 1896–1954.* Cynthia Colville (Lady in Waiting to Queen Mary) to Violet Markham 24 August 1942.
68. Imperial War Museum Mrs E. Mascall, wartime diary p. 182.
69. **Means R., Smith R.** 1985 *The development of welfare services for elderly people.* Croom Helm, p. 25.
70. Voluntary hospitals were being paid by the Government to keep beds available for air raid casualties and so it was to their advantage to keep the beds empty, rather than allow those who were not war victims to use them.
71. Means R., Smith R. *The development of welfare services for elderly people.* pp. 28–31.
72. Imperial War Museum Miss Kay Phipps. Extract from letter to Kay Phipps 27 February 1943.
73. Means R., Smith R. *The development of welfare services for elderly people.* p. 17.
74. Ibid. pp. 29–105.
75. **Longmate N.** (ed) 1971 *How we lived then: A history of everyday life during the Second World War.* Hutchinson, pp. 341–42.
76. Mass Observation *An enquiry into British war production: Part 1 People in production.* pp. 282–3.
77. Braybon G., Summerfield P. *Out of the cage: Women's experiences in two world wars.* p. 226.
78. Inman P. *Labour in the munitions industries.* p. 224.
79. Mass Observation *An enquiry into British war production Part 1 People in production.* p. 254.
80. As a result of the Orders and pressure from Factory Inspectors, by April 1942, 3,538 factories which employed over 250 people provided canteens, and 3,115 factories which employed less than 250 workers provided canteens. There were 144 dock canteens and 739 building sites provided with canteens. In addition 803 canteens were in the course of erection in factories in which they could be required under the terms of an Order.
81. Titmuss R. *Problems of social policy.* p. 478.
82. Public Record Office (PRO) LAB 20/2 HPC (41) 28. 24 February 1941 F. M. Tribe.
83. PRO LAB 20/2 J. A. Barlow to F. N. Tribe 3 March 1941.
84. **Industrial Health Research Board** 1945 *Why is she away? The problem of sickness among women in industry.* MRC.
85. For example, Addison P. *The Road to 1945.*
86. For instance, **Eckstein H.** 1960 *Pressure group politics: The case of the British Medical Association.* George, Allen and Unwin.
87. **Macnicol J.** 1980 *The movement for family allowances, 1918–45: A study in social policy development.* Heinemann; **Deacon A., Bradshaw J.** 1983 *Reserved for the poor: The means test in British social policy.* Martin Robertson, pp. 35–48.

88. **Jefferys K.** 1987 British politics and social policy during the Second World War. *Historical Journal* **30:** 123–44.
89. PRO LAB 20/2 HPC (41) 28. 24 February 1941 F. M. Tribe.
90. Beveridge W. *Social Insurance and Allied Services.* pp. 153, 158.
91. **Jefferys K.** 1991 *The Churchill coalition and wartime politics, 1940–45.* Manchester University Press, pp. 118–29.
92. PRO MH 77/26 Ernest Brown to Ernest Bevin (undated).
93. PP 1943–44 vol. 8 A National Health Service Cmd 6502 p. 10.
94. *The Economist* 3 February 1945 p. 144.
95. HC Deb vol. 398 cols 427–518; 535–633, 16–17 March 1944.
96. Churchill College, University of Cambridge. Willink papers Box 2 file IV Unpublished autobiography.
97. Macnicol J. *The movement for family allowances, 1918–45: A study in social policy development.* p. 202.

Chapter 6
HIDDEN FROM VIEW: 1945–68

INTRODUCTION

For nearly a decade following the 1945 general election there were strong continuities with the war and even pre-war years, both in people's day-to-day lives and in the public controversies over the future shape of the health services. The National Health Service (NHS) was to display many of the characteristics of its forebears. In contrast to the immediate post-war years, the years from the mid-1950s to the late 1960s are distinguished by the degree of party political agreement over health-related issues. After 1951 the political storms subsided; for the rest of the decade and throughout the 1960s cross-party agreement on all substantive health service issues was the norm rather than the exception. During this decade and a half standards of living rose and the number of consumer goods multiplied: a spending spree on cars, televisions and holidays was underway. Young people had higher disposable incomes than ever before and this was reflected in the youth-led popular music and fashion industries. Yet, class, gender and ethnic inequalities and tensions remained, albeit more effectively masked than in the past. The gulf had never been wider between public harmony and private conflict over a range of influences on people's health and their sense of well-being: domestic violence, the double burden of paid work and domestic work, double standards between men's and women's morals, class inequalities in standards of health, and the experience of immigrants. In the late 1960s tensions which had long been bubbling below the surface suddenly erupted.

The euphoria of Victory Europe (VE) and Victory Japan (VJ) Day did not signal a bright new dawn of health and happiness for the people of Britain. The bombing raids ceased and the troops gradually returned home, but day-to-day struggles associated with the war continued remorselessly. Basic foods, sweets, chocolate and

117

clothes were all subject to the ubiquitous ration book. In July 1946 bread rationing was introduced for the first time. The size of the ration fluctuated. In 1948 a weekly ration consisted of 13 oz of meat, 1½ oz of cheese, 6 oz of butter and margarine, 1 oz of cooking fat, 8 oz of sugar, two pints of milk and one egg.[1] In the bitterly cold winter of 1946–47 fuel rationing was especially hard to bear. Rationing, which did not disappear completely until 1954, lowered spirits and contributed to the drabness of post-war Britain, but it was the housing crisis, the single most important domestic issue in the 1945 general election, which caused widespread hardship.

The wartime bombing, the lack of new building during the war and the shortage of building materials after it, meant that many people had to wait years for their own home. It was not uncommon for couples to start married life (as their parents before them) living with their in-laws. Homes were often of a low standard: dilapidated tenement blocks, old houses converted into cramped flats and back-to-backs dotted the landscape. In 1951 one-third of homes still had no bath. However, there was one positive aspect of wartime life which continued into the peace. Demobilised men found work in civvy streeet. Women's experiences in the labour market were less straightforward. On the one hand they were not dismissed *en masse* as had been the case at the end of the First World War, and indeed in 1947 the Government launched a campaign to lure women back into industry; but on the other hand, nursery places were hard to come by, and 'experts' were now issuing dire warnings about the consequences for young children's health and well-being if their mothers went out to work.

Despite the deprivations and austerity of post-war Britain, it was the plight of the hungry and homeless on the Continent which mobilised the public's sympathy. The 'Save Europe Now' campaign, launched in the autumn of 1945 by Victor Gollancz, a Jewish publisher, exposed the abysmal housing conditions, low standard of living and starvation rations of Germans. Notwithstanding rationing and shortages in Britain, various organisations sent parcels of food and clothes to Germany, and schoolchildren collected for the defeated enemy. During the vacations groups of students went over to Germany to help rebuild homes from the devastation and rubble.

A very different response, one of either hostility or indifference, greeted the European refugees shipped over to Britain by the Government in order to relieve the acute shortage of workers such as nurses and cleaners. The first scheme, Balt Cygnet, brought over a thousand women to work in hospitals. Known as European Volunteer Workers (EVWs), it was assumed that when their labour was no longer required they would be sent back to the Continent. Deportation was never carried out, although there were attempts to return Ukranians suffering from ill health. Before they were allowed to join a scheme refugees underwent a rigorous medical examination, in particular for VD, TB and pregnancy. Professionals, such as doctors and dentists, had to retrain before they were allowed to practice.[2] While EVWs were coming over to shore-up existing hospital provision, the future of the health services in general were the subject of intense debate.

THE CREATION AND EARLY WORKINGS OF THE NHS

In 1945 the Labour Party was returned to office with a commitment to a universal, free and comprehensive health service. The proposals put forward by Aneurin Bevan, the new Minister of Health, departed from the 1944 White Paper in one important principle; the voluntary hospitals were to lose their charitable status and be taken over by the government; in other words, they were to be nationalised. Bevan's plan, which he put to the Cabinet in October 1945, included other changes too: it gave more control to the Ministry of Health and greater encouragement to health centres and group practices in areas where there was a shortage of GPs. There was to be a salaried element in GPs' pay along with a capitation fee. Hospitals were to be reorganised, with the hospital governing system under regional boards, accountable to the Ministry of Health.[3]

Bevan faced considerable opposition from within the Cabinet, from the medical profession and from the Conservative Party. A row broke out in Cabinet between those led by Herbert Morrison (Lord President of the Council between 1945 and 1951) who wanted voluntary and municipal hospitals to remain under local authority control, and the majority of the Cabinet, led by Bevan, who wanted to end the charitable status of the voluntary hospitals and bring all hospitals under central government control. Bevan won the day, to go on to fight the medical profession, in particular those wealthy doctors at the head of the BMA who resented greater state control and the salaried element in doctors' pay.

While much has been made of Bevan's fight with the doctors, less attention has been paid to the hostility of the Conservative Party to Bevan's proposals. As the NHS Bill was passing through Parliament the Conservative Party maintained that it accepted the Bill in principle but opposed the clauses which departed from the 1944 White Paper. This claim was misleading as the main departure which it opposed was the nationalisation of the voluntary hospitals, which was a matter of principle. The party was privately concerned that it should gain some credit for the Act; it wanted to avoid any widespread impression that the Government was proposing a great step forward in the health services and all the Conservatives could do was latch on to questions of money.[4] Nevertheless, a number of Conservatives mounted an attack on Bevan and the Bill. In terms of parliamentary tactics, the Conservative position was a disaster, for the party gained no real concessions and saddled itself with a popular image it had wanted to avoid. The party appeared to become the mouthpiece of vested interests, while failing to present a coherent alternative policy.[5] The party's fiercest attack was on the incorporation of the voluntary hospitals into the new NHS. Conservatives believed that while there should be regional planning boards, the ownership and administration of voluntary hospitals should be left in private hands. Attacks were also launched on the proposed health centres, referred to as one of the Bill's 'grave blemishes'. The Conservatives put forward amendments to the Bill's second and third readings. Opposition was far more than a matter of detail, for the Second Reading Amendment read:

this House, while wishing to establish a comprehensive health service, declines to give a Second Reading to a Bill which prejudices the patient's right to an independent family doctor, which retards the development of the hospital services by destroying local ownership, and gravely menaces all charitable foundations . . . which weakens the responsibilities of local authorities without planning the health services as a whole.[6]

The Conservative Party outside Parliament was also keen to preserve the voluntary hospitals.[7]

Historians such as David Dutton, David Marquand, Dennis Kavanagh and Peter Morris argue for the existence of a post-war consensus over the setting up of the NHS. Their definitions of consensus include a framework of common assumptions about the role of the state and a commitment to collective provision of comprehensive welfare services.[8] These criteria did not exist either at the planning or implementation stages of the NHS. If one takes into account both the antipathy of much of the Conservative Party and medical profession during the war and in 1946 during the passage of the NHS Bill, it is difficult to maintain the view that the creation of the NHS was based on a political consensus. Between 1945 and 1951 disagreements within the Cabinet, between the Government and the medical profession and between the Government and Conservative opposition all belie the notion that the NHS received a unanimously warm welcome. Charles Webster, official historian of the NHS, has certainly thrown cold water on the idea of a consensus over the creation of the NHS. Moreover, public opinion at the time detected little of the consensus with which certain historians have characterised the period. In the early 1950s opinion polls revealed that a majority of the nation saw a good deal of difference between the major parties; it was only later in the decade, when Conservative governments did not dismantle the welfare state, that political parties were popularly perceived as pursuing similar policies.[9]

Kenneth Morgan, who underlined the lack of continuity between wartime Conservative plans and post-war Labour ones, listed the main aspects of the 1946 National Health Service Act which became operational in July 1948: the nationalisation of the hospitals; new regional hospital boards; the creation of health centres; a better distribution of doctors around the country; and new salary provisions for doctors, including provisions for specialists to treat private patients in NHS hospitals.[10] Although there were real fears that the doctors might refuse to work in the new system, at the last moment Bevan successfully won them over with a conciliatory gesture. On 7 April 1948 Bevan confirmed that a full-time salaried service would not be introduced, so the capitation element would continue, and doctors would be free to air their opinions publicly on the running of the NHS.[11] As a result of disagreements at the planning stage of the NHS, compromises were reached which automatically built weaknesses into the system, and ensured that the NHS was mainly a national *hospital* service. In the early years of the NHS little effort was put into preventing ill health.

Whatever else might have divided Labour politicians before the introduction of the NHS, they were unanimous in their commitment to a service free at the point of use. Within the Conservative Party there was no such agreement. Paradoxically, it was the Labour Government which rapidly came to be racked by self-doubt, controversy and crisis over the issue of funding, and the Conservatives who subsequently ruled for thirteen years without major internal or public controversy over funding policy. The Labour government, faced with the realities of office, had introduced some NHS charges and this policy was to be continued in the 1950s by Conservative governments. Disagreements over the funding of the NHS related almost entirely to the overall costs of the service. Little attention was paid to the distribution of resources between primary (non-hospital-based) and secondary (hospital-based) services, between teaching and non-teaching hospitals, or between regions.[12]

As soon as the NHS came into operation its costs became a political hot potato. The bald facts are that in 1949 prescription charges were authorised by the Government but never implemented and in 1951 charges for spectacles and teeth were imposed, resulting in the resignation from the Government of Aneurin Bevan (by now Minister of Labour and National Service), Harold Wilson (President of the Board of Trade), and John Freeman (Financial Under-Secretary at the War Office).

During the planning stages of the NHS it was erroneously assumed that there was a set amount of illness in the country and that while the introduction of a free health service might at first lead to a big jump in use because of the backlog of untreated complaints, in the long-term the costs would stabilise or even fall as the nation became healthier and required less treatment. When, therefore, in December 1948 Bevan told his Cabinet colleagues that his original estimate was going to be overshot it was not felt that there had been a major miscalculation in the projected costs of the service.

After the devaluation of the pound in the autumn of 1949, the Government made a major effort to economise. There was to be either a cutback in services or the imposition of prescription charges. The Cabinet decided on presciption charges. Bevan justified the introduction of prescription charges to the Parliamentary Labour Party on the grounds that there were 'cascades of medicine pouring down British throats – and they are not even bringing the bottles back!' But why was he willing to accept prescription charges in 1949 when in 1951 he resigned over the Government charging for spectacles and false teeth? One of his biographers (John Campbell) suggests that in 1949 Bevan still believed that the Labour Government could lead the country along the road to socialism and prescription charges were a short detour. On a personal level, Bevan admired Stafford Cripps, Chancellor of the Exchequer in 1949, and hated Hugh Gaitskell who replaced him. Moreover, Bevan agreed to waive his belief in a free health service on the first occasion because old age pensioners were to be exempted, and as this would reduce the revenue from prescriptions from £10 million to £6 million Bevan hoped that the administrative cost of collecting the charges would not make their imposition worth the Government's while. The prescription charges were presented, by both Clement Attlee, the Prime Minister, and Bevan, as a means of protecting the Health Service against abuse.[13]

In 1951 problems over the NHS's budget came to a head. The defence budget had leapt up since the summer of 1950 when Britain became embroiled in the Korean War, and this had consequences for welfare, especially health, expenditure. Early in 1951 the new Minister of Health, Hilary Marquand, accepted the need for charges on spectacles and false teeth, and the imposition of prescription charges, already accepted in principle back in 1949. When the charges were announced in the Chancellor's Budget speech, Aneurin Bevan, Harold Wilson and John Freeman resigned.

The key question is whether the imposition of charges was contrary to the principle of a health service free at the point of use. Bevan argued that health expenditure was being sacrificed at a time of escalating defence spending in response to American pressure. As John Campbell has pointed out, there were already some charges within the Health Service: for instance, for regular transport to hospital in rural areas, and for treatment after a road accident. These charges were not, however, symbols of the principle of a free service in the same way as dentures, spectacles and prescriptions: for Bevan it was a matter of principle, even though there were inconsistencies in that principle. With hindsight we can see that Bevan's argument was borne out by later events. Defence expenditure was overestimated, while the income from prescription charges made little impact on the overall costs of the Health Service, and the massive leaps in expenditure in the first three years of the NHS were the result of a backlog of needs, not a sign that Health Service costs were careering out of control.[14]

One long-term consequence of a Labour government accepting prescription charges was that the Labour Party was never able to criticise, with any moral authority, future Conservative governments for extending charges, and indeed Conservatives were quick to point to a precedent which had been set by Labour.[15] The Labour movement's fear that the Conservatives would dismantle the NHS when returned to office proved unfounded.

By the time the Labour government fell in 1951 the Conservatives' problem was to find a distinctive policy which would not be open to the criticism that the Tories were undoing Labour's achievement. The Guillebaud Committee was set up to report on how the NHS might be managed more effectively. In 1956 its report gave the Conservatives no ammunition for an attack on the NHS, rather the reverse, for the report concluded that the NHS gave value for money and it would not be possible to make any substantial savings. Minor savings were made by implementing Labour's provision for prescription charges, and by increasing spectacle and dental charges. (In 1964 Labour abolished prescription charges, and in 1967 reintroduced them.)

THE IMPACT OF THE NHS

The NHS was viewed by both its supporters and its critics as the flagship of British socialism. Aneurin Bevan certainly believed that the creation of the NHS was a watershed in health service provision. After 1948 the financial worries associated with medical treatment vanished. The importance of a free service, especially for children, young workers and the vast majority of married women who had not been covered by National Health Insurance, should not be underestimated.

It would seem that women, who had not normally been covered by National Health Insurance, and who had probably been hardest hit by poverty, gained most from the NHS. The full extent of women's ill health had never before been revealed. One woman doctor who qualified on the day the NHS came into operation recalled women queuing with thyroid deficiency, gynaecological problems, painful varicose veins, or with menopausal difficulties.[16] The biggest increase in visits to the GP came from the elderly and from women aged up to thirty-five.[17] The day-to-day running of the hospitals might not have appeared very different, but the new funding arrangements for the old voluntary hospitals, now part of a state system, brought enormous relief, as flag days to raise money for the hospitals passed into memory: ('begging and rattling' became a thing of the past).[18] One consultant physician welcomed the NHS because he felt it would improve the distribution of specialist skills (in particular anaesthetists, paediatricians, gynaecologists and orthopaedic surgeons) around the country.[19]

This picture of a distinctive health service which made a clean break with the past needs some modification. Most historians now point to significant continuities in health-care provision. The creation of the NHS did not in itself lead to the building of any new hospitals, the training of extra doctors or the evolution of new drugs and treatment.[20] The anecdotes cited above, giving the impression that people who had previously not been able to afford the doctor now flocked to their GP, needs to tempered by the knowledge that those who were brought up in pre-NHS days have been less inclined than their children to use the service, and that over the years the working class have under-used NHS facilities.[21] The provision of health care improved dramatically, but inequalities in access and use remained.

Bevan's compromises had sown the seeds of future problems and left in place many features of the old health-care system. As a result of the compromises which he made with the medical profession, teaching hospitals were given a special status, and a disproportionate allocation of resources, private practice and pay beds in NHS hospitals was permitted; doctors, but no other health workers, were allowed to sit on management bodies; and the proposed health centres, which would have played a major role in preventative work and co-ordination of services, were shelved because of doctors' fears that they would become subject to local authority control. Regional inequalities were built into the system by allowing teaching hospitals to continue to hold a special status. Emphasis on a hospital service rather than on primary and preventative community care, co-ordinated through health centres, meant that the NHS was increasingly out of step with the changing health needs of the population; it never encompassed all aspects of health care. The most serious omission was that of an occupational health service. Mortality and morbidity statistics show a continuity in trends, although their usefulness in this context is limited. Much illness does not show up in official statistics, and it is difficult to judge how quickly a new health-care system would change a country's standards of health: should one allow a decade or a generation? This in turn raises the problem of how to disentangle the impact of a health-care system from other influences, such as standards of living or the environment, on standards of health. The main decline in mortality rates had occurred by the end of the Second World War, before the creation of the NHS. Life expectancy continued to improve. By the time the NHS came into operation the major infectious diseases were already under control. Deaths from TB had fallen as a result of rising living standards and the introduction of a new drug, streptomysin; from the early 1950s further protection was provided by the introduction of BCG vaccination. Even so, Scottish TB rates were slow to drop and remained high compared with other countries. Infectious diseases could now be treated more effectively with antibiotic or chemotherapeutic drugs. Immunisation against diphtheria was already underway before the NHS came into operation. Soon, there was to be immunisation against polio, measles, and rubella. Rising standards of living, together with medical advances, meant that people were better able to withstand infectious diseases. Where standards of living were slowest to rise, infectious diseases, such as TB, were more persistent.

As deaths from infectious diseases declined, medicine turned its attention to the new major killers, such as cancer, coronary heart disease and bronchitis. While the old infectious diseases fell only slowly in Scotland, the new killers rose quickly. Medicine increasingly intervened with surgery, radiotherapy and chemotherapy. These techniques, which can produce unpleasant side effects, sometimes cure and sometimes delay death.

THE PERSISTENCE OF INEQUALITIES

In a country with a free health service available to all, full employ-ment and state welfare benefits throughout life, it was generally assumed that significant class inequalities in the standard of living, and poverty (with its attendant ill-health) were virtually eradicated. In the 1950s and 1960s lone voices questioned this reassuring pic-ture.[22] Only later in the 1970s and 1980s did the persistence of class-related inequalities in standards of health become a full-blown academic and public debate.

The quality of people's homes continued to exert a strong influence on their health. Families struggled along in condemned properties until the mid-1950s when the slum clearance programme (on the back-burner since the outbreak of war) took off. Blocks of high-rise flats provided no solution to the housing problem and many became unpopular while families were still moving into them. Isolation, lack of amenities, broken lifts and vandalism created new housing problems. Building programmes and renovation did not make up for the housing shortage, and throughout the 1950s and 1960s homelessness proved an ever-growing problem with its risks of mental ill health, and of children being taken into care. The problem remained largely hidden until the 1966 television play *Cathy come Home* aroused the nation's conscience. Campaigns followed, spearheaded by Shelter, the newly formed campaign against homelessness.[23]

In the early years of the NHS evidence of class inequalities in standards of health was patchy. A study of all babies born during one week in 1958 showed that a baby's birth weight was closely linked to its parents' social class, and that normal length (thirty-eight to forty-one week) pregnancies were most common in class 1 and steadily declined thereafter.[24] Over the years many more studies were to appear which highlighted the class-related inequalities across a wide range of areas.[25] From the late 1940s to the early 1960s inequalities between men in the highest and lowest occupational groups widened. During the 1960s the health of men in class 5 improved relative to those in other classes but the gap still remained wider than it had been in the 1949–53 period. Variations in standards of health for women of different classes have not been as great as for men but, in the 1950s and 1960s, the gap between women of different classes increased.[26] As the Registrar-General equates occupation with class for the purposes of his analysis, it is worth considering the links between occupation and illness at this time.

As the negative effects of unemployment receded in a period of virtually full employment, poor working conditions were still perceived as playing a major part in men's ill health. A 1952 study of men working in heavy industry in Wallsend found that they identified their work as having a more harmful effect on their health than any other single factor. Fumes, damp conditions, dirt, noise, heat and artificial or inadequate lighting at work, were all seen as producing tiredness and nervous strain. Other aspects of their lives, such as damp housing, a dirty environment, and domestic troubles were all thought by the men themselves to have less effect on their overall health.[27]

Clocking-on for work was a hazardous business. Every year tens of thousands of workers sustained an accident at work (of which about one-third went unreported). Hundreds of people lost their lives at the workplace. Roughly half of these deaths were due to very simple causes, such as a fall or a vehicle moving; they were not the result of a too rapid embrace of sophisticated technology.[28]

The most comprehensive occupational health schemes continued to be private ones in large factories. Such schemes varied considerably. In some cases they were limited to the occasional examination of high-risk workers, in other cases they comprised a broad spectrum of medical treatment: nursing and first aid services; examining new entrants to industry; examining all workers; examining workers returning from sick leave; minor surgical treatment; infra-red and ultra-violet ray treatment; massage; chiropody; ophthalmic and dental treatment; and the keeping of sickness records. Treatment was usually given in the firm's time, while dental and ophthalmic services were arranged under the NHS. In new factories the youngest and oldest workers often received special attention. Interestingly, for a period when poverty supposedly went unacknowledged, 'Signs of malnutrition are watched for in young workers and at one factory this is related to cases where the home environment is known to be below normal.' The shortage of labour at this time is reflected in the efforts of medical examinations to extend the working life of older workers, either by improving working conditions or by transferring them to different work.[29]

One new initiative was the grouping together of firms to provide a health scheme. The first such scheme, which began in Slough in 1947, was jointly funded by the individual firms, the Nuffield Foundation and the Nuffield Provincial Hospital Trust; it covered roughly 145 firms and 14,400 workers. The aim was to provide a service which would meet the health needs of both large and small firms in the area. Hazards were investigated and workers rehabilitated and resettled after illness or injury. Initially, the scheme provided an emergency casualty service and facilities for medical examinations.

While privately funded schemes were developing, the Government set up a Committee, chaired by Judge Dale, to look into the future of a state occupational health service. In 1951 the Dale Committee reported that there should be no change in the organisation of industrial medicine. Despite this negative response from government, the medical profession continued its calls for an occupational health service integrated with the NHS.

Welfare schemes in general, and medical ones in particular, tended to be found in large firms or nationalised industries which employed only a minority of the workforce. Most workers were employed in small-scale undertakings without an occupational health scheme, and it was for these workers that the TUC wanted medical facilities. In the early 1950s nearly half of factories employing 250 or more workers had a medical service whereas only 1 per cent of smaller factories had any kind of service. Part-time workers, the majority of whom were women, were least likely to benefit from firms' welfare schemes, yet they increasingly struggled under the double burden of paid and unpaid work.

DOUBLE STANDARDS

Women did not return to their homes in the same numbers as after the First World War: a labour shortage meant that they were actually needed in industry and in professions such as teaching and nursing. Yet women remained predominantly in low-paid, unskilled and low-status work.[30] The cult of domesticity and 'femininity' caught women in a double bind of paid work, domestic work and child care. Experts, such as John Bowlby, warned that young children needed their mothers at home with them if they were to grow up into healthy and normal citizens. Child delinquency could, allegedly, be traced to a lack of maternal attention and affection. A woman's decision to enter the labour market was not merely a private one, for it had implications for the social fabric of society. There is no agreement over the extent to which distinct gender differences were blurred by mid-century. In the early 1950s Michael Young suggested that during and after the war wives' housekeeping allowances did not keep pace with their husbands' earnings. A 1952 opinion poll suggested that housekeeping allowances rose less in poorer than richer families, less in older than younger ones, and less in the south of Britain than in other areas. State welfare, such as family allowances, school meals and milk, and food supplements all helped women's budgets, but from 1950 women were hit harder than men by increases in the cost of food and clothing.[31] Elsewhere, Young was to argue that relations between men and women were becoming closer as ties weakened between women across the generations.[32] Both these assertions have been challenged. For instance, in one traditional mining town in the 1950s it was found that men and women still maintained quite separate responsibilities and social lives. The wife spent money on the family and household items, the husband spent money on himself. A wife was expected to keep the home clean, warm and comfortable, and to cook a good meal. If she could not do all of these things on the money allocated to her, then 'marital discord' would follow.[33] What this 'discord' actually entailed was not stated, and indeed the whole question of domestic rows and violence received little public attention or academic recognition at this time. When marriage and the family were being upheld as the ideal for which all women should strive, the violent side of marriage was not something which social scientists and social commentators chose to focus on. Yet, violent attacks by men on women in the home poses the most serious challenge to the notion that women and men were living in greater domestic harmony.

Women continued to suffer from the fear, and the reality, of violent attacks in their home. Evidence from the East End of London suggests that domestic violence was still regarded as an unfortunate fact of life which had to be endured. Domestic violence was probably the greatest threat to women's safety, it remained within the 'private' domestic sphere, neighbours most typically turned a blind eye and it was certainly not revealed to outside researchers.[34]

Gender divisions in the home meant that even when married women were engaged in paid work, they were burdened with domestic work and they, rather than their husbands, would look after dependent relatives (either children or parents). Even though men spent more time at home than in the past and undertook 'odd jobs' around the house, the sexual division of labour remained. In some working-class homes girls were still expected to give domestic work priority over attending school. One Glasgow woman, born in 1942, recalled that from the age of eight she had to stay at home for a month to help her mother with the cooking and washing every time a new baby arrived. Another woman, the eldest of twelve, had to stay away from school one day every one or two weeks so that her mother could get all the washing done.[35]

Caring was still viewed as a private and individual problem for women: community support services remained inadequate. There was a chronic shortage of nurses working in public health. Health visitors, responsible for pregnant women, nursing mothers and young children, and occasionally the aged sick and follow-up services for those who had received hospital treatment, such as diabetics, were in constant demand.[36] Too much can therefore be made of the extent to which professionals, such as health visitors and social workers, were used to teach women how to avoid and overcome problems such as 'child delinquency', for which women were blamed. There were too few, rather than too many, professionals in the support services, and it was the elderly, the majority of whom were women, whose health needs were left unmet.

Older women also suffered from the lack of adequate hospital provision for the aged sick. The shortage of suitable geriatric units encouraged the development of a new approach which aimed at rehabilitating the elderly so that they could return to as normal a life as possible. In the early 1950s special efforts to rehabilitate the elderly were made in Dundee and Glasgow. A growing awareness of the problems of loneliness for older people was accompanied by an expansion of meals-on-wheels and old people's clubs. However, many of the needs of the elderly and the handicapped (such as sheltered housing, frequent domiciliary visits, transport and informal company) failed to be met by either the housing or health services. It was only slowly dawning that the needs of the elderly required the co-operation of various types of services, and that they should be as much a part of community services as the care of the young.[37] The elderly not only received a poor service from the NHS, but they were also falling behind by the rising standards of living of those in paid work.

A double standard flourished, not only in the expectation that women would undertake an unpaid caring role, but also in all matters pertaining to sex. These responsibilities inevitably affected women's well-being. In the early post-war years sexual promiscuity was still an important factor by which a woman was judged by neighbours and acquaintances. The double standard for women and men was still strongly in evidence. For instance, a 1956 study of birth control written by the chair of the Birmingham Family Planning Association (FPA) displayed a highly judgemental attitude towards women, but not towards men. She referred to women as feckless, lazy, muddle-headed and incompetent, and commented that 'women least competent to rear a family are exactly the ones most easily discouraged from persevering with contraceptives'.[38]

When assessing the extent to which there was a sexual revolution in the 1960s, commentators have tended to use surveys of respondents' sexual behaviour, but these are not always reliable. An alternative way of measuring the scope of change is to look at attitudes towards prostitutes and towards unmarried mothers, and when this is done, it is hard to detect a crumbling of double standards for men and women.

The 1950s witnessed a moral panic over prostitution on the streets of London. Hysteria peaked in 1951 at the time of the Festival of Britain, and again in 1953 during the Coronation of Elizabeth II.[39] The mood of the country revealed deep-rooted sexism. The fact that women were resorting to prostitution and then being singled out for condemnation is both an indicator of the economic difficulties facing some women and of the double standards applied to male and female sexual behaviour. The number of arrests for prostitution increased, but it is impossible to know whether this reflected an increase in the number of prostitutes or a clamp-down by the police.[40]

Women, whether or not they were married, could receive financial assistance from the state (National Insurance, or if uninsured National Assistance) during and after their pregnancy. In 1947 a shortened form of birth certificate was introduced, stating the name of the child, but not, as in the full version, her or his parentage; so illegitimacy was not thereby disclosed. While this may reflect a weakening of the urge to stigmatise unmarried mothers and their children[41] the overwhelming condemnation of society still fell heavily on the unmarried mother, whether or not her baby was given up for adoption.[42]

During the war it was assumed that it was preferable for the natural mother to keep her child, but in the post-war years this argument was challenged by respected academics, such as John

Bowlby, who argued that unmarried mothers bringing up their own children generated cycles of deprivation through families. Much time was spent investigating the alleged abnormalities of unmarried mothers' personalities and experiences, such as broken homes, severe disruption in early life, delinquency, promiscuity or neuroses. There was an unceasing search for an explanation for the behaviour of a group of women still widely regarded as different. As religious taboos against pre-marital sex became less relevant to many people, uninformed prejudices against unmarried women and their children were reinforced by a range of spurious pseudo-scientific research which labelled illegitimate children as unsocialised, aggressive, disturbed or delinquent.[43]

In the early 1950s roughly one-fifth of unmarried pregnant women entered Mother and Baby Homes where they lived for a period both before and after the birth of the baby. Some of the babies were then handed over for adoption, not infrequently after pressure from social workers and relatives. The existence of these Homes might be seen as a practical expression of a willingness to help unmarried mothers, but many aimed to increase rather than relieve a woman's suffering, not only to punish her but also to act as a terrible deterrent to other women. In the late 1960s a survey of a number of Mother and Baby Homes found almost all of them to be gloomy, dismal, bleak and shabby with worn and clumsy furniture, some of which was broken or unsafe to use. The depressing atmosphere, which affected the morale of both staff and residents, confirmed the impression of the women when they entered the Home that it was comparable to a workhouse or a prison. In certain Homes the depressing conditions were the result of a management policy to inflict further suffering on the women. The existence of these Homes, whether run by local authorities, religious groups or other organisations, suggests that society condoned such institutions and believed that they should be punishment centres. Rules and regulations varied from Home to Home. The range of forbidden activities included going outside the Home (in one case this included the garden) without permission, bus rides, visits to certain shops or parts of town, meetings with friends or even parents. Most Homes had set visiting times, one matron sometimes opened the women's letters and another would occasionally stand over them while they opened their post. In two-thirds of the Homes the research team did not feel that matrons provided sympathy or support for the women. Many of the residents, although resenting the rules, chose not to go out because they did not wish to be seen by censorious or gossipy neighbours and acquaintances.[44] In the late 1960s it was still the case that if birth control failed or was not used it was women who paid the price.

SEX AND LEISURE

The responsibility for birth control still rested with women. One health visitor who worked in London after the war commented that while she offered mothers information on birth control, their husbands would not bother to buy condoms or would refuse to use them. Embarrassment would also have deterred some men from buying condoms. In chemists' shops contraceptives were hidden behind the counter. One man who worked in a chemist's shop in the late 1950s could not recall anyone asking for contraceptives in a normal voice; indeed many drew attention to themselves by their shifty manner.[45]

By the 1950s most women were using some form of contraception, although this varied according to factors such as age and religion. The reasons for severely pruning family size were the same as in the 1920s and 1930s. Women were less willing to tolerate the hard conditions of their mothers whose lives were remembered as one long round of drudgery and ill health. The trend towards smaller families continued into the post-war years and this was probably the single most important factor in raising the standard of women's health. In the early post-war years the housing shortage, the lack of domestic help, inadequate maternity provision and the greater availability of birth control information meant that as well as there being a strong desire among women for smaller families, the means were available for them to make a choice over the size of their families. From the mid-1950s a higher standard of living was within the grasp of more and more families.[46] The post-war expansion of grammar school places for girls widened their horizons beyond boys and marriage to boys, marriage and a career.

A survey at the end of the 1960s found 83 per cent of mothers approved of contraceptives: 'I think it's a good thing. We ourselves take every precaution – well if you understand it you can enjoy your sex life and not worry about having children you can't afford.' Another woman commented 'I agree with it. It's no good for you or the children having them all the time like that. It wears you out and you haven't the patience with them.' The proportion of couples not using contraceptives was higher in the lower social classes than in the higher ones.[47] Attitudes were changing more slowly among poor people who would, anyway, have found it more difficult to afford contraceptives or to organise trips to the family planning clinic.

Attitudes towards birth control had undergone a gradual transformation and women were gaining greater access to contraceptives. By the 1950s the FPA was running 500 family planning clinics in conjunction with local authorities. In 1961 a reliable oral contrapective for women, 'the pill', became widely available. It was launched in a blaze of publicity,[48] and hailed as one of the greatest leaps forward for women in their struggle for independence. Even so, since the advent of the 'pill' controversy has been generated over its side effects, which include a greater risk of developing certain cancers and circulatory diseases.

Until the 1967 National Health Service (Family Planning) Act local authorities could only offer contraceptive advice and supplies to married women for whom further pregnancies would be a danger to their health. (Since 1964 the Brook advisory centres had welcomed unmarried women.) The 1967 Act authorised, although did not require, local authorities to assist all women (including the unmarried) with contraceptive advice and supplies on social as well as medical grounds. A year after the Act was passed about one-quarter of local authorities were providing a full family planning service. The Act, which had been a back-bench private member's Bill, was not as controversial as might have been expected, partly because birth control was no longer as emotive an issue as in the past, and partly because the Abortion Act of the same year deflected much potential outrage.

The 1967 Abortion Bill aroused stiff opposition, but was ultimately successful for a variety of reasons: fear of over-population and a public acknowledgement that fertility control was socially desirable; rising teenage pregnancies; demands from women to exert a greater control over their bodies and lives; the thalidomide tragedy, which helped to extend definitions of the quality of life to wider social issues; a diminishing willingness to tolerate back-street abortions; and a recognition that the number of legal abortions were already rising. In 1961 2,300 abortions were carried out under the NHS, by 1967 the number had risen to nearly 10,000 and there were a similar number carried out in private clinics. Estimates of the number of 'back-street' abortions ranged from 15,000 to 100,000.[49]

The Abortion Act allowed an abortion to be conducted if two doctors certified that a child would be a danger to the woman's physical or mental health, or if an abnormal child was expected. It was accepted that the social and medical grounds on which an abortion might be carried out could not be separated. As an early abortion is physically safer than a full-term pregnancy, there is always a medical justification for an abortion. The wide regional variations in the number of abortions caried out under the NHS may be an indication of divergent attitudes around the country or of the influence of individual doctors on the operation of the Act. (Abortion is still illegal in Northern Ireland.) By ending the need for back-street abortions the risks to women's health which accompany an unwanted pregnancy have been significantly reduced. Childbirth was, anyway, becoming safer as women were ever more likely to go into hospital to give birth, and to have fewer children.[50]

Extra-marital sex existed throughout the century, although it was heavily condemned in public. The pill, contraceptives becoming more easily available and the Abortion Act do not seem to have heralded a sudden change in sexual activity. In the mid-1960s a study of fifteen- to nineteen-year-olds found that two-thirds of boys and three-quarters of girls had not had sexual intercourse. Nor did this study find any evidence to suggest that pre-marital sex led to, or encouraged, adultery in marriage.[51] Another study carried out in the late 1960s found no evidence to support the view that there had been a radical change in sexual activity. Of those interviewed, 92 per cent opined that sexual fidelity in marriage was important. The fact that the pill was available did not alter these views,[52] and despite negative media images of campuses and communes, sexual mores were not undergoing a rapid transformation.

The 1960s image of a free-and-easy lifestyle did, however, reflect a genuine increase in the amount of leisure which most people now enjoyed. A holiday, for instance, came to be regarded as essential to one's well-being, as a means of escaping the drudgery and tedium of day-to-day life. The 1938 Holidays with Pay Act did not come into operation until after the Second World War. At first people continued to stay at seaside resorts in traditional hotels or bed and breakfast accommodation; however, in the 1950s holiday camps (where meals and entertainment were laid on) were much in vogue. During the 1960s holidays abroad became the expectation of the many, not the privilege of the few. Men and women in paid work all had a release from the work environment and its routine, and the pleasure gained from a holiday long outlasted the actual holiday itself: planning a holiday and then reminiscing over photographs became one of life's greatest pleasures. Holidays, apart from self-catering and camping ones, gave women a break from cooking and cleaning, and fathers on holiday were more likely to help look after the children.[53]

NURSING

Double standards, which meant that women were still expected to bear the burden of domestic work and health care for the family, were paralleled in the public sphere where the majority of nurses were women. Nurses are the single largest group of NHS employees. Despite the number of nurses, the impact of nurses' organisations, such as the Royal College of Nursing (RCN), on NHS policy-making was negligible. In 1946 the Wood Committee was set up to review the projected NHS's requirements in the recruitment and training of nurses. It recommended a shorter training period and better working conditions as a solution to the nursing shortage. The briefer training period was to be achieved by raising the educational entry requirements of nurses and by removing much of the repetitive work. The RCN, which had not been consulted, was extremely critical of this suggestion. The 1949 Nurses' Act adopted some, although not all, of the Wood Report's recommendations. It dealt with the funding of nurses' training, tightened up the registration of nurses, amalgamated the men's and women's register, and laid down a system for introducing changes to training courses. In some ways, however, gender stratification became more rather than less pronounced. Midwives, who carry a high status in nursing and probably exercise more discretion than other nurses, actually lost a degree of their autonomy under the NHS, for now they were legally subordinated to doctors. This subordination continued even after 1967 when they were permitted to undertake a number of highly skilled and responsible tasks, such as administering perineal anaesthesia; managing and removing epidural catheters; administering intravenous infusions; performing and suturing episiotomies, and testing a baby's blood.[54] Following the report of the Salmon Committee on Senior nursing staff structure, three tiers of management were created: top nursing managers who were to participate in determining hospital policy; a middle tier who were to put the policy into action, and a third tier of on-line managers who were to have executive functions. Although male nurses comprise only a small proportion of the nursing profession they have come to dominate nursing management.

Neither the creation of the NHS nor the 1949 Nurses' Act alleviated the chronic shortage of nurses, which in turn meant empty beds, overcrowded wards and long hours of work. Instead of making the profession more attractive by improving wages and working conditions, the Ministry of Health trawled for recruits in the New Commonwealth and Pakistan (NCWP), presumably on the assumption that immigrants would be more willing to put up with low wages and poor conditions. Enoch Powell, Minister of Health from 1960 to 1963, who first encouraged people from the NCWP to come and work in the NHS assumed that their stay would be temporary, and when they returned to their country of origin they would be replaced by a new wave of temporary immigrants. Many of the immigrants also assumed their stay would be a short one.[55] The availability of this source of cheap labour avoided decisions which would have increased the NHS's labour costs, and it helped to keep nurses' pay low and working conditions poor. The consequences for industrial relations of this failure to improve pay and conditions in the NHS began to show from the mid-1950s among mental nurses, who were especially badly off, and from the 1960s among other nurses.

IMMIGRANTS

At the end of the Second World War the Royal Commission on Population commented in its report that immigration on a large scale into a fully established society, such as Britain, could only be welcomed unreservedly if the immigrants were of 'good human stock' and were not prevented by their religion or their race from intermarrying with the host population and becoming merged into it.[56] Indeed an ability to merge with the indigenous population was to remain the chief yardstick by which immigrants were often judged; equality of status, such as health parity between different ethnic groups, was not an issue for the host population. In 1945 the Fabian Society described ideal immigrants as people of European stock, aged between twenty and thirty, and therefore of an economically active and fertile age, who were physically and mentally 'sound'.[57] When the supply of EVWs dried up, the desire for Christian Europeans was outweighed by the demands of the labour market for healthy workers. Britain now turned to the NCWP to bolster its economy.

The need for fit and economically active immigrants was underlined by the screening out of the 'unhealthy'. After 1962 medical examinations at the point of entry were introduced for immigrants from the NCWP, with the exception of dependants and returning residents; from 1965 dependants were also subject to examination.[58] The early post-war immigrants tended to come on their own rather than with their families, but the fear that single male immigrants would spread VD led to calls for immigrants to be admitted in family groups.[59]

Immigrants who arrived in Britain with high expectations received a rude awakening. A Jamaican woman, who came to England to work in the NHS, had thought of England as 'a kind of fairy godmother, the most extraordinary place on earth'. She was disabused of that idea almost as soon as she got off the plane.[60] An Indian man who came to England in 1962 experienced a constant feeling of alienation as he saw signs in north London shop windows 'No Blacks, No Indians'.[61] Racial attacks were a day-to-day experience for many immigrants, and in the 1950s and 1960s attacks with bricks and knives were commonplace in certain areas. Women took their sons shopping with them for protection,[62] and even walking down the street could be a frightening experience for a young girl subjected to racist taunts.[63] Most people were probably unaware of these daily dangers to a minority of the population, although in the summer of 1958 tensions snapped and riots, which received wide press coverage, broke out in the Notting Hill area of London.

Often it was difficult to know how far racism was the sole cause of physical and emotional attacks. The racism behind workmates shunning a black woman (born in this country) because she was 'not like one of them' is clear-cut.[64] In 1962 an incident which received widespread publicity was more ambiguous. During his second day at work a black bus conductor was attacked by a group of youths shouting racist abuse. The bus conductor lost an eye and his job. An article about his plight in *The Guardian* produced a flood of letters and donations, and it did seem to raise the consciousness of a section of the white population to the precarious situation in which many immigrants found themselves. However, one of the attackers later commented in a radio interview that he thought the trouble would have started anyway, regardless of the colour of the bus conductor.[65]

Evidence about the health of immigrants may be culled from a number of sources, providing us with a contrasting and often contradictory picture: research carried out at the time into the health of immigrants, which concentrated largely on the psychologically traumatic and destabilising effects of the process of migration; the testimony of those who were themselves immigrants, or who were white health workers coming into contact with immigrants; and secondary literature on immigrants and the Health Service.

Research into the health of ethnic minorities concentrated on infectious diseases and mental health, used very small samples, and was based on the assumption that immigrants from the NCWP were an additional burden on the NHS. The findings were often contradictory.[66] Cultural differences and changing ideas about mental illness necessitates great caution in dealing with research findings.

Most researchers claimed that mental illness rates were higher among West Indians than indigenous whites. The explanation for this difference was frequently located in the actual process of migration. This analysis fitted in with the findings of social scientists and psychiatrists who focused on the relationship between psychiatric illness and migration, and who usually concluded that migration led to increased mental illness because of the strange and often hostile environment in which the immigrants found themselves. Changes in diet and climate, exposure to new diseases, worry about children still in the country of origin and the absence of close family were all seen as being an inevitable part of the migratory process which could adversely affect people's health.[67] In 1964 it was argued that changes in West Indians' lives led to psychological problems: a woman neded to be emotionally supportive as well as a source of income; this was especially difficult for immigrant women who were isolated from friends and relatives. At the same time many West Indian men felt threatened by the increased economic independence of women and resented being called upon to act as babysitters. They reacted by drinking, promiscuity and emotional illness, which in turn led to an increased desire among the women for independence; hence a vicious circle of conflict was established.[68]

Many of the problems which immigrants themselves (as well as some researchers) felt were adversely affecting their health were not directly linked to the migratory process. Moreover, some of these problems have continued to affect second and third generation ethnic minorities, for whom the migratory process could not provide the causal link with poor health.

The difficulty of finding housing meant that immigrants frequently lived in overcrowded accommodation, often with inadequate heating and bathrooms. They faced all sorts of anxieties: the fear of pregnancy; the hostility of the majority population; the need to undertake paid work while being responsible for their children; exhaustion; employment problems; low rates of pay and poor working conditions – all of which could contribute to ill health. It was suggested that relatively high TB rates among ethnic minorities were probably the result of their poor working conditions[69] – conditions which were made worse by minorities' experiences of the NHS.

The negative experiences of black women when dealing with the health services have been graphically described. It has been argued that white male doctors were preoccupied with black women limiting the size of their families, and indifferent to those health issues of greatest concern to black women. Many doctors persuaded black women to accept contraceptives which carried a lower risk of pregnancy, but a higher risk to their health, and abortions were offered with unseemly haste.[70]

In contrast, Catherine Jones has presented a mixed but, on the whole, positive picture of health service provision for immigrants. Local authority health departments lacked information about newly arrived immigrants. When good relations existed between the health departments and immigrant community, new immigrants were traced through the immigrant grapevine; compulsory school medical examinations for new entrants and health visitors' reports on births could all provide information, but it was never comprehensive. Once immigrants had been identified, it could prove difficult to persuade them to be examined, especially if this was interpreted as discriminatory. Jones claims that health departments attempted to 'educate' immigrant mothers at clinics and that there was an abundance of special language literature covering a wide range of health issues. However, no interpreters were employed for a number of years; instead, children were used to interpret for their parents. If the problem was a 'very personal one' then children might not be used.[71] One district nurse recognised the limitations of such a practice but concluded that if one really needed to communicate with an Asian woman it was always possible. (How this was achieved remains a mystery).[72]

Jones identified three broad areas which created health-related problems. First, differences between immigrant practices and indigenous ones, for instance, dietary variations. Second, there were intrinsic limitations in the health services. They could not, for example, improve the poor housing of many immigrants. Third, there were race relations problems, such as medical procedures which were perceived to be discriminatory. Yet, Jones concludes that the most common view among health workers was that they should fall over backwards not to give offence.[73] One reason for the divergent views of black immigrants and white health workers was that health workers' own needs coloured their assessment of ethnic minorities' health needs. One nurse working in a Bradford hospital in the 1950s commented on the fact that Asian men were no problem to nurse because many of them did not speak English and they were, therefore, very quiet on the wards.[74]

It was frequently alleged that immigrants came to Britain in order to misuse the NHS, yet the NHS was heavily dependent on immigrant nurses and doctors.[75] They worked in hospitals, so supporting the area of health care given top priority by all governments.

Propaganda encouraging black women to come and train in Britain appealed to women in countries such as the West Indies, where nursing enjoyed a high status. Black women who applied for training in Britain were often unaware of the existence of three grades of nurses: State Registered Nurse (SRN), State Enrolled Nurse (SEN) and auxiliary nurse. Only the first of these qualifications was recognised in many immigrants' countries of origin. Although women from the NCWP were promised that if they trained as SENs they would later be able to take a shortened SRN course, in practice this proved difficult. With only an SEN qualification, black nurses faced poor promotion prospects and they also found it more difficult to return to their country of origin and work in nursing. Many black nurses also felt that racism affected their promotion prospects.[76]

THE WORKINGS OF THE NHS: SHORTCOMINGS AND DEVELOPMENTS

The dissatisfaction of NHS employees with their pay and conditions remained largely hidden, as did other fundamental weaknesses of the system. The creation of the NHS supposedly gave the public health services the opportunity to devote themselves to important aspects of primary health care, such as prevention and welfare (by relieving them of hospital administration which they had gained under the 1929 Local Government Act), but after 1948 public health went into a downward spiral with only a limited and ill-coordinated role within the NHS. Medical Officers of Health (MOHs) dealt with services outside the hospital; they were primarily co-ordinators of community health services and their work was mainly administrative.[77] As a result of the NHS Act they had lost responsibility for maternal and child welfare and now dealt almost exclusively with environmental health. Environmental health was well down on all governments' lists of priorities.

Rudolph Klein has emphasised that the NHS was essentially a national *hospital* service.[78] Although the hospitals received the lion's share of expenditure the constant pressure on funds meant that in the early years of the NHS maintenance and capital development were cut back. Even though concern over the shortage of hospital facilities had long been expressed, the creation of the NHS did not inaugurate a hospital-building programme. The NHS inherited old, poorly maintained hospitals with out-of-date services and poor staffing arrangements.[79]

From the mid-1950s, and throughout the 1960s, the emphasis in NHS planning was on a building and modernisation programme for hospitals. In 1955 Iain Macleod, Minister of Health from 1952 to 1955, announced a hospital-building programme which was to become the focus of both Conservative and then, in the 1960s, Labour health policy.[80]

The Conservatives' 1962 Hospital Plan was welcomed by Kenneth Robinson on behalf of the Opposition; the policy, taken up by the Wilson governments from 1964 to 1970, gave priority to hospital-building. The 1962 Hospital Plan recommended ratios of beds to population in different regions according to the use of the bed; for example, it distinguished between beds for acute, maternity, geriatric and mentally handicapped patients. The location of hospitals was a major concern of the Plan which recommended large District General Hospitals (DGHs), providing comprehensive and up-to-date treatment. The interdependence of many branches of medicine and the breadth of modern facilities which required large catchment areas for the smaller specialisms, such as radiotherapy and neurosurgery, as well as in-patient and out-patient treatment for maternity, short-stay psychiatric units and geriatric units could all be embraced by the DGH. The new hospitals reflected current thinking about the design of hospitals. The Nuffield Provincial Hospital Trust undertook research into hospital design and recommended single rooms of four to six beds grouped together, rather than the old Nightingale wards with their long corridors and lack of privacy.

In the 1960s intensive-care units were developed in which all the bodily functions could be performed artifically by machines. While these techniques are hailed, especially by the popular press and by those who have staked out high-status careers in the field, as the vanguard of medical advance, others have been more critical of scarce resources being used for techniques which are extremely expensive and benefit relatively few people. From the 1960s kidney dialysis was available, at first in hospitals and later at home. The machine removes waste products from the body, performing the function of the kidneys. However, it is an unpleasant and inconvenient system, and people on dialysis never feel completely well. Kidney transplants are, therefore, more attractive; although the technique was available from the 1960s there has always been a shortage of kidneys for transplant. Since the 1970s heart transplants have been undertaken and since the 1980s liver transplants have been performed. A widening array of drugs formed an integral part of this hospital-based treatment.

After 1948 people were able to accept treatment without the worry of whether or not they could afford the drugs' bill, but the ever-growing international pharmaceutical industry (really underway since the 1930s) was a mixed blessing. Conservative and Labour governments were both constrained from placing the pharmaceutical industry under state control because of the valuable contribution the industry played in maintaining British exports and thereby the balance of payments. Doctors were asked to avoid excessive prescribing and in 1957 voluntary price regulation was introduced. Still the NHS's drugs' bill soared.

The expansion of the pharmaceutical industry increased the risks of unsafe drugs, but until the problem reached a tragic climax between 1958 and 1961 when a number of babies were born with shortened limbs after their mothers had taken the thalidomide drug when pregnant, little public discussion had taken place on the subject. Ironically, the alleged safety of the thalidomide drug was a key element in its promotion. Basically an error arose because the drug did not cause side effects when one dose, however large, was injected into rats. The dangers from more than one dose had not been adequately investigated, even though it was known that drugs which are not toxic after one dose may be toxic if taken over a longer period.[81] As a result of the thalidomide tragedy, in 1963 a Safety of Drugs Committee was set up to scrutinise new drugs and monitor reactions to them. One of the most significant aspects of the pill-popping generation was the growing use of drugs to manage mental illness. At the same time this bucked the trend by leading the move away from hospitalisation.

The motives behind the running-down of mental hospitals, along with attempts to keep patients outside hospitals and in the community, have been much debated. The traditional view is that the development of tranquillisers in the 1950s meant that it was no longer necessary to incarcerate many of the mentally ill; this breakthrough in treatment was coupled with a humanitarian reaction against the worst aspects of institutional care. Anthony Scull, leading the assault on this interpretation, argued that turning patients out of mental hospitals was primarily an economy measure; mental institutions were among the most dilapidated of all hospitals, and their running-down preceded the effective use of drugs. Patients were turned out of institutions without any real evaluation of the effects this would have on them or on the community. The expansion of state welfare and state benefits meant that it was possible for those who would previously have been institutionalised to survive in the community.[82] Scull later modified his argument in the light of evidence from Peter Sedgwick and others that deinstitutionalisation preceded the acute fiscal crisis and that if one puts changes in Britain in a broader international context there is no automatic relationship between financial problems and a shift towards community-care policies.[83]

The shift from institutional to community care has been linked more closely with developments in psychiatric work. On the one hand it has been argued that the NHS created a parity of esteem between psychiatry and other branches of medicine,[84] but on the other hand, that mental health workers continued to be professionally isolated.[85] Clive Unsworth believes that the NHS did have an impact on mental health services by highlighting just how out of step they were with current medical thinking. Once the 1948 National Assistance Act had dismantled the last vestiges of the old Poor Law it was inevitable that mental health could not continue indefinitely within the framework of the 1890 Lunacy Act. Unsworth argues that reforms embodied in the 1959 Mental Health Act were seen as a consummation of the welfare state. The Act recognised mental disorder as an illness to be treated, and it gave the medical profession greater discretion in administering that treatment; the hospital was to be marginalised in the field of mental health.[86]

One other attempt to counter the emphasis on hospital treatment lay in the effort to raise the status of general practice and to integrate it more effectively with other health services. From the early years of the NHS, general practice was seen to be in need of an overhaul, partly to improve the professional status of GPs, and partly to meet more effectively the health needs of the population. The main suggestion concerned the co-ordination of different services under the umbrella of health centres.

The early purpose-built health centres were on new housing estates and provided surgeries for GPs with some common services and some local health authority services; in other respects they varied enormously. The 'show piece' health centre was Woodberry Down at Stoke Newington, planned by the London County Council before 1948, and comprising six surgeries for GPs, two for dentists, antenatal, postnatal and child welfare clinics, a school health clinic, child-guidance clinic, and an ophthalmic clinic. Consulting rooms and offices were attached for health visitors, midwives and school nurses, as well as a room for minor operations and a hall for health education lectures. A day nursery was established on the same site.[87]

Woodberry Down never acted as a catalyst for an expansion of health centres because critics of health centres claimed that it was not cost-effective.[88] Despite an upsurge in demand it was not until there had been a major review of the family doctor service in 1966 that the number of health centres grew significantly.

The re-emphasis on health centres was in part the result of gradually changing views about what it meant to be 'healthy'. From the 1940s there was a greater emphasis on seeing the patient in her/his total environment, which required the expertise of social workers and health visitors. Further, the changing nature of illness during the course of this century has meant that infectious diseases have declined, while chronic, degenerative illnesses are more common and require long-term care rather than acute hospital services. Yet, in the early post-war years expectations about what the NHS could achieve for an individual's standard of health were high. This optimism was accompanied by the view that one should feel well most of the time. Expectations of standards of health had risen, but this was often the triumph of hope over experience. Immigrants in particular found that their high hopes were not matched by the reality of their day-to-day lives and sense of well-being. The indigenous population, especially women, recognised that their health was much better than that of their mothers', mainly because they had fewer children to wear them down, but their expectations were also rising. A quarter of a century after the introduction of the NHS a fresh wave of cynicism and dissatisfaction with the health services had emerged. Stormy times lay ahead as criticisms of the NHS surfaced and many of the hidden influences on people's health came to light. Private miseries became public issues.

NOTES

1. Figures quoted in **Marwick A.** 1982 *British society since 1945.* Pelican, p. 74.
2. **Tannahill J.** 1958 *European volunteer workers in Britain.* Manchester University Press, pp. 19, 20, 26, 32, 44, 70, 80–2, 94–5, 101, 133.
3. **Morgan K.** 1985 *Labour in power, 1945–51.* Oxford University Press, p. 154.
4. Bodleian Library, Oxford. Conservative Research Department (CRD) 2/27/1 Brief on health service 14 March 1946.
5. **Hoffman J.** 1964 *The Conservative party in opposition, 1945–51.* Macgibbon and Kee, p. 235.
6. HC Deb vol. 422 col. 356, 2 May 1946.
7. For example, **London Municipal Society** 1946 *LCC elections 1946. The LCC hospital and medical services.* LMS, p. 7; **LMS** 1946

LCC Elections 1946 Hospitals and medical services. Lecture by
Dame Barrie Lambert, pp. 5–8.

8. **David Marquand** 1989 The decline of post-war consensus. In **Gorst A., Johnman L., Scott Lucas W.** (eds) *Post-war Britain, 1945–64: Themes and perspectives*. Institute of Contemporary British History, p. 1; **Kavanagh D., Morris P.** 1989 *Consensus politics from Attlee to Thatcher*. Basil Blackwell, p. 4; **Dutton D.** 1991 *British politics since 1945: The rise and fall of consensus*. Basil Blackwell. See also **Lowe R.** 1990 The Second World War consensus and the foundations of the welfare state. *Twentieth Century British History* **1:** 152–82. See citations in above references for other contributions to the debate.

9. **Bogdanor V., Skidelsky R.** 1970 *The age of affluence, 1951–1964*. Macmillan, pp. 71–2; **Webster C.** 1988 *The health services since the war vol. 1 Problems of health care. The National Health Service before 1957*. HMSO, pp. 389–93.

10. Morgan K. *Labour in power, 1945–1951*. p. 157.

11. HC Deb vol. 449 cols 164–6, 7 April 1948. Aneurin Bevan, Minister of Health.

12. Webster C. *The health services since the war*. p. 292.

13. **Campbell J.** 1987 *Nye Bevan and the mirage of British socialism*. Weidenfeld and Nicolson, pp. 182–4.

14. Ibid. pp. 246–7.

15. Bodleian Library Oxford CRD 2/27/9 6 February 1961 p. 2.

16. **Holdsworth A.** 1988 *Out of the doll's house: The story of women in the twentieth century*. BBC Books, p. 102.

17. Survey of sickness quoted in **Chamberlain M.** 1981 *Old wives' tales: Their history, remedies and spells*. Virago, p. 138.

18. Bradford Heritage Recording Unit (BHRU) H0003 Male clerical worker born 1913.

19. **Addison P.** *Now the war is over: A social history of Britain, 1945–51*. Jonathan Cape, p. 107.

20. **Watkin B.** 1978 *The National Health Service: The first phase, 1948–74 and after*. Allen and Unwin, p. 1.

21. See Chapter 8.

22. For example **Tony Lynes** 1962 *National Assistance and national prosperity Occasional papers on social administration*. Codicote Press; **Titmus R.** 1964 Introduction. In **Tawney R.** *Equality*. George Allen & Unwin pp. 18–22.

23. **Burke G.** 1981 *Housing and social justice: The role of policy in British housing*. Longman, pp. 66, 70; **Malpass P., Murie A.** 1987 *Housing policy and practice*. 2nd edn. Macmillan Education, p. 73.

24. Quoted in **Reid I.** 1981 *Social class differences in Britain*. 2nd edn. Grant McIntyre, p. 122.

25. See Chapter 8 for a discussion of class-related inequalities in health.

26. **Townsend P., Davidson N.** 1982 *Inequalities in health: The Black report*. Penguin, pp. 66–9.

27. **Wiggans K.** 1952 Job and health in a shipyard town *Sociological Review* **44:** 80–2.

28. PP 1966–67 vol. XXXI Annual Report of the Chief Inspector of Factories for 1966 p. 93.

29. PP 1956–57 vol. XII Annual Report of the Chief Inspector of Factories for 1955 pp. 143–51.
30. **Lewis J.** 1984 *Women in England, 1870–1950: Sexual divisions and social change.* Wheatsheaf, pp. 152–3, 205.
31. **Young M.** 1952 Distribution of income within the family *British Journal of Sociology* **3**: 313–20.
32. **Willmott P., Young M.** 1957 *Family and kinship in East London.* Routledge & Kegan Paul.
33. **Slaughter C.** 1956 Modern marriage and the roles of the sexes *Sociological Review* New Series **4**: 214–17.
34. See for instance **Cornwell J.** 1984 *Hard-earned lives: Accounts of health and illness from East London.* Tavistock, pp. 44–8.
35. **Straw P., Elliott B.** 1986 Hidden rhythms: Hidden powers? Women and time in working-class culture *Life stories* no. 2, pp. 36–7.
36. See, for example, PP 1951–52 vol. XV Report of the Ministry of Health for 1950–51 p. 66.
37. PP 1955–56 vol. XX Report of the Ministry of Health for 1954 p. 196; PP 1960–61 vol. XVII Report of the Department of Health for Scotland p. 39.
38. **Florence L.** 1956 *Progress report on birth control.* Heinemann, pp. 62–3, 80.
39. **Weeks J.** 1989 *Sex, politics and society: The regulation of sexuality since 1800.* 2nd edn. Longman, p. 240.
40. **Smart C.** 1981 Law and the control of women's sexuality: The case of the 1950s. In **Hutter B., Williams G.** (eds) *Controlling women: The normal and the deviant.* Croom Helm, p. 50.
41. **Yelloly** 1964 Social casework with unmarried parents: A critical evaluation of its theoretical aspects in the light of a study of extra-marital pregnancies. MA thesis University of Liverpool, p. 23.
42. **Pochin J.** 1969 *Without a wedding ring: Casework with unmarried parents.* Constable, p. 19.
43. Yelloly, Social casework with unmarried parents. pp. 31–3, 148.
44. **Nicholson J.** 1968 *Mother and Baby Homes: A survey of Homes for unmarried mothers.* George Allen & Unwin, pp. 61–88; **Spensky M.** 1992 Producers of legitimacy: Homes for unmarried mothers in the 1950s. In Smart C. (ed) *Regulating womanhood: Historical essays on marriage, motherhood and sexuality.* Routledge, p. 110.
45. **Thompson D.** 1975 Courtship and marriage in Preston between the wars *Oral History* **3**: 40 The author includes a comment about his experiences in the 1950s.
46. **Standing Joint Committee of Working Women's Organisations** 1946 *Working women discuss population, equal pay, domestic work.* Standing Joint Committee of Working Women's Organisations, pp. 3–6.
47. **Cartwright A.** 1970 *Parents and family planning services.* Routledge & Kegan Paul, p. 25.
48. **Leathard A.** 1980 *The fight for family planning: The development of family planning services in Britain, 1921–74.* Macmillan, pp. 94–104.
49. **Brookes B.** 1988 *Abortion in England, 1900–67.* Croom Helm, pp. 134, 152; **Lewis J.** 1992 *Women in Britain since 1945: Women, family, work and the state in the post-war years.* Basil Blackwell, p. 57.

50. See Chapter 7 for criticisms of the increasing medicalisation of childbirth.
51. **Schofield M.** 1968 *The sexual behaviour of young people*. Penguin, pp. 19, 224–33.
52. **Gorer G.** 1973 *Sex and marriage in England today: A study of the views and experience of the under 45s*. Panther, p. 189.
53. For a brief review of the subjects see **Urry J.** 1991 Holiday-making in Britain since 1945 *Contemporary Record: The Journal of Contemporary British History* **5**: 32–44.
54. **Dingwall R., Rafferty A. M., Webster C.** 1988 *An introduction to the social history of nursing*. Routledge, pp. 116–19.
55. **Bryan B., Dadzie S., Scafe S.** 1985 *The heart of the race: Black women's lives in Britain*. Virago, p. 22.
56. PP 1948–49 vol. XIX Royal Commission on Population *Report* HMSO Cd 7695, p. 124.
57. **Fabian Society** 1945 *Population and people: A national policy*. Fabian Society, p. 50.
58. **Field F., Haikin P.** 1971 *Black Britons*. Oxford University Press, p. 82.
59. **Lenton J., Budgen N., Clarke K.** 1966 *Immigration, race and politics: A Birmingham view*. Bow Group, p. 30; **Patterson S.** 1969 *Immigration and race relations in Britain 1960–67*. Oxford University Press, p. 356.
60. **North Kensington Community History Series** 1987 *Women remember*. North Kensington Community History, p. 9.
61. **Green J.** 1990 *Them: Voices from the immigrant community in contemporary Britain*. Secker and Warburg, p. 312.
62. North Kensington Community History Series no 2 (no p. nos).
63. **Heron L.** 1985 *Truth, dare or promise: Girls growing up in the fifties*. Virago, pp. 220–1.
64. National Sound Archives BBC LP28603 Back 2 (NSA T10484R).
65. National Sound Archives BBC T/29328 (NSA T10483R).
66. See for example research quoted in **Bagley C.** 1968 Migration, race and mental health: A review of some recent research *Race* **9**: 347–8.
67. **Patterson S.** 1969 *Immigration and race relations in Britain 1960–67*. Oxford University Press, p. 358.
68. **Kiev A.** 1964 Psychiatric illness among West Indians *Race* **5**: 48–53.
69. Quoted in Bagley C. Migration, race and mental health. *Race* **9**: 348; **Donovan J.** 1986 *We don't buy sickness, it just comes: Health, illness and health care in the lives of Black people in London*. Gower, pp. 15–16; **Rex J., Moore R.** 1967 *Race, community and conflict: A study of Sparkbrook*. Oxford University Press, pp. 20–4.
70. Bryan B., Dadzie S., Scafe S. *The heart of the race*. pp. 101–5.
71. **Jones C.** 1977 *Immigration and social policy in Britain*. Tavistock, pp. 198–200.
72. BHRU H0027 Female district nurse in Bradford area, born 1926.
73. Jones C. *Immigration and social policy in Britain*. pp. 202–4.
74. BHRU H0066 Female nurse born 1935.
75. This is pointed out in Lenton J., Budgen N. and Clarke K. *Immigration, race and politics*. p. 29.

76. Bryan B., Dadzie S., and Scafe S., *The heart of the race*. pp. 38–40.
77. **Lewis J.** 1986 *What price community medicine? The politics, practice and policies of public health since 1919*. Wheatsheaf, p. 57.
78. **Klein R.** 1983 *The politics of the National Health Service*. Longman, p. 7.
79. **Allsop J.** 1984 *Health policy and the National Health Service*. Longman, pp. 25–6; Webster C. 1988 *The health services since the war vol. 1*. p. 261.
80. PP 1961–2 vol. XXXI A hospital plan for England and Wales Cmd 1604; **Watkin B.** 1978 *The National Health Service: The first phase, 1948–74 and after*. George Allen & Unwin, pp. 59–61.
81. **Sjostrom H., Nilsson R.** 1972 *Thalidomide and the power of the drug companies*. Penguin, pp. 8, 43–4.
82. **Scull A.** 1984 *Decarceration: Community treatment and the deviant – A radical view*. 2nd edn. Polity, pp. 1–2 and *passim*.
83. Discussed in **Unsworth C.** 1987 *The politics of mental health legislation*. Clarendon, p. 260.
84. **Jones K.** 1972 *A history of the mental health services*. Routledge & Kegan Paul, p. 275.
85. **Butler T.** 1985 *Mental health, social policy and the law*. Macmillan, pp. 125–7.
86. Unsworth C. *The politics of mental health legislation*. pp. 230–1, 251.
87. PP 1952–3 vol. XIII Report of the Ministry of Health for 1952 p. 91.
88. Webster C. *The health services since the war vol. 1* pp. 385–6.

Chapter 7

OPEN SORES: THE LATE 1960s TO EARLY 1990s

INTRODUCTION

For a number of years, the ways in which social relationships in the home, at work, on the street and in the doctor's surgery affect health and well-being had been obscured from the public eye. In the late 1960s a combination of academic research and political activism refocused our gaze; and interest in the impact of class position, gender and ethnicity on health experiences was aroused. Private concerns developed into public issues. Demands for individuals to exercise greater control over their bodies and their lives were accompanied by a partial backlash against the onward march of medical technology; the long-buried scepticism about the ability of the medical profession to improve the quality of people's lives resurfaced. On the one hand, numerous self-help groups emphasised individual autonomy and governments laboured the importance of individual responsibility. On the other hand, a great deal of research highlighted socio-structural factors, such as standards of housing, and educational and employment opportunities, which affect health and well-being, and which are often beyond an individual's power to control.

Over the past quarter of a century the incentive for change has come from within and beyond the health services. As in the past, this impetus has reflected current preoccupations and assumptions not only about the desirability of certain types of health services, but also about the type of society in which we wish to live. The 1970s was a decade of stock-taking, when earlier assumptions and administrative developments were seriously questioned. Out of this reassessment grew a greater emphasis on prevention rather than cure, community care rather than hospital treatment, and more discussion about the needs of the elderly and the handicapped. However, no clear breaks were made with the past and the needs of disadvantaged groups continued to be inadequately met. Similarly, there has been increasing concern about environmental issues and the hazards of work, but few new initiatives from governments. Changes have taken place when particular groups have attempted to gain more control over meeting their own health needs.

During the 1980s there was renewed pressure on women to care for relatives without payment, so re-emphasising double standards for men and women; a new wave of blaming the victims of disease (such as homosexuals with AIDS) for their own ill health; growing racist hatred, and rising unemployment with its attendant ill-health. These trends underline the way in which broad social influences (prevailing attitudes and social structures) impact on health and well-being.

SOCIAL STRUCTURE

In the 1970s and 1980s the effects of the stratification of society on standards of health were most commonly gauged by analysing mortality rates according to occupational class. During the 1970s and 1980s class differences in mortality and morbidity rates remained constant throughout life: at any age people in each of the Registrar-General's five occupational classes had a higher death-rate than those in the class above them.[1] The biggest gap was in the early years of life. In the 1970s babies of the unskilled were twice as likely to die at birth and in the first month of life as babies born to professionals. Babies in class 3 were at one and half times times greater risk than babies of professional parents. From the age of one month to twelve months for every death of a baby boy in class 1 there were two in class 3 and three in class 5. Even bigger differences existed for baby girls. The most striking class differences were in deaths from respiratory diseases and accidents. Both these causes of death are closely associated with the socio-economic environment and are therefore preventable by environmental changes. Between the ages of one and fourteen, differences between classes narrowed: there was one death in class 1 for every two in class 5. Again, the causes were environmental. Accidents showed the sharpest class gradient. Boys in class 5 were ten times more likely to die in fires, or from falls or drowning than boys in class 1, and seven times more likely to be killed as pedestrians. Less distinct class gradients were also to be seen in infectious and parasitic diseases.

For those aged between fifteen and sixty-four class gradients in accidents and infectious diseases continued, but were less pronounced. Inequalities in non-infectious diseases, such as cancer, heart disease and respiratory diseases continued throughout life. Men and women in class 5 were two and a half times more likely to die before retirement than those in class 1. Even when allowance is made for the fact that there are more older people in unskilled than professional jobs, the figures were still double. The statistics for pensioners showed less difference between the classes, but the figures are not so significant, as even those in class 1 are not immortal.[2]

Evidence for the 1980s, quoted in the Health Education Council's *The Health Divide*, points to increasing inequalities. This is true across a range of illnesses and for almost all causes of death. It is also applicable to a range of health indicators relating to illness, fitness and well-being. In the 1970s the one exception to this trend was the dramatic decline in the death-rates of babies one month to one year old in all classes, but especially in class 5, so that a reduction in health inequalities actually occurred.[3] The reason for the decline is not certain, but it may well have been due to the decreasing family size of those in class 5.

Analysing structural inequalities in society through occupational class is one-dimensional; in recent years a rich seam of evidence about health inequalities has been mined by quarrying the relationship between health and poverty, housing and working conditions. During the 1980s relative poverty increased. Between 1979 and 1987 the percentage of children living in a family on or below 140 per cent of the supplementary benefit level increased from 18 per cent to 30 per cent of all children. During the same period the proportion of children living in families with incomes below 50 per cent of average incomes increased from 12 per cent to 26 per cent. Women suffered disproportionately. Low pay was the single biggest cause of poverty, and two-thirds of those on low pay were women. While some writers see women's poverty as a new phenomenon of the late twentieth century, others have argued that the gendered nature of poverty is a long-standing feature of our society.[4] There is ample evidence from earlier chapters to support the latter thesis. Poor housing and poverty are the lethal combination.

In recent years a number of studies have appeared which are concerned with deprivation and health. Sarah Payne has provided an excellent analysis of this research. Studies published between 1986 and 1990 found that people living in damp homes were likely to have poor health, in particular, asthma, respiratory disease, chest problems, depression, diarrhoea and vomiting. Damp, mould and cold were linked to respiratory illnessess; noise and a lack of safe play areas for children affected mental health. Even when behavioural factors, such as smoking, and structural factors, such as occupational class, were allowed for, the link between damp, cold homes and ill health remained.[5]

Women suffer disproportionately from bad housing conditions. They are the ones who normally shoulder the burden of noise, cold, dangerous appliances and an absence of safe play areas for children.[6] Mildred Blaxter, in particular, has drawn attention to the impact of the local environment on health and illness.[7] Housing, the quality of the environment and standards of health are closely linked. Noise from transport and building work, litter, dirty streets, isolation, unsafe public spaces, poor street lighting, poor public amenities such as inadequate transport, libraries, community centres, nurseries and shops – all contribute to poor health. Women, especially, suffer from the effects of bleak estates where there is nowhere to hang out the washing, no safe play spaces and no cheap supermarkets.[8]

Women in poor accommodation suffer from a higher rate of miscarriages, and their babies are more likely to die than those of women in decent homes. Homeless women are more likely not to attend antenatal clinics until late in pregnancy and then to have premature babies, babies with low birth weights and babies with congenital abnormalities. The homeless have higher rates of emergency and hospital treatment compared with local residents, and later rates of consultation for primary health care. A 1980s survey of women with children in bed and breakfast accommodation found health problems relating to depression, anxiety, stress and poor diets.[9] Homemaking is a hard task for poorly housed women, and an impossible one for homeless women. Unpaid work in the home may take its toll on health and, depending on a person's position in the labour market, so can paid work.

HEALTH AND SAFETY AT WORK

The number of women in paid work has continued to grow. On the one hand this has meant that more and more women have responsibilities both at home and at the workplace, and on the other hand that women are more likely than in the past to have their own money, and are less reliant on a husband handing over his wage packet. As well as going out to paid work many women work from home. This offers flexibility but it may also increase the depressing risks of isolation, and mean that wages are low because there is no trade union to press for higher pay. Low-paid workers are likely to have a low standard of living and therefore low standards of health. Women are much more likely than men to be employed in part-time work. Part-time workers rarely enjoy a firm's perks, such as pensions and sick pay schemes; they are unlikely to have promotion prospects or to have the same degree of job security as full-time workers. Increasingly, however, full-time workers suffer from the disruption of high job-turnover and redundancies. The shift away from the old manufacturing industries to the service sector, coupled with technological changes, has meant that old familiar work practices are disappearing and those at the bottom of the employment ladder are likely to face worries associated with the uncertainty of change as well as new and possibly unknown work hazards.

In May 1970 Barbara Castle, as Secretary of State for Employment, appointed a committee of inquiry, under the chairmanship of Lord Robens, to review provisions for the safety and health of people in the course of their employment and to consider whether any changes were necessary in the scope or nature of major legislation, or in the nature and extent of voluntary action, and to consider whether further steps were required to safeguard the public from industrial, construction and commercial hazards. A great deal of evidence was presented to the committee about health hazards in industry, especially about the extensive use of potentially harmful substances; this concern was usually coupled with demands for a considerable extension of statutory occupational health provisions. Nevertheless, the committee failed to recommend a comprehensive, co-ordinating statutory occupational health service. Its main proposals were for the self-regulation of industry within a broad statutory framework of minimum standards.[10]

By the summer of 1972 the Labour movement had laid the foundations of the social contract which was to come into its own in 1974 when the Labour Party returned to government. The social contract included a broad agreement on an occupational health service with statutory powers financed by a levy on industry. Like the Robens Report, the labour movement favoured a statutory system of joint safety organisations in industry. The legislation, originally introduced by the previous Conservative government and carried through by Labour, closely followed the recommendations of the Robens Report and did not include a statutory occupational health service. It did include joint statutory safety committees in industry. How successful were these committees in reducing the accident rate? At first it seemed that the new system was working well. In the first six years of the Act's operation fewer people were killed and injured at work in both absolute and relative terms. After 1981 this trend was reversed. The reasons for the worsening hazards of work in the 1980s are complex.

In 1982 the Chief Inspector of Factories commented that firms were increasingly relying on outside contractors and this had been accompanied by a reduction in maintenance manning levels. In the 1980s the increase in small businesses also had negative implications for health and safety at work, as narrow profit margins meant that employers were more likely to try and shave their overheads by cutting corners where health and safety were concerned. So people who did not work in large or predominantly unionised firms, or who did not do so on a direct employment or regular basis, were most at risk from hazardous working conditions. Those workers who felt vulnerable to unemployment were likely to find this stressful and to be more willing to take, and keep, jobs with known hazards. It is unlikely that in these circumstances policies to prevent workplace hazards were going to be very successful, despite government policy statements placing great importance on 'prevention'.[11]

With increasing numbers of people exposed to radiation at work and concern over nuclear accidents affecting not only those employed in the nuclear industry, but also entire populations, the problem of industrial hazards took on global dimensions. By the late 1980s all the main political parties were committed to reducing pollution and developing environmentally friendly strategies, although they may not have seemed the most urgent problems for those groups, such as the poor and many from ethnic minorities, who have to battle against a range of health hazards.

ETHNIC MINORITIES' HEALTH

It is ironical that so little official concern has been expressed over the well-being of Britain's ethnic minorities when they play such an important role in sustaining the NHS. However, since the 1980s there has been a quickening interest among academics and health workers in the overall well-being of some of the country's ethnic minorities, and in health initiatives, in some cases led by ethnic minorities themselves. Issues surrounding the health of ethnic minorities are now aired beyond the confines of academic (particularly psychiatric) journals and the subject is firmly on many local agendas.

The health of ethnic minorities has been studied largely from the point of view of particular illnesses, especially those which are thought to be specific to an ethnic group, but it is as well to remember that such illnesses will affect a relatively small number of people; the day-to-day health concerns of ethnic minorities are not so different from those of the majority population.[12] For instance, in the mid-1980s it was found that the needs of elderly Asians were much the same as those of other working-class elderly people living in the inner cities. The older Asians found hospital medical care adequate, and they appreciated it; however, they disliked the lack of privacy, the food and the failure of the hospitals to accommodate certain Asian customs and preferences. Moreover, they found certain practices demeaning and discriminatory.[13]

There are also a range of social circumstances and relationships which have a bearing on the well-being of ethnic minorities which the majority population do not experience. If we are going to understand the varied and distinctive influences on ethnic minorities' health we need to form a picture of the daily lives of ethnic minorities' different members (young, old, men, women; first and second generation). There is not the space here to paint as large and complicated canvas as the subject deserves, so two details must suffice.

First, as Alix Henley has pointed out, immigrant Asians may suffer from separation, loneliness, language barriers and a change in climate and routine. Haley suggested a number of ways in which different members of a family suffer stress. A man may suffer stress if he is no longer his own boss but working in a low-status job, without other men in his family. He may feel that the family's success in Britain is his responsibility, and he may also be under financial pressure, especially if he is sending money back to relatives in Asia. He may no longer command the authority he would traditionally expect, which may be especially hard to bear if he feels that his children are growing away from him while at the same time the family in Britain is growing away from the family in Asia. A wife may only be in the country on suffrance, and may have joined her husband after a period of separation. Shopping and the weather may present unforseen problems. If she is in paid work outside the home she will no doubt have the double burden of also having to cope with the domestic work while seeing ethnic majority women with greater freedom, and she may come to resent the traditional role expected of her. On the other hand, she may remain behind closed doors, isolated and without the female companionship she previously enjoyed or expected. Children can also be squeezed between conflicting cultures. Elderly Asians share many of the problems of the ethnic majority, but in addition they may not be offered the respect they would automatically enjoy in Asia; they may be short of money, and dependence on the family may increase tensions, especially if housing is inadequate, and if local authorities do not make appropriate provision in their meals-on-wheels services and day centres.[14]

Second, during the 1980s an increasingly menacing cloud has hung over the daily lives of many black people as racist attacks in the street, in the home and at school have blighted lives. During the 1980s a range of evidence appeared which strongly suggested an upward spiral in bombings, arson and other physical attacks.[15] In 1981 the Home Office produced the first official estimates of racially motivated offences and found that Asians were fifty times more likely than whites to be the victims of racially motivated crimes and West Indians thirty-six times more likely to be victims than whites. In 1984 a Policy Studies Institute survey suggested that racial attacks could be ten times higher than the official estimates because so many incidents went unreported. Racial harassment was common throughout the country; few areas were actually safe for black residents, but harassment was especially severe in the London area. On some estates families were met by hostile reception committees when they moved into a house. One family in 1981 and another family in 1985 were the victims of fatal arson attacks. Endless anecdotes tell the same story: an Asian woman's children were physically attacked when they went out to play; they were tied to railings and left, stripped and put in dustbins, or had their heads banged against brick walls.[16] In 1988 the Commission for Racial Equality commented that although the evidence was anecdotal, there were a sufficient number of reports to conclude that children from a range of ethnic minorities suffered frequent acts of racial harassment, and experienced insecurity and anxiety from the threatening atmosphere associated with the fear and actuality of racial insults, graffiti and violence.[17]

As well as coping with overt racism, the way society, including the NHS, is organised can operate to the disadvantage of particular groups, creating a glass ceiling which prevents advancement in relative standards of health. In the 1970s and 1980s low take-up of NHS services was widespread among certain ethnic groups. Interaction with the health services was inhibited by a range of problems. In the 1980s maternity services were under-used by Asians, Afro-Caribbeans and travellers for a variety of reasons: lengthy waiting times might act as a deterrent, some women did not want to be examined by a male doctor, and allowances were not necessarily made for different customs and practices. Hospital food and dietary advice may have been inappropriate, and information and explanations could be lacking.

The attitudes of NHS staff were also seen as a potential problem. Black people were under-represented at senior levels and patients might encounter prejudice from staff. Staff might not be aware of the significance of different beliefs and lifestyles.[18] Certain ethnic groups are still stereotyped, just as they have been throughout the century. A Pakistani woman living in Bradford recalled that when her husband complained of back pain to his GP the doctor's response was to dismiss it with the words 'All Pakistanis complain about backache.' (Her husband subsequently underwent three operations on his back.) She admitted that Asian doctors can neglect patients too, but in this case the problem stemmed from racist stereotyping.[19]

In the 1980s ethnic minority groups tended to receive little support from local authority social services; Asians under-used the home help service and many meals-on-wheels services did not cater for their diet. It was still the exception to find day centres with interpreters, staff training in the needs of different ethnic groups or the appointment of staff from various ethnic backgrounds to work with their own ethnic group. While respite care and care attendants to replace carers in the home are slowly developing, few are drawn from a broad range of ethnic backgrounds.[20]

Communication problems can form barriers, yet understanding is vital if correct diagnoses are to be made, and treatment instructions understood. In the past, interpreting services were notoriously *ad hoc*, although this is changing.[21] Many health authorities have a list of staff who speak another language, but they are not always available when required. There have also been numerous complaints about racial discrimination, such as racist comments, poor or no explanations, inadequate examination or offhand treatment.

The main race-related initiatives of the Department of Health and Social Security (DHSS) were the funding of voluntary organisations, and the funding of management and training projects such as Training in Race and Health. Health authorities have provided interpreting services, sickle cell screening, link workers, community health workers, and staff training. In the 1980s community health initiatives also expanded. There have been neighbourhood-based community health projects employing community workers; community-based initiatives taken by health professionals such as health visitors and health education officers; projects to look at particular health issues; resource and information projects, such as women's health information centres; health-related work undertaken by organisations with wider interests, such as health courses for pensioners; advocacy projects to change health services, and self-help groups.[22] In the mid-1980s an Asian Mother and Baby campaign, sponsored by the DHSS aimed to improve antenatal and postnatal care for Asian women, and to develop a more sensitive service. A campaign was launched to inform Asians about early antenatal care, diet and the care of pregnant women, and women fluent in Asian languages were employed as linkworkers to bridge the gap between health professionals and Asian mothers.[23] At the beginning of the 1990s the Department of Health commissioned the establishment of a major data base on ethnic minorities' health to provide information on good practice in health services and to help encourage and develop new services.[24]

FEMINIST STRATEGIES

From the 1970s many aspects of women's health have enjoyed a high profile. Factors adversely affecting women's well-being, such as domestic violence, are now more openly discussed. Even so, what goes on in the family is still seen as a 'private' matter. Moreover, although the increasing percentage of babies born to unmarried mothers reflects a decrease in the stigma of single parenthood, moralising about the behaviour of others is still alive and well.[25] Women themselves have attacked the dominant medical ideology, by emphasising the control and influence they can have over their own well-being and by establishing Well Women Clinics (WWCs). From within the medical profession Wendy Savage, a Senior Lecturer and Honorary Consultant in Obstetrics and Gynaecology at the London Hospital, challenged the high technology approach towards women's health favoured by the medical profession. Yet, women's ability to gain autonomy is still severely limited by the two old chestnuts: poverty and caring for others.

Jan Pahl has argued that as the welfare state developed and increasingly intervened in what had previously been private family matters, there was a growing parallel concern for privacy in the home and the rights of the private individual. Much mental and physical assault, which was both severe and prolonged, went unrecorded. Governments continued to stress the importance of two-parent families, and it was not until the early 1990s that English Courts began to recognise rape in marriage as a crime. In the 1980s Pahl unearthed injuries ranging from cuts and bruises, broken bones, damaged eyesight, a ruptured spleen, stab wounds and a fractured skull.[26] Concern over such injuries had been publicly voiced by the women's movement for over a decade.

In the late 1960s and early 1970s the women's movement, inspired by international and especially American developments, provided a fresh analysis of gender relationships, including violence against women. In 1971 the first women's refuge in Britain was opened at Chiswick; and on its heels many more refuges opened in different parts of the country. They provided a means of escape from violence, a place of safety and a sense of solidarity with other women. The setting up of refuges in itself helped to focus public attention on the violence suffered by many women in the home.

Women have differed both in their analyses and strategies for combating male violence: there is no agreement as to whether the violence of men stems from violent personalities or from a society which promotes male domination. The Chiswick refuge emphasised the personal inadequacies of both batterer and battered and the intergenerational transmission of violence in the home. The Chiswick solution involved institutionalised care for all the family, and psychiatric treatment. Other refuges, which in 1974 formed the National Women's Aid Federation, saw the problem as stemming from violent men; they sought legal changes to protect women and to provide them with their material needs, such as adequate housing.[27]

Violence against black women remained hidden longer than violence against white women. In the late 1980s evidence began to emerge that violence against black women was as extensive as violence against white women. Like white working-class women, black women often suffer violence over long periods because of their weak position in the labour market and their limited housing options.[28] Violence is still, as in the past, often associated with poverty, inadequate housing and alcohol abuse.[29]

Financial rows can lead to domestic violence, and when money is short a family's health is likely to suffer from poor eating habits. It is clear from research carried out in the mid-1980s that in a poor family it is crucial for the health and well-being of all its members for resources to be managed in an equitable fashion.[30] In a two-parent, low-income family it is probably advantageous for the woman to control the finances because research has shown that when women control the budget a higher proportion of it is spent on food and day-to-day living expenses.[31] This research is reinforced by other work from the 1980s which suggests that low-income and male control of the purse-strings are the two factors which most effectively limit the adoption of a healthy diet. First, as men tend to have more traditional tastes in food than women they are less likely to adopt and enjoy a new, healthy diet. Second, if different kinds of food are bought and not enjoyed, they are likely to be wasted or spark off rows. In low-income families it is more important to avoid waste than to try and convert a stressed family to different food. Indeed, health educators, in trying to change the diets of poor families, may merely increase the worries of a women rather than lead to any action.[32]

From the late 1960s there was a more assertive approach to health matters on the part of women. The women's movement spearheaded demands for changes in the medical profession's approach to women's health, and encouraged women to learn more about their bodies so that they could exercise greater control over their health. Women's groups stressed the importance of prevention rather than cure, and practical changes which women could bring about for themselves. This pressure from women manifested itself in the growth of WWCs.

A WWC set up in 1973 in Islington, North London, was probably the first of its kind. It expanded the already existing facilities of cervical cytology clinics, incorporating a more holistic approach to women's health which included physical, emotional and social needs. A health visitor and doctor performed medical examinations; women were taught how to carry out a basic self-examination and they were encouraged to discuss their problems. The clinic did not provide treatment although it could refer women to other health services.[33] A decade later WWCs had sprung up around the country. By 1987 a hundred health authorities claimed to have a WWC.

Katy Gardner, a GP who has worked in a WWC, saw them as an attempt to provide an open-access system for any woman to have a check-up and discuss her health with sympathetic health workers.

She believes that WWCs should be provided by the NHS as part of its general practice and primary health care service. Separate WWCs are necesssary because a separate clinic indicates the importance of 'health' as well as 'illness', and appointments of at least twenty minutes allow time to talk. The ideal, although not the reality, for WWCs according to Gardner, was that they should reach women who did not normally visit a doctor, who were intimidated by male doctors, or who had doctors who were not interested in women's health issues. The clinics aimed to teach women about self-help breast examination, remedies for thrush and prevention of cystitis; to screen women for cancer of the breast, cervix or ovary; to act as a sympathetic referral agency for any problems that were mentioned; to raise the consciousness of women about health care; to put pressure on the medical profession to improve their service for women; to publicise themselves through Community Health Councils, women's groups and trade unions; and, finally, to become involved in health education – especially in the procedures of well woman examinations and in the concept of self-help and prevention.[34] The role of most WWCs in practice remained far more limited. Many WWCs were Family Planning Clinics with a name-change, and hostility still exists within the medical profession to a feminist approach to women's health.[35]

Were WWCs successful in attracting 'high-risk' women? In 1982 an evaluation of a Manchester WWC found that the most common problems of women attending the clinic were 'specifically female' and it was these problems which were least likely to be receiving treatment elsewhere. Critics of them claimed that the care offered by WWCs could be provided by FPCs or clinics undertaking cervical smears. Yet, the Manchester WWC found that the profile of attenders did not match those at FPCs. Over half the women attending the WWC were over forty-three years old, and it attracted a higher proportion of working-class women than normally attended FPCs. However, although it was claimed that women attending the clinic were from 'high-risk' groups who usually had little contact with preventative services, Peggy Foster pointed out that among women attending this clinic only 5 per cent had never had a smear test while over 80 per cent had had one within the previous five years, which suggests that the clinic was not in fact attracting women in a high-risk category.[36]

The most public and dramatic conflict between a woman doctor and the medical profession came in April 1985 when Wendy Savage was suspended for allegedly being a danger to her patients. In February 1986 she was exonerated by a public inquiry into her competence and five months later reinstated. Savage believed in minimum surgical intervention during labour and birth (in other words she favoured normal delivery, wherever possible), but she was swimming against the tide of rising Caesarians and an increasingly high technology approach to obstetrics. According to Savage, pregnancy is normal unless there are clear indications that something is wrong. Pregnancy is not an illness and women should not be labelled 'high-risk' on the basis of statistical rather than individual information, as this leads to far too many women attending hospital clinics rather than having the more personal care of a doctor or midwife closer to home. Savage believes that a woman should feel in control of the birth process. The court case, which Savage won, helped to bring an important aspect of women's reproductive rights to the fore.[37]

However, despite women's efforts to highlight their own health needs, much of their time is still spent looking after others. In 1988 the first national survey of adults looking after elderly and disabled people at home was published. It revealed that the number of such carers had previously been very considerably underestimated. In 1988 about six million people (one adult in seven) were looking after an elderly or disabled person. Most of these carers were women (about 3.5 million, compared with 2.5 million men). In most families it was typically one person alone who took on the job of carer with little or no support from other family members, friends, neighbours or formal agencies. Most carers were middle-aged, while a growing number were elderly. It was a long-term commitment, usually lasting a number of years, and one taken on by a growing number of people as the proportion of elderly people in the population increases.[38]

Women have traditionally cared for other family members, but the role is becoming an ever more burdensome one for a number of reasons: the growing percentage of the elderly in the population; the expanding number of people with chronic illnesses and disabilities; the rise of smaller and more mobile families; the changing role of women, which means that more have paid work outside the home, alongside their unpaid informal caring tasks in the family; women's changing expectations (of the choice they should exercise over the balance between paid and unpaid work, childbearing, childrearing and running around after a husband); and, finally, government policy of keeping people out of institutions means that formal care facilities are dwindling. (During the 1970s unpaid caring began to be recognised in the state benefit system, but the following decade saw a reduction in the already limited entitlements which those who cared for dependent relatives could claim.)[39]

THE SHIFT FROM SECONDARY CARE TO PRIMARY CARE

From the mid-1970s there was wide-ranging discussion and limited action over the move away from secondary, hospital-based treatment, to primary, community-based, health promotion and care. The shift away from secondary care was partly a reaction against high-technology medicine. The medical profession's tight grip over health strategies was being prised open at a time when the changing nature of illness made medical intervention less appropriate. The increase in chronic illness meant that long-term care and support were needed for both the patient and the family.

The increasing proportion of elderly in the population, for whom high-technology hospital treatment is largely irrelevant, need back-up resources in the community so that they can continue to live in their own homes. Geographical mobility and the changing role of women mean more, not less, formal support systems are required. However, the need for formal support often goes unrecognised, particularly for certain ethnic groups, when it is assumed that they prefer to look after their own without formal support. In fact, the isolation of carers and dependants from ethnic minorities can be worse than for the majority population who are not hemmed in by cultural barriers and racism. Moreover, much acute care in hospitals is dependent on post-operative care in the community. If the back-up services exist, many services such as day surgery and out-patient treatment, which cut down the 'hotel costs' for hospitals, are possible.

In recent years, more emphasis has been laid on looking after the physically and mentally handicapped and ill in the community. In part this is a reaction against the unpleasant aspects of life in an institution; medical conventional wisdom was very strongly in favour of de-institutionalisation as were a whole generation schooled in 1960s and 1970s thinking about the way in which the medical profession, and especially mental health practitioners, were creating their own disease. The timing of the switch is best explained by governments' belief that community care is cheaper. Anne Borsay has questioned the assumption that care in the community is cheaper than institutional care. She has pointed out that while studies which have costed care in the home have been unanimous that it is cheaper, there are methodological problems, such as comparing like with like, and calculating the costs of unpaid support, which these studies do not address adequately. Borsay does not think that it is possible to calculate the costs of community care accurately, but governments behave as if it is so. Personal family costs may in the long run affect governments' costs in terms of additional social needs.[40] Although the humanitarian motive behind de-institutionalisation has been questioned (see Chapter 6) most seem agreed that it is preferable. However, in the mid-1980s Janet Finch mounted a swingeing attack on care in the community which she rightly criticised for being gendered to the disadvantage of women. More controversially, she argued that the only feasible means for women to escape from the burden of unpaid caring was for institutional care to be expanded.[41]

The 1970 Chronically Sick and Disabled Person's Act made local authorities responsible for providing a number of specialist services, but because the Act's wording was vague, local authorities interpreted it differently. The 1986 Disabled Person's Act removed a number of loop-holes by specifying that local authorities had to assess the needs of disabled people, if requested to do so. Disabled people had the right to appoint an advocate when negotiating with social services, and disabled children had the right to have their future needs assessed before leaving school. Carers also had the right to have their needs taken into account, but only when, and if, their dependants were being assessed.[42] Underpinning the policy of keeping as many long-term patients out of hospital as possible was an emphasis on the role that individuals can play in improving their health.

HEALTH EDUCATION

From 1968, when the Health Education Council (HEC) was created until it was reconstituted in 1987 under the DHSS as the Health Education Authority, the HEC was the focus of health education in Britain. According to Ian Sutherland, the HEC was beset with ethical, organisational and resource problems which undermined its effectiveness. The work of the HEC became explicitly political, and this brought it into conflict with certain vested interests which were closely linked to government interests. In April 1987 tensions between the Government and the HEC came to breaking point; the latter was disbanded and replaced by a Health Education Authority, directly under ministerial control.[43]

While political parties preach prevention they are constrained by political calculations from pursuing a wholeheartedly preventative policy. The negative influence of the tobacco industry on antismoking measures is a case in point. Both Conservative and Labour parties have traditionally been loathe to act against the tobacco industry, which has mounted effective campaigns against government interference. Groups who work to discourage smoking are the British Medical Association, the Royal College of Physicians (RCP), Action on Smoking and Health (ASH) and various environmental and cancer groups. In 1971 ASH was set up by the RCP to keep the issue of smoking and health alive, and to press for policies to discourage smoking, such as taxing tobacco more heavily and banning advertisements. ASH encourages research and education, forms local groups, has a network of media and political contacts and monitors the activities of the tobacco industry. Pitted against its educative and preventative work is the tobacco industry's advertising death-machine. The Tobacco Advisory Council, the Tobacco Workers' Union and some retailers which pressure governments not to act have a major weapon because of the money which the Treasury receives in taxes from tobacco. If any government attacks the tobacco industry there is the threat of job losses and rising unemployment, as well as the loss of exports. So, there are strong economic arguments which are then linked to arguments about individual freedom of choice to discourage government interference. Fear of losing votes can also influence governments not to take action.[44]

Health education campaigns have aimed to prevent illness by changing an individual's behaviour. Yet, good health depends on social and economic well-being, reflected in, and reinforced by, a healthy lifestyle. It is contradictory to talk about a healthy lifestyle for the poor, the lonely, the frightened or the ill-housed, because all these conditions are themselves unhealthy. In an effort to get around this problem, preventative programmes have attempted to identify high-risk groups, such as children likely to be suffering abuse. Certain occupations have screened those believed to be at risk because of the hazardous job they do, or they examine applicants for jobs to sift out those whom it is believed might be more susceptible to certain hazards. Such action does not actually remove the cause of illness; rather it is a compromise.

AIDs policy has lurched between targeting the whole population and targeting those groups (such as homosexuals and drug addicts) which are perceived to be most at risk. AIDS is an infectious disease caused by a virus, Human Immunodeficiency Virus (HIV), which attacks the body's immune system so that infections, which are normally not harmful, become deadly. The virus is transmitted through blood and certain other body fluids. The bulk of British victims are homosexuals, although AIDS has spread to the hetero-sexual population, in particular, to intravenous drug users and to those receiving infected blood transfusions.[45]

Virginia Berridge has argued that AIDS policy has passed through three phases. First, between 1981 and 1986 AIDS gradually became a policy issue. Policies were thrashed out at the local level through gay groups while the scientific and medical worlds were developing their expertise in the field. Jeffrey Weeks has criticised the tardy response of governments during this period, which he blames on the emergence of the New Right. In defence of the Government's position it has been argued that there is no reason to assume that a disease primarily affecting the 'respectable' heterosexual community would have produced a smarter governmental response. Between 1986 and 1987 the threat of AIDs became a national emergency with a major health education campaign under the slogan 'Don't Die of Ignorance' filling television screens and letter boxes. As the threat of an immediate epidemic in the heterosexual population receded, the campaign shrank back to play a more normal part in the policy process with most immediate implications for homosexuals and intravenous drug addicts.[46]

As Nicholas Dorn and Nigel South have pointed out, until the 1980s the problem of hard drug abuse was left to the medical profession. Known addicts could receive doctors' prescriptions and in certain cases undergo rehabilitation programmes. In the 1960s there were relatively few 'hard' drug users and they tended to be concentrated in the South East of England. By the 1980s the drug scene had changed dramatically. Drug abusers now lived all over the country, and the supply of hard drugs was big international business, systematically organised. These changes, coupled with the link between intravenous drug users and AIDS, meant that an anti-drugs policy became a central concern of governments. A relatively narrow medical approach was replaced by a broader strategy which was much more concerned with the criminal activities of those who supplied the drugs. The problem came to be regarded as one of national and international law and order. In the mid-1980s the Government's strategy for tackling the drug problem (in order of priority) was to reduce supplies from abroad, to tighten controls on drugs produced and prescribed in Britain, to police effectively, to strengthen deterrence, to improve prevention and to provide treatment and rehabilitation.[47] As in so many other areas of health care and health promotion, the role of the medical profession was moved to one side. Even so, resources are still heavily weighted towards traditional hospital services.

THE HEALTH SERVICES

In the course of the 1980s, Conservative governments attempted to apply the managerial techniques of private industry to the NHS, and encouraged the growth of a private health-care industry. This emphasis on managerial and admininstrative change can be traced back to the Labour governments of the 1960s. In the early 1970s the NHS underwent a major reorganisation, since when further attempts to rearrange the NHS's management structures have taken place periodically.

In the late 1960s and early 1970s the official reasons given for reorganisation were to integrate the different health services more effectively; to prioritise services for the elderly, mentally handicapped and disabled; to improve the NHS's management structure; and to make the services more democratic. Despite extensive reorganisation, the Government remained dissatisfied with management in the NHS, and in 1983 Roy Griffiths, Managing Director of Sainsbury's, was asked to prepare a report: *NHS Management Inquiry*. Griffiths was critical of consensus management and the absence of one person at each level who was accountable for action. He suggested that general managers should be appointed to improve efficiency. This suggestion was adopted, but still criticisms continue, the main one being that it is not possible or appropriate to run a health service as if it were a supermarket.

PRIVATE HEALTH CARE

The issue which perhaps more than any other politicised health policy in Britain in the 1980s was that of private health care. The growth of private health care has challenged assumptions about the desirability of a free and universal health-care system. As the poorest sections of society, which include a substantial number of women and ethnic minorities, are least likely to be covered by private health insurance, they will not gain from any of the supposed benefits of the system; if private care is better than the NHS, then the gap in the quality of health care between the poorer and better-off will widen. Moreover, it is not obvious that there are any benefits to unpaid carers in a growing private system. By focusing attention and praise on private care, fundamental issues relating to health inequalities and chronic illness are swept under the bed.

From the early 1970s the left wing of the Labour Party had been increasingly vocal in its condemnation of pay beds in NHS hospitals. From 1972 Labour Party policy aimed to phase out pay beds and to stop part-time consultant contracts in the NHS. In 1974 health workers began to take strike action to speed-up the process. In 1975, when the Labour Government made it clear that it intended to abolish pay beds, there was an outcry from a section of consultants and the private industry. A compromise was reached whereby pay beds were to be phased out, and the future of private health care assured. The long-term effect of this policy was to boost private health-care facilities outside the NHS.[48]

In the 1980s chains of private hospitals run for profit extended throughout the country. Factors, unrelated to the 'free' working of the market economy, gave private health care a fillip. Griffith et al have detailed the numerous ways in which the post-1979

Conservative governments promoted commercial medicine. First, they tried to undermine the status of the NHS by encouraging health authorities to use the new private hospitals, which ministers publicly endorsed by, for instance, attending their openings; moreover, governments regularly sought the opinions of those at the head of the private sector and arranged cut-price private medical care for civil servants. Second, there were increases in, and extensions of, prescription charges. Third, health authorities were encouraged to raise funds through public appeals which, Griffith et al believe, blurred the distinction between charity on the one hand and medical provision as a *right* on the other hand. Fourth, the Government wanted NHS management to imitate private industry. (Following the Griffiths Report, top NHS management posts were created to introduce commercial management practices into hospitals.) Fifth, health authorities were urged to 'contract out' domestic, catering and laundry services. (Since 1983 there has been mandatory tendering.) Finally, measures were introduced to make it more attractive for consultants to undertake private work.[49]

At the same time as Britain has seen an expansion in commercial medicine a declining proportion, about one-fifth, of those who use its facilities pay for it directly: in the 1980s (with a downturn in 1981) private health insurance grew. As the cost of private health insurance increased it became more common for groups, such as trade unions and companies, rather than individuals, to take out private cover. On the whole, those with private health insurance are the better-off and healthiest sections of society. Although the types of treatment covered by insurance have grown, no one receives 100 per cent cover, and for many aspects of health care it is still assumed that the NHS will be used. It is largely true to say that the chronically sick, the geriatric, psychiatric patients and pregnant women will not be covered by private insurance.

It has been argued by the promoters of privatisation that contracting out non-medical services such as catering, laundry and cleaning reduces costs and improves efficiency. There is strong evidence, however, that the reasons behind this strategy and its operation are in practice not motivated primarily by principles of economy. The 1979 Conservative Government returned to power with the promise of curtailing the power of trade unions. The 1978–79 winter of discontent in the health services contributed to the defeat of James Callaghan's Labour Government in the May 1979 general election. In the 1980s the push for privatisation came from Conservative governments on ideological grounds, not from the free working of the market economy. In the 1970s contracting out had actually been on the decline.

Since 1979 Conservative governments have argued that contracting out increases efficiency. We may well ask if this is in fact the case.

Kate Ascher has provided evidence which suggests that in contract award decisions the need to economise plays only a small part. Other factors, such as the attitudes of one or two administrators, the stance of the health authority or the strength of trade unionists often determines the outcome.[50]

A number of arguments have been put forward in favour of privatisation. First, as mentioned above, it is suggested that private services are more efficient, less wasteful of resources and so more economical than the NHS. Second, private services are thought to be more innovative because they are less bureaucratic than the NHS. Third, greater specialisation is possible; expertise can be developed in particular areas, as private services do not have to cater across the board for everyone. Fourth, it is argued that private medicine takes some of the strain off the NHS. Finally, private provision is regarded as flexible and attuned to people's needs. If people do not like the service they are getting, they can go elsewhere, so they have more choice. According to Seldon, the fundamental weakness of the NHS is that although it appears to be free because people do not pay for it when they use it, in actual fact it is not free – it is paid for out of National Health Insurance and taxes but, because it appears to be free, it destroys people's bargaining power with the medical profession. If a person pays directly for her/his health care, or indirectly through insurance, she/he is more willing to go elsewhere if dissatisfied with a doctor. Seldon also thinks that it is wrong to assume that there will never be anything better than the NHS.[51]

Supporters of private care have not had it all their own way. Furious opposition was mounted to the expansion of private medicine on a range of grounds, often intimately linked to the fact that American companies have spearheaded the growth of private medicine in Britain. Joan Higgins has underlined the small but significant involvement of American companies in British health care. Never before has there been substantial overseas investment in the direct provision of health and welfare in Britain. In 1979 there were three hospitals with 366 beds owned by American companies in Britain; by 1986 the figures had shot up to thirty-one acute hospitals with 2,239 beds. In the course of the 1980s, AMI, the largest foreign company in Britain in the health and welfare sector, opened acute hospitals, clinics for drug and alcohol addicts, health centres, and it started acting as a co-ordinator for kidneys for transplant (which in 1984 caused a public outcry). In 1985 it started running a secure unit for the severely mentally disturbed, and the following year it opened a rehabilitation unit for victims of road accidents. Opposition has been mounted on a number of fronts to AMI and other American companies. Higgins argues that apart from opposition to more private medicine *per se* there was scepticism about the American companies' aims and methods, anti-Americanism, competitive aggression, and fears about the impact on British health and welfare services. There was opposition to building plans for new hospitals, and to American companies buying existing facilities and institutions; there was also criticism of the aims and methods of American companies and hostility from the existing British-run private sector.[52]

Notwithstanding criticisms of the private sector, the NHS is taking on board certain of its features. Norman Johnson has detailed the ways in which these changes are restructuring the welfare state. In 1988 health authorities were urged to investigate new ways of turning their facilities into money-spinners, for instance, by leasing space in hospitals to fast-food chains and other retail outlets, and by selling advertising space. Internal markets now operate as hospitals become independent of the District Health Authority and form self-governing trusts which control their own budgets, appoint staff and negotiate pay and conditions. GPs can also apply for practice budgets to pay for hospital services, practice staff, prescription costs and improvements to the practice facilities.[53]

A number of writers have pointed out that reassessing the relationship between the private and public sector and searching for ways of containing public expenditure on health care are not unique to Britain. Throughout Europe spiralling costs have injected an added urgency into the search for cost-effectiveness and the need to monitor and appraise services. All European countries are grappling with the problem of apparently infinite demand but finite resources. This is especially problematic at a time when medical technology is immensely costly, and when there is an expectation that if one country has a technique other countries should rapidly acquire it. Paradoxically, while medicine is becoming ever more financially burdensome, there is a backlash against both the ubiquitous high technology and the power of the medical profession. The onward march of medical technology is seen as diverting attention from socio-structural aspects of society which are the real determinants of patterns of health. As the domination of medicine is increasingly challenged in public (private scepticism is nothing new, of course) attempts are being made to devolve decision-making to the individual or local community level. Appropriate formal health-care structures have never been more urgently required. Social mobility, the increased participation of women in the paid labour force and women's changing expectations all militate against the feasibility of caring for an ageing population in small family circles.[54]

At present, the Conservative government is reviewing the organisation and finances of the NHS, supposedly to provide the twenty-first century with a leaner, fitter health care service. Although government policy is hailed or condemned, depending on one's political stance, as the biggest overhaul since the NHS was created, in conception it is part of a tradition which conceives health policy in a very narrow sense. It also fails to come to terms with many of the problems which are perceived by health practitioners and health commentators to be the fundamental health issues of our time. These are not dissimilar to those identified by earlier generations, namely poor health associated with people's class, gender or ethnic background.

NOTES

1. See Chapter 8 for the Registrar-General's breakdown of occupations into five classes, and for the academic debate over the relationship between class and health.
2. **Townsend P., Davidson N.** 1982 *Inequalities in Health: The Black Report.* Penguin, pp. 51–6.
3. **Whitehead M.** 1988 *Inequalities in health: The health divide.* Penguin, p. 258.
4. **Blackburn C.** 1991 *Poverty and health: Working with families.* Open University Press, pp. 17–18, 22–3.
5. **Payne S.** 1991 *Women, health and poverty: An introduction.* Harvester Wheatsheaf, pp. 119–38.
6. Ibid.
7. **Blaxter M.** 1990 *Health and lifestyles.* Routledge, p. 87 and *passim*.
8. Payne S. *Women, health and poverty.* p. 136.
9. Ibid. pp. 119–38.
10. **Committee on safety and health at work** 1972 *Safety and health at work: Report of the committee, 1970–72.* (Robens) HMSO.
11. **Dawson S., Willman P., Clinton A., Bamford M.** 1988 *Safety at work: The limits of self-regulation.* Cambridge University Press, pp. xvi–xix; For the impact of unemployment on people's health see chapter 8.
12. **Donovan J.** 1984 Ethnicity and health: A research review. *Social Science and Medicine* **19**: 668.
13. **Barker J.** 1984 *Research perspectives on ageing: Black and Asian old people in Britain.* Age Concern, p. 26.
14. **Henley A.** 1979 *Asian patients in hospital and at home.* King Edward's Hospital Fund, pp. 21–9.
15. **Gordon P.** 1990 *Racial violence and harassment.* The Runnymede Trust, pp. v, 7–9.
16. **Commission for Racial Equality** 1987 *Living in terror: A report on racial violence and harassment in housing.* CRE, pp. 7–12; see also **Independent Commission of Enquiry into racial harassment** 1987 *Racial harassment in Leeds, 1985–6.* Leeds Community Relations Council, pp. 15–28.
17. **Commission for Racial Equality** 1988 *Learning in terror: A survey of racial harassment in schools and colleges in England, Scotland and Wales, 1985–87.* CRE, pp. 5–16.

18. **Pearson M.** 1985 *Racial equality and good practice in maternity care. Training in Health and Race.* Health Education Council, pp. 7–15.
19. Bradford Heritage Recording Unit C0070 Female born 1951.
20. **Hicks C.** 1988 *Who cares: Looking after people at home.* Virago, pp. 190–200.
21. **Commission for Racial Equality** 1987 *Memorandum submitted by CRE in response to primary health care: An agenda for discussion.* CRE, pp. 9–10.
22. **McNaught A.** 1987 *Health action and ethnic minorities.* National Community Health Resource, pp. 12–23.
23. **Rocheron Y.** 1988 The Asian mother and baby campaign: The construction of ethnic minorities' health needs. *Critical Social Policy* **22,** for criticisms of the campaign.
24. *Ethnic minorities.* 1991 HMSO, p. 60.
25. **Lewis J.** 1992 *Women in Britain since 1945: Women, family, work, and the state in the post-war years.* Blackwell, pp. 31–2, 45.
26. **Pahl J.** 1985 *Private violence and public policy: The needs of battered women and the response of the public services.* Routledge & Kegan Paul, pp. 3–4.
27. **Dobash R., Dobash R.** 1992 *Women, violence and social change.* Routledge & Kegan Paul, pp. 1, 16, 90, 117–19.
28. **Mama A.** 1989 *The hidden struggle: Statutory and voluntary sector responses to violence against black women in the home.* Race and Housing Research Unit, pp. 299–301.
29. Pahl J. *Private violence and public policy.* pp. 9–10, 37–41.
30. **Graham H.** 1984 *Women, health and the family.* Wheatsheaf, pp. 102–5.
31. **Pahl J.** 1989 *Money and marriage.* Macmillan, pp. 151–2.
32. **Wilson G.** 1989 Family food systems, preventive health and dietary change: A policy to increase the health divide. *Journal of Social Policy* **18:** 173, 183.
33. **Thornley P.** 1987 The development of Well Women Clinics. In Orr J. (ed) *Women's health in the community.* John Wiley and Sons, pp. 97–9.
34. **Gardner K.** 1981 Well women clinics. In Roberts H. (ed) *Women, health and reproduction.* Routledge & Kegan Paul, pp. 129–43.
35. **Foster P.** 1989 Improving the doctor–patient relationship: A feminist perspective *Journal of Social Policy* **18:** 346.
36. Ibid. **18:** 345.
37. See **Savage W.** 1986 *A savage enquiry: Who controls childbirth?* Virago.
38. **Hicks C.** 1988 *Who cares: Looking after people at home.* Virago, p. 1 and author's note, no p. no.
39. **Land H.** 1991 Time to care. In **Maclean M., Groves D.** (eds) *Women's issues in social policy.* Routledge, pp. 9–10; In the second half of the twentieth century, women, especially married women, have increased their participation in the formal labour market significantly.
40. **Borsay A.** 1986 *Disabled people in the community.* Bedford Square Press, p. 1.
41. For a full discussion of this debate see **Baldwin S., Twigg J.**

1991 Women and community care – Reflections on a debate. In Maclean M., Groves D. (eds) *Women's issues in social policy.* Routledge, pp. 117–35.

42. Hicks C. *Who cares: Looking after people at home.* pp. 229–30.
43. See **Sutherland I.** 1987 *Health education – half a policy: The rise and fall of the Health Education Council.* National Extension College, Cambridge.
44. **Popham G.** 1981 Government and smoking: Policy-making and pressure groups *Policy and politics* **9**: 331–47.
45. **Robertson R.** 1987 *Heroin, AIDS and society.* Hodder and Stoughton, pp. 76–9.
46. **Berridge V., Strong P.** 1991 AIDS in the UK: Contemporary history and the study of policy. *Twentieth-century British history* **2**: 152–8.
47. **Dorn N., South N.** 1987 *A land fit for heroin? Drug policies, prevention and practice.* Macmillan, pp. 36–42.
48. **Higgins J.** 1988 *The business of medicine: Private health care in Britain.* Macmillan, pp. 64–72.
49. **Griffith B., Iliffe S., Rayner G.** 1987 *Banking on sickness: Commercial medicine in Britain and the USA.* Lawrence and Wishart, pp. 45–6.
50. **Ascher K.** 1987 *The politics of privatisation: Contracting out public services.* Macmillan, pp. 266–7.
51. **Seldon A.** 1980 *The litmuss papers.* Centre for Policy Studies, p. 2.
52. Higgins J. *The business of medicine.* pp. 124–62.
53. **Johnson N.** 1990 *Reconstructing the welfare state: A decade of change, 1980–90.* Harvester/Wheatsheaf, pp. 79–81.
54. **Culyer A., Mills A.** 1989 *Perspectives on the future of health care in Europe.* Centre for Health Economics, University of York, pp. 1–5; **Hatch S., Kickbusch I.** 1983 *Self-help and health in Europe: New approaches to health care.* WHO Regional Office for Europe Copenhagen, p. 12.

Chapter 8

INEQUALITIES IN HEALTH EXPERIENCE: THE DEBATE

INTRODUCTION

Throughout Europe there is a growing interest in inequalities in standards of health, although in many cases the evidence is less comprehensive than for Britain.[1] Inequalities exist throughout Europe despite a range of health-care systems which, like the British system, have come in for sustained criticism. At the same time faith weakens in the ability of medicine to make a major contribution to well-being. 'Health' is now broadly defined; and the wide social influences (relating to class, gender and ethnic relationships) on standards of health are receiving increased attention. This last chapter offers a taster of the debate currently underway in Britain.

CLASS

Before reviewing the debate over class inequalities in health, it is as well to be aware of the problematic nature of measuring class. There are a variety of class schemas on offer to operationalise the concept of class.[2] Those writers discussing class inequalities in standards of health usually use the Registrar-General's five-tier classification, not least because it is the system by which official statistics are compiled. It is based on a man's, or single woman's, occupation. A married woman is classed according to her husband's occupation, so the term has an inbuilt gender inaccuracy. The first two classes are middle class and the bottom three are working class.[3] The Registrar-General's class schema has been the subject of much criticism alongside the more theoretically sophisticated class schemas.[4] For men and women occupation is only one of the components constituting class position;

it is a crude measure of class experience, particularly for women. A woman's class is more accurately measured when housing tenure, car ownership, her occupation and her husband's occupation, are all taken into account.[5] Putting people into class categories inevitably creates a stepping-stone effect, although in the real world class inequalities are part of a gradual gradient. Before 1911 only some working-class men were covered by Friendly Societies, and between 1911 and 1948 only certain sections of the working class were covered by National Health Insurance. With the growth of private health care in the 1980s a minority of the working class will be covered by private health insurance by, for instance, their trade unions. Housing tenure has always been diverse within the working class, varying according to region, ethnicity, income and family size. Income, housing, family size, ethnic origin and the nature of employment have all fractured working-class experience. In short, there are serious methodological weaknesses in the official data relating to class and health.

In the early post-war years it was assumed that because the NHS was free at the point of use the working class had gained most from it. Removing the financial worries associated with medical care was thought to be of greatest benefit to the working class. As the NHS was (and is) funded mainly out of general taxation, the middle class shouldered the financial burden: their higher earnings meant that they paid more in taxes than the low paid.

In 1968 Richard Titmuss challenged the assumption that the working class were benefiting most from the NHS. He argued that those with more money made better use of the Health Service. The working class had actually gained least from the NHS.[6] However, Titmuss's evidence was somewhat dated and confined to a narrow range of health-care services. Martin Rein soon attacked Titmuss's claims, maintaining that lower socio-economic groups made more use of GPs and in-patient hospital services. He did not believe that this was due to the greater amount of illness among lower socio-economic groups. He concluded, 'The British experience suggests that the availability of universal free-on-demand, comprehensive services is a crucial factor in reducing class inequalities in the use of medical care services.'[7] Like Titmuss, however, he was drawing on a narrow range of evidence.

Over the last twenty years, an array of evidence has been presented to support one or other side. In 1970 M.R. Alderson suggested that there were far too many variables when overall consultation rates were examined, and instead the use of specific services should be taken into account. Alderson looked mainly at preventative services and found that the middle class used these services more than the working class. Although the initial data were not always very up-to-date,[8] evidence has subsequently accumulated proving that the middle class make much greater use of preventative services, such as antenatal care, cervical screening and immunisation. Evidence about the use of other services remains more controversial. In the 1970s when GP consultation rates were linked with self-reported illness it was found that higher socio-economic groups made more use of GP services.[9] Strong evidence exists from the 1970s that there are class inequalities in the use made of a range of services.

Cartwright and O'Brien suggest a number of reasons why the middle class makes better use than the working class of NHS resources. First, the geographical distribution of resources favours middle-class areas. Throughout the course of this century the distribution of health care resources has tended to vary inversely with need. Before the establishment of the NHS local authority provision was usually worst in areas of poorest health. When the NHS was set up there was no redistribution of health-care resources to right the longstanding geographical imbalance. Since the 1976 Report of the Resource Allocation Working Party (RAWP) there have been efforts to distribute resources according to health needs, but success has been patchy. Moreover, physical access difficulties for certain groups, such as those living in rural areas and the elderly continued.[10] However, the impact of the distribution of health-care resources on standards of health should not be overstated. In 1980 it was pointed out that Scotland had the highest infant mortality rates but the shortest GP lists and more health visitors, consultant obstetricians and consultant paediatricians than any other area of the country.[11]

Second, the middle class are more knowledgeable than the working class about health and medicine, which is a reflection of their higher levels of education. They are more critical and display greater self-confidence when dealing with the medical world. Third, the nature of GP consultations works to the advantage of the middle class who receive longer consultations and discuss their problems more extensively with the GP. One piece of research in the 1970s found that a middle-class patient's average consultation lasted 6.2 minutes and a working-class patient's 4.7 minutes.[12] Patients who walk out of the doctor's surgery satisfied with the consultation are more likely to follow the doctor's advice. Satisfaction is related to the amount of information, including explanations, given by doctors. Patients who receive most information are more satisfied and compliant with medical advice than those receiving minimum explanation. Pendleton's and Bochner's study showed that 'lower-class' (they used three classes) patients do not receive as much information and explanation. They were also the social group expressing least satisfaction with all aspects of medical care. The implication of these findings is that if a doctor wants lower-class patients to be better satisfied and follow medical advice, the doctor should offer them more information.[13]

174

Before the establishment of the NHS the costs of seeking treatment were both direct and indirect. The direct financial costs of treatment and formal health care were removed by the NHS, but not the indirect costs of transport, taking time off work and, particularly for women, looking after the rest of the family. The creation of the NHS did nothing to alter attitudes towards certain patients or destroy stereotyping. When assessing the quality of care, the value-added element of a user-friendly health service remains largely hidden.

In recent years interest has shifted away from the relative use made of services to the relative standard of health, or health status, of people in different groups. The first problem we encounter in this debate is how to measure the amount of health or illness in the population. If we lean too heavily on mortality rates this can detract both from the amount of chronic illness in society and from illnesses which do not kill people but lower their well-being. As death certificates only record the last occupation of a deceased man, or in the case of a married woman normally her husband's last occupation, they give no indication of a man's occupations over a lifetime, or of a wife's occupations. Morbidity rates are also problematic as not all illnesses are reported. Perceptions vary as to what it means to be ill and this will affect the amount of illness reported. Long-term changes in people's sense of well-being are hard to gauge as many people in the past would not have consulted a doctor on account of the financial or non-monetary costs. Earlier this century working-class women took for granted that they would frequently feel unwell. A number of studies have compared self-reported illness with clinical examination and they have all found that disease is under-reported, particularly among the lower classes. General Household Survey (GHS) self-reported illness statistics are influenced by individual perceptions of illness. The costs of being ill are higher for the working class: they may lose pay if they take time off work to visit a doctor, and transport may be relatively more costly and inconvenient. They may be less likely, therefore, to define a symptom as an illness.

In the mid-1970s Blaxter summarised self-reported illnesses from the GHS. She divided illnesses into acute (restricting activity over two weeks), chronic (limiting activity compared with others of the same age) and handicapping. The main difference between classes lay in the amount of chronic, rather than acute, illness. Blaxter's data also showed greater class differences in morbidity than in mortality rates.[14] This data contradicts Martin Rein's claim that class mortality is not an index of class morbidity and that just because people in the lower classes tend to die younger does not mean that they suffer more illness when alive.[15]

Although there are problems with using mortality and morbidity statistics, taken together they provide us with a general impression of the health of British society. The key question is: why have class differentials in health status been so persistent? One argument runs that class inequalities are not as great today as they were when the NHS was set up. Class 5 has shrunk and many who were in class 5 are now in class 4.[16] At the same time the middle class has grown. Moreover, by using occupational class as a means of analysis it is not obvious which particular aspects of deprivation, for instance housing, poverty or working conditions, relate to ill health.[17] However, class differences exist between all the classes, not just between class 5 and the other classes. A class gradient still exists, running through classes 1 to 5. The fact that class inequalities exist is not altered by the fact that the number of people in each class may be changing.

Second, it is argued that the unhealthy sink to the bottom of the class pile. So, it is not people's class position which determines their health status, but their health status which influences their class position. In Chapter 2 mention was made of the fact that poverty could aggravate ill health and push people into greater poverty. There is some evidence to suggest that this may still have some (but not a great deal of) influence on class inequalities in standards of health.

Third, the attitudes and behaviour (or culture) of individuals and families has been put forward to explain class differences. In the early part of this century physical and moral inadequacies were linked together as integral aspects of lower working-class life. In Chapters 2 and 4 we saw the emphasis laid on personal habits in improving health. Eugenicists pointed to what they claimed to be a disproportionate number of inadequate and feeble people among the lower working class. Today there is still a school of thought which holds that those who are unthinking, reckless, fickle and lead irresponsible lifestyles will make themselves ill and will therefore be more likely to die young. Some people stuff themselves with unhealthy, especially fatty, food; they smoke like chimneys and drink like fish. During their non-working hours they are 'couch potatoes', refusing to take enough exercise. They fail to use preventative services, such as antenatal care, vaccination and family planning clinics. This range of unhealthy behaviour is due either to a lack of education or to a disproportionately high number of feckless people in the working class.

Critics of a cultural explanation of ill health argue that it is highly judgemental, subjective and simplistic. Throughout the century those critics who have pointed to the unhealthy behaviour of others have failed to understand the constraints operating on poor people's lifestyles or to recognise the strategies developed to cope with influences beyond an individual's control. Moreover, it is difficult to say exactly what constitutes a healthy lifestyle for everyone. For instance, manual workers who are spectators rather than participants in sports may well exert more physical energy at work. There is no evidence, anyway, that sports participation reduces health inequalities associated with class, gender or age.[18] Access to healthy food and sports facilities often depends on personal resources. It may be that people are forced to behave in an unhealthy fashion because they do not have adequate resources (educational and material) to choose their lifestyle. A health education strategy which aims to improve standards of health can, therefore, be quite inappropriate when a lack of resources is the major constraint on behavioural changes. Indeed, emphasising the importance of altering a lifestyle may be positively harmful if it merely adds to existing stresses.

Fourth, and challenging the cultural approach in particular, it is argued that class inequalities in health status are related to the social and economic structure of society. Such an explanation is favoured by Townsend and Davidson in *The Black Report*, and others have since supported their case. Ill health is directly related to poverty and economic deprivation. Those near the bottom of the class scale are more exposed to hazards at work, such as toxic dangers and accidents. Evidence from the 1930s and 1980s has demonstrated that those workers with the most comprehensive range of work-related health hazards are likely to suffer most in periods of high unemployment. Unemployment is higher among lower classes, and there are stresses and strains related to unemployment. For whatever reasons (and it may include the fact that unemployment brings ill health to light), the unemployed appear to be in worse health than those in work. Those on lower incomes have less money for a healthy diet. People with fewer resources typically live in homes of a poorer structural quality and are surrounded by environmental hazards. Poor housing has long been recognised as a health hazard. Infectious diseases have spread more rapidly in overcrowded and dilapidated homes, and women have been worn down by the problems of home-making under such conditions. By mid-century, as slums were being replaced by tower blocks, one problem was being solved by the creation of another. The whole local environment is now acknowledged as influencing health and well-being.

Inequalities in health and illness have also been placed in the context of the capitalist method of production. Lesley Doyal lists four causal connections between capitalism and illness: accidents at work are directly linked to the process of capital accumulation; industrial pollution is worse because of the profit motive; harmful goods are sold and consumed because they are more profitable than harmless ones, and the nature of the competitive, alienating capitalist system increases stress.[19] However, these characteristics, which Doyal attributes to capitalist societies, have been present in all industrialised societies; Eastern Europe is a notorious example.

Finally, the most recent (and most interesting) research links structural and behavioural influences on standards of health. There is not a single 'correct' explanation of health inequalities, but a range of influences interact in a complex fashion. Clare Blackburn argues that poverty shapes health in a number of ways. First, the poor have fewer material resources and suffer more health hazards in their housing and diet. These hazards affect their physical health. Physical symptoms are linked to emotional behaviour, such as irritability. Second, poverty increases the number of stressful life events and makes them hard to resolve. Money brings choice and influence to solve problems. Those without the personal or social resources to deal with stress and conflict may cope by smoking, heavy drinking or drug abuse. Psychological processes interact with physical and behavioural ones. Blackburn underlines the fact that behaviour does not take place in a social vacuum; health choices which are made to preserve one aspect of health may damage another one.[20] Mildred Blaxter has also analysed the web of influences on people's health. She has shown that social and economic circumstances, including the extent of social support, exert a greater influence on health than people's behaviour. She argues that unhealthy behaviour does not reinforce disadvantage as much as healthy behaviour increases advantage.[21] Emphasising behavioural changes to the poorest members of society will do nothing to break the vicious circle of poverty and ill health; emphasising a healthy lifestyle to the most advantaged members of society will reinforce the virtuous spiral of rising standards of living and good health.

EMPLOYMENT AND UNEMPLOYMENT

As the working class suffer disproportionately from unemployment and unhealthy working conditions, the debate over class inequalities in health is linked with the controversy over the impact of employment and unemployment on health. The ill-effects of unemployment on people's health have been discussed for a number of decades, but now the debate also includes the hazards of paid work in periods of both economic growth and recession. Work affects health both directly and indirectly. The environment of work may contribute to ill health by exposing workers to physical, chemical and psychological hazards. Paid work provides money and status, which influences lifestyle, diet, housing and health.

Some links between health and illness are easier to make than others. Accidents at work are the most direct link, although accident statistics underestimate the real accident rate as many accidents are not reported. The symptoms of an industrial disease may not show up for many years after a worker has been exposed to a hazard. In the early 1990s controversy flared up over the possibility that fathers working at the Sellafield nuclear reprocessing plant passed cancer onto their children who have since died.

Work-related stress is also difficult to prove. Vicente Navarro has argued that the intensification of work as well as new kinds of work organisation lead to fatigue and stress; new technological developments may lead to new risks from accidents and toxic materials. Deskilling and the fragmentation of jobs gives individual workers less control over their own work which creates dissatisfaction, absenteeism, indifference or hostility to management. This process leads to alienation, which in turn involves unease, stress, anxiety, dissatisfaction, disease, disability and even death. Several studies have shown that certain types of illness have a higher incidence among workers with little control over the work process than among those with control. However, as workers with least control over their jobs are also likely to be those in the worst-paid jobs and lowest down the class scale, it is difficult to identify the exact cause of the poorer health. Navarro also argues that the effects of psychologically unrewarding work spreads to life outside work and influences an individual's lifestyle.[22] It seems more likely that income is a stronger determinant of lifestyle. The problems which Navarro blames on capitalism are apparent in all industrialised countries. When social class and employment are considered in conjunction with gender, then patterns of illness become less distinct. Among women with children, middle-class women seem to have less illness if they are in paid work, and working-class women more illness if they are in paid work.[23]

The debate over the relationship between health and employment has now shifted its focus to the relationship between employment, unemployment and health. From the 1930s evidence has existed that work can have a negative impact on health during a recession.[24] Broadly, there is less security for those in employment: the fear of losing one's job can be as big a worry as the loss itself; one person's unemployment can have a negative effect on the whole family; employers can keep wages down more easily; in order to keep one's job, or earn some extra money, there is a greater willingness to take risks at work, to leave unsafe practices unreported, and to work in hazardous processes. Firms under harsh economic competition, and especially small businesses, will have less money to spend on a safe and healthy working environment. Workers who have been out of work for long periods are more accident-prone when they regain employment. Yet, it is usually only in times of war that governments attempt to grapple seriously with the hazards of work. It is important to differentiate between types of employment, for certain jobs are far more likely than others to be hazardous in a recession. While some workers suffer from job insecurity and unemployment in a recession, others will be enjoying a rising standard of living. The impact of a recession on people's health will, therefore, vary accordingly. There is a wide-ranging debate over the effects of a recession on those out of work.

Despite many shocking newspaper headlines and pronouncements from various quarters linking unemployment and ill-health, the connection is not an easy one to explain. There have been no major long-term investigations into the relationship between health and unemployment and, even if full data existed for Britain, there are various methodological problems involved in this kind of research. One problem is that the unemployed are likely to claim in surveys that they are unemployed for reasons of ill health, perhaps because they feel this to be less stigmatising. Although there is evidence to show that the unemployed are less healthy than those in work it is difficult to show whether unemployment is the direct cause, or a contributory factor. Notwithstanding these problems, it is possible to identify a connection between unemployment and ill health.

The link between unemployment and ill health is strongest in mental illness.[25] What is not so clear is whether people go through distinct 'phases' when they become unemployed. In the 1930s and in the 1980s definite phases of a mental syndrome were identified. For instance, in the 1980s Fagin and Little identified four phases: the initial shock of losing one's job is followed by a 'holiday' feeling of optimism and internal denial of the situation. This is followed by anxiety and stress when, within a few weeks, the unemployed frantically start looking for work. Finally there is a mood of resignation and depressing adjustment to the situation.[26] Sinfield has attacked the creation of models into which the mental state of the unemployed is placed, arguing that people do not react in a set pattern to unemployment. For instance, the impact on the short-term and long-term unemployed is likely to be quite different.[27] His argument is supported by evidence that the young unemployed regard unemployment in a very different light from their parents' generation.[28] As well as individual factors others, such as age, class, gender and location (whether one is surrounded by others who are unemployed) all affect the way an individual responds. Further, unemployment may reinforce existing situations. So, for instance, if a marriage is slightly rocky, unemployment will make it worse, but if the marriage is relatively strong, unemployment may enhance it.[29]

The unemployed seem to be in worse health than those in work and their children have poorer health and development.[30] What is hardest to untangle is whether the unemployed have poor health and other problems because they are unemployed, or whether the unemployed are more likely to have been previously employed in occupations which harmed their health, or the unemployed become poorer when out of work and it is the poverty, rather than the state of unemployment, which brings a range of problems in its wake.

There is a longstanding school of thought which holds that paid work outside the home brings benefits other than financial ones, and it is for this reason that unemployment is devastating. In the early 1930s it was suggested that work imposes a time-structure on the day, it provides social contact beyond the family, it gives a sense of purpose and social achievement, it assigns social status and requires a regular lifestyle. More recently it has been argued that work acts as a traction, pulling people along and pacing their week so that, for instance, more is done on a Monday than on a Sunday. The unemployed have less scope for making major decisions and less chance of developing new skills, and the unemployed suffer frequent humiliation.[31] However, this argument needs to be tempered by a recognition of the varied nature of work. For many people work is boring, with no scope for developing new skills or making decisions. Not all work offers a sense of achievement. Time and again it appears to be the poverty associated with unemployment which undermines the health and well-being of individuals and families.

The link between suicide and unemployment has received intense media coverage. Both suicide and para-suicide (self-mutilation rather than failed suicide) are linked with unemployment. There are higher rates of suicide among the unemployed. It is not clear whether the suicide is the result of being unemployed or of the poverty associated with unemployment. There is some evidence that those with a previous history of mental illness are the ones who appear in the suicide statistics when unemployed. The link between unemployed women and suicide is not nearly so strong as it is with unemployed men, although very little research has been undertaken into the impact of unemployment on women.

It has been suggested that unemployment leads to death, irrespective of the suicide rate. Partly this is because the unhealthiest section of society (class 5) are more likely than others to be unemployed. The deterioration in mental health associated with unemployment may also contribute to an early death by aggravating physical illness and depression, and weakening people's will to recover. The poverty associated with unemployment may also contribute to an early death. Living in poverty means stress, poor diet and a range of unhealthy influences. Ill health can strike the whole family, not just the unemployed member.

It is usually only as members of unemployed men's families that women's health has been considered. Little research has been undertaken into the impact of unemployment on women, but there is some evidence to suggest that there are negative psychological effects.[32] While some writers have assumed that women's work lies in the home, not in the paid labour force, at the same time the work undertaken by women in the home has not been thought worthy of serious academic consideration. Yet, throughout the twentieth century unpaid work, especially that work undertaken by women in the home, has had its effect on health. Further, the double burden of paid work outside the home and unpaid work in the home has been especially acute for married women during the two world wars and in the post-war years. It is only fairly recently that academics have incorporated the effects of housework into their equations, and even now they tend only to appear in feminist analyses and not in the major tomes on work, unemployment and health.

WOMEN'S HEALTH AND GENDER INEQUALITIES

Two linked debates surround women's health. First, why are women apparently less healthy than men during their lives, but then outlive men? Second, what are the implications for women of women's and men's unequal experiences as providers and users of health care? Running through both these debates are feminist challenges to conventional medical wisdom about the nature of women's illnesses. Women's scepticism about medicine is nothing new of course; it existed at the turn of the century, when women of different classes had their own health strategies independently of, and often in conflict with, medical orthodoxy.

   Some writers suggest that the image of women as less healthy than men is, in fact, a false one. First, women report more illness to their GPs than men because it is easier for them to do so. It can be hard for men to take time off paid work, whereas visiting a GP with children is part of a woman's unpaid work. Moreover, women's reproductive role brought them into closer contact with the medical profession as reproduction came to be increasingly monitored and treated as an illness (although in the 1980s there was shift away from the medicalisation of women's childbearing role). Finally, a free NHS has made it easier for women to use the health services. It should be remembered, of course, that during the first half of the century women would have been less likely than men to seek medical treatment because financial considerations acted as a deterrent. Second, the Victorian stereotype of frail and feeble women languishing under the male doctor's stethoscope has continued to influence assumptions about women's health and capabilities. Women were regarded as the weaker sex, both physically and mentally. Any behaviour which deviated from the stereotype of the ideal woman could be an indication of insanity. Male doctors' stereotypes of women mean that women are more readily thought of as having mental health problems than men. Third, it is possible women express their stresses through illness, while men express theirs through excessive bad temper, drinking and violence.

Further flaws have been identified in the data used to make claims about the differing illness rates of men and women. Feminists have challenged the traditional, medical view of illness so that there is no longer any agreement over what it means to be 'ill'. Researchers have used different methods of asking people about their illnesses, and there is no agreement over whether all kinds of illness, disability and health-care use should be given equal weight.[33] Less research has been undertaken on women's than men's social inequalities; and women's social and economic environment is reflected even less well than men's in the Registrar-General's definition of class by occupation. The differing experiences of ethnic minority and ethnic majority women are also woefully under-researched.[34]

In contrast to those who are dismissive of evidence that women's health is worse than men's, others have argued that women suffer poorer health because their lifestyles and social roles mean that they spend a great deal of time looking after relatives, and too little time taking good care of themselves. Women have been doubly burdened by paid and unpaid work. Throughout the century women have played an important role in promoting good health and in providing health care and, until recently, this role has been largely taken for granted. As we have seen in previous chapters, when women have allegedly not performed these tasks adequately, commentators have been quick to heap blame on them. Hilary Graham has drawn attention to the important health and hygiene work expected of women in the home: washing children, cleaning, teaching children basic hygiene and setting standards so that children learn from their mother's example. Women are also responsible for the more obvious health care, such as taking children to the doctor, dentist and optician, and ensuring babies are immunised. Even when there are two parents, both in paid employment, the woman is more likely to take time off work to care for the family. This unpaid health care becomes an especially heavy burden for women when there are relatives with long-term illnesses. The toll it takes, both physically and mentally, has been highlighted by various writers.[35] We have also seen how poor or inappropriate housing adversely affects women more than men.

A mother is the emotional crutch of a family, and it is hardly surprising, therefore, if she appears to suffer disproportionately from loneliness, depression and emotional strain. Indeed, mothers will

183

often support the health of their families, at the expense of their own health. There is evidence that single mothers often put off seeking medical help for themselves because they fear that the income and care which they provide for children might suffer. We have seen in previous chapters that women are more likely to be in poverty than men, even if they are part of the same household, and that this poverty affects their health. When money is short women will cut back on food in order that their children and husbands have enough to eat.

Power relations within the home, which work to the disadvantage of women, mean that women are more likely to suffer abuse than men. The family has been viewed as a private haven from the cut and thrust of the public world, and as the means by which cultural values are transmitted and children socialised. As such, it has been lauded as the bastion of British culture and the preserver of the nation's health and well-being. Until recently its negative aspects have been underplayed, and the differing experiences of members of the same family overlooked.

Finally, health-care systems, both before and after the introduction of the NHS, have frequently been absent or inappropriate to women's needs. The services offered to women have not always been those which they most urgently required. Free medical treatment and free contraceptives were both slow to develop for women. Yet, as inter-war birth control campaigners emphasised, childbirth was far riskier than any activity upon which a man might be engaged. Women form the majority of the frail elderly in the population but appropriate long-term care and support in the community for the growing elderly population has not materialised. Often women have been urged to follow lifestyles which were not in their own best interests: such as married women giving up paid work and unmarried mothers giving up their babies for adoption. In short, women have more stressful lives than men, and this is reflected in their poorer health.[36]

Part of the feminist challenge to long-standing assumptions about women's appropriate role in society is an attempt to 'reclaim' the body. Issues surrounding obstetrics and gynaecology are especially contentious because all the patients are women and most of the consultants are men. Ann Oakley has described the process by which medical technology has been used to remove women's control over reproduction. The fight to reclaim control over the birth process and for women to choose whether or not to have children, which involves demands for both birth control and abortion, have been two of the main issues for white feminists and women's groups.[37] Mention was made in the last chapter of Wendy Savage's struggle with the medical establishment over the birth process. In contrast, black women have focused on their right to *have* children rather than to limit the size of their families under pressure from a white-dominated medical profession.

There is growing concern among feminists that doctors are actually increasing their control over women through the new reproductive technologies. For instance, decisions over which women should receive infertility services lie beyond women's control. Some health authorities do not provide a service and among those that do, the service is rarely a free one, so that better-off women are more likely to be able to take advantage of it.[38]

It has to be remembered, of course, that many women have benefited from, and welcome, medical advances in gynaecology and obstetrics. As in other areas of health care, it is important to recognise that some women welcome developments which others condemn, and the experience of women using gynaecological and obstetrical services will vary. Women have differing expectations from a service; what is important, therefore, is to build as much flexibility and genuine choice as possible into the system.

Feminists have also developed critiques of attitudes within the medical profession towards women's mental health. Elaine Showalter has argued that whereas in the nineteenth century women were labelled as 'hysterical', since the Second World War 'schizophrenia' has become more closely linked with women's mental health. Fallacious assumptions about natural female passivity and obedience have now been exposed. Medicine now treats women, not so often by locking them up, as by drugging them up. Greater reliance is placed on anti-psychotic drugs, tranquillisers and anti-depressants for women.[39]

The differing experiences of ethnic minority and ethnic majority women complicate the debate over both class and gender differences. Historical research into the health of Britain's ethnic minority women is slowly emerging and has been discussed in earlier chapters, but there is a serious lack of published quantative and qualitative research on black women's health. Studies have tended to focus on maternity services for Asian women. The majority of research into black women's health has not come from black British women themselves. White feminists have taken gender analysis as their starting point, and often underlined the common oppression of women, and the family as an important site of that oppression.[40] Black women have criticised this mode of analysis as irrelevant to their experiences. In contrast to white women, black women have identified racism as the main cause of their oppression. Whole areas of black women's life experiences are absent from the pages of social history books as well as from publications on current social issues. How, for instance, do black women fare as unpaid carers? General comments about the need for health services more sensitive to black women's needs are not backed up with a list of well-researched specific requirements.[41] Lack of research, as well as methodological problems with the research undertaken, is a common problem for a range of issues relating to the health of ethnic minorities.

THE HEALTH OF ETHNIC MINORITIES

This section will review the debate about the health experience of ethnic minorities, both in terms of the wider social factors which affect their health, and the kind and quality of treatment they receive. 'Ethnic minority' refers to a group who share a cultural heritage, who are not part of the majority and who may suffer various forms of discrimination. 'Black people' refers to those of Afro-Caribbean, and sometimes Asian descent. The first problem encountered when discussing the health of ethnic minorities is the dearth of information. Qualitative evidence is often highly polemical. No systematic evidence exists about the health experience of ethnic minorities in Britain. Such information as does exist tends to be either out of date or localised. Research on ethnic minorities' health focuses on the health of immigrants from the New Commonwealth and Pakistan (NCWP). Virtually no research has been undertaken into the health of other ethnic minority groups, such as Irish immigrants who have the worst mortality rate of any ethnic group in Britain; the pages of health journals and books will be scoured in vain for any explanation, analysis or even recognition of this fact.[42] It is difficult to find information about the mortality and morbidity rates of those ethnic minorities who are not immigrants but second-or third-generation residents. When the health of immigrants has been taken seriously it has often been because either it is feared that they are bringing infectious diseases into the country, or they are undermining the British way of life, however interpreted. Earlier this century inter-racial sex and mixed-race children were seen as a threat to the future strength of the British race.

There are a few diseases specific to an ethnic group; for instance only Afro-Caribbeans suffer from sickle cell disease. Certain illnesses are more common among particular ethnic groups, although in some cases immigrants appear to fare better than the indigenous population.[43] A number of explanations have been posited for the unequal health experience of ethnic minorities in Britain.

The oldest argument blames genetic factors for the relatively poor health of ethnic minorities. It is assumed that genetic predisposition can be equated with racial characteristics. This is a meaningless link, as race is a social concept with no specific biological meaning.

Nevertheless, the supposed link was made earlier in the century, and more recently, to explain the high TB rates of Asians in Britain. It makes no allowances for the fact that Asians are over-represented lower down the class scale, that they tend to live in the worst housing and in overcrowded conditions, all of which increase the likelihood of contracting the disease.[44]

Second, differing health experiences are seen as a reflection of cultural differences. It is assumed that the health of ethnic minorities can be improved by health education and a change to a more Western lifestyle. Jenny Donovan has shown how such an approach lends itself to victim-blaming; either the culture or the individual is at fault.[45] Rickets, high infant mortality rates and mental ill health, have all been explained in terms of the cultural 'inadequacies' of ethnic minorities. For those who see racism as the root cause of their poorer standards of health a cultural explanation is superficial and misleading. Ethnic minorities are more prone to these conditions because of racism. A cultural explanation is dangerous because it serves not only as explanation but also as justification for ethnic minorities' poor health. Moreover, because it is employed by the medical profession it is vested with a fallacious scientific objectivity.

Third then, it is argued that racism exists in the NHS and is experienced by ethnic minorities as both consumers and employees. Immigrants and ethnic minorities have experienced hostility through-out the century. In the 1900s Jewish immigrants, and in the 1930s Jewish medical students and doctors were treated with hostility; and in post-war Britain ethnic minorities have propped up an ailing health service while their own health has been undermined. Although social, political and economic factors adversely affect working-class health and access to services, working-class people who are members of an ethnic minority have disadvantage reinforced by racism. Poor housing and bad working conditions affected poor immigrants as well as the indigenous population early this century, but the Jewish immigrants were doubly disadvantaged by the racism of the majority population. It is argued that the NHS discriminates in the way it treats patients. Racism is subtle because it occurs in an institution which is supposedly 'caring' and there to serve the patients. This institutional racism exists because efforts are not made to avoid the general racism which pervades all British institutions and to provide a service equally adequate for all patients, whatever their ethnic background. It has further been claimed that a major problem within the NHS is that the medical profession lacks knowledge about diseases specific to the black community and there is a lack of government-funded research in this field. There has been a general lack of attention to health needs specific to black people.[46]

The ignorance of the medical profession not only causes discomfort, but may also be dangerous. Without adequate knowledge, doctors are likely to make wrong diagnoses. For example, this is true of sickle cell anaemia, which is a genetically transmitted disease affecting those of Caribbean and African origin. Further, an Asian person's problems may be misunderstood unless a health worker is aware of the way in which Asians use the term 'feeling hot'. Many Asians use the term to cover a range of feelings, such as giddiness, sweating and tiredness. It does not necessarily mean that they have a temperature.[47]

Various evidence exists from the early 1980s of institutional racism within the NHS. For instance, it was the practice to translate only health education leaflets into Asian languages. It was rare to find hospital handbooks in Asian languages; and it was difficult to obtain information about health rights, such as how to get a second opinion or how to make a complaint. When Brent and Harrow Family Practitioners' Committee had DHSS leaflets about optical and dental services translated into Asian languages, there was strong pressure to leave out some of the information about how to make a complaint. Even so, this translation initiative was exceptional.[48] While Brent community health council saw the racism of the NHS resulting from explicitly racist attitudes, others suggest the racism is less explicit but no less real. In effect the NHS is racist by default. Existing policies may indirectly result in ethnic minority patients receiving less favourable treatment.[49]

Perceived racism has meant that some ethnic groups, when resources have permitted, have developed strategies for providing health care and welfare facilities more appropriate to their needs. The extensive welfare services developed by the Jewish community in the late nineteenth and early twentieth century are a case in point. However, at this time state personal health services were in their infancy and rudimentary for the whole population. This is no longer the case and therefore state services should take full account of the needs of the various ethnic groups in British society; this can only be done if all ethnic groups are involved in the policy-making and policy-implementation processes.

The position of ethnic minority workers within the NHS is also seen to be the result of racism. As a result of the NHS's recruitment policy in the 1950s people from the NCWP are employed as doctors, nurses and ancillary workers. Within the medical and nursing professions such workers are to be found predominantly in the low-status specialisms and on the lowest rungs of the ladder. This, it has been argued, is the result of the NHS's racist employment policies.

While many ethnic minorities have problems dealing with a health service which is insensitive to their needs, it is also the case that the weakest members of the majority population, those needing geriatric and mental health care, are the ones most likely to be treated and cared for by those of a different culture. These patients may also suffer from communication problems as a result of cultural differences. The problem can work both ways.

Fourth, focusing on diseases or illnesses specific to, or more prevalent among, ethnic minorities, and on institutional racism can divert attention from the socio-economic structure of society and the political influences on ethnic minorities' ill health.[50] The main determinants of health lie beyond the NHS, so, to concentrate on racism within the NHS as the main explanation for the unequal access to services and poor health status of ethnic minorities means that deprivation caused by poverty, poor housing and the wider racism of British society, which all contribute to ill health and a lowered sense of well-being, are marginalised. It is clear from previous chapters that hostility and violence against ethnic minorities has less to do with the actual size of the minority, or its rate of growth, than with the prevailing political climate. Thus, hostility was probably greatest during the era of the two world wars, although the 1980s witnessed an increasing number of ugly incidents. Ironically, when hostility from the majority population towards those perceived to be different or foreign is intense that same majority population can demonstrate sympathy for the plight of others, so long as they are safely beyond Britain's shores.

While it is true that health issues pertinent to the needs of ethnic minorities have been ignored, it is also true that the health needs of other groups, such as women, have also been marginalised and racism is not the major explanation here. Racism can aggravate the health experience of ethnic minorities but it is not necessarily the central cause of it. This then brings us back to the interlocking class, gender and ethnic determinants of health in twentieth-century British society. While an individual's health can be improved by medical intervention, raising the standard of health of entire populations lies largely beyond the bounds of medicine. Social factors are the main cause of improvements in standards of health and of inequalities in health.

Three main themes of class, gender and ethnicity as they relate to health have run throughout this book. While standards of health have risen for all groups in society and the health services have played an ever-growing role in our lives, there has been no spectacular U-turn in the unequal health experience of different groups. Nevertheless, class, gender and ethnicity are crude categories which current researchers are unpicking. Historians are walking a tightrope: on the one hand drawing out the personal and particular circumstances which affect us individually, while at the same time not losing sight of the impersonal and general features of our society which still provide the interlocking tripod of class, gender and ethnicity on which our health rests.

NOTES

1. **Fox J.** 1989 *Health inequalities in European countries.* Gower.
2. **Goldthorpe J. H.** in collaboration with **Payne C.** 1987 *Social mobility and class structure in modern Britain.* 2nd edn. Clarendon; **Stewart A., Prandy K., Blackburn R. M.** 1980 *Social stratification and occupations.* Macmillan.
3. Class 1 Professional (e.g. accountant, doctor, lawyer).
   Class 2 Intermediate (e.g. manager, nurse, teacher).
   Class 3 Skilled non-manual (e.g. clerical worker, secretary, shop assistant).
   Class 3 Skilled manual (e.g. bus driver, butcher, carpenter).
   Class 4 Semi-skilled (e.g. agricultural worker, bus conductor, postman).
   Class 5 Unskilled (e.g. cleaner, docker, labourer).
4. **Marshall G., Rose D., Newby H., Vogler C.** 1988 *Social class in modern Britain.* Hutchinson.
5. **Roberts H.** 1990 Women's health counts. In Roberts H. (ed) *Women's health counts.* Routledge, p. 31.
6. **Titmuss R.** 1968 *Commitment to welfare.* George Allen and Unwin, p. 196.
7. **Rein M.** 1969 Social class and the health service *New Society* **14:** 807–10.
8. **Alderson M. R.** 1970 Social class and the health service *The Medical Officer* **124:** 50–2.
9. **Forster D. P.** 1976 Social class differences in sickness and general practitioner consultations *Health Trends* **8:** 29; **Blaxter M.** 1976 Social class and health inequalities. In **Carter C., Peel J.** *Equalities and inequalities in health.* Academic Press, p. 116.
10. **Whitehead M.** 1988 *Inequalities in health: The health divide.* Penguin, pp. 267–8.
11. **Hubley J.** 1980 *Poverty and health in Scotland – A review.* Paisley College of Technology Local Government Research Unit Working Paper no. 10, p. 10.
12. **Cartwright A., O'Brien M.** 1976 Social class variations in health care and in the nature of general practitioner consultations. In **Stacey M.** *The sociology of the NHS: Sociological Review Monograph No. 22.* University of Keele, pp. 77–98; quoted in **Foster P.** 1979 The informal rationing of primary medical care. *Journal of Social Policy* **8:** 500. See this article for other aspects of non-monetary rationing of health care.
13. **Pendleton D., Bochner S.** 1980 The communication of medical information in general practice consultations as a function of patients' social class. *Social Science and Medicine* **14a:** 669–73.

14. **Blaxter M.** 1976 Social class and health inequalities. In Carter C., Peel J. *Equalities and inequalities in health.* Academic Press, p. 117.
15. Rein M. Social class and the health service *New Society* **14:** 807.
16. **Klein R.** 1991 Making sense of inequalities: A response to Peter Townsend. *International Journal of Health Services* **21:** 177.
17. **Carr-Hill R.** The inequalities in health debate: A critical review of the issues. *Journal of Social Policy* **16:** 535; Klein R. Making sense of inequalities: A response to Peter Townsend. *International Journal of Health Services* **21:** 178.
18. **Roberts K., Brodie D.** 1992 *Inner-city sport: Who plays and what are the benefits?* Giordano Bruno Culemborg, The Netherlands, p. 139.
19. **Doyal L.** 1983 *The political economy of health.* Pluto Press; see also **Navarro V.** 1976 *Medicine under capitalism.* Croom Helm.
20. **Blackburn C.** 1991 *Poverty and health: Working with families.* Open University Press, pp. 44–6.
21. **Blaxter M.** 1990 *Health and lifestyles.* Routledge, pp. 230, 233 and *passim.*
22. **Navarro V.** 1982 The labour process and health: A historical materialist interpretation. *International Journal of Health Services* **12:** 5–29.
23. **Whitehead M.** 1988 *Inequalities in health: The health divide.* Penguin, p. 244.
24. **Nichols T.** 1986 *The British worker question: A new look at workers and productivity in manufacturing.* Routledge & Kegan Paul, pp. 199–201.
25. For a broad review of the subject see **Smith R.** 1988 *Unemployment and health: A disaster and a challenge.* Oxford University Press.
26. **Fagin L., Little M.** 1984 *The forsaken families: The effects of unemployment on family life.* Penguin, pp. 40–57.
27. **Sinfield A.** 1981 *What unemployment means.* Martin Robertson, pp. 37–41.
28. **Roberts K.** 1984 Youth unemployment: An old problem or a new life-style? In **Thompson K.** *Work, employment and unemployment: Perspectives on work and society.* Open University Press, pp. 238–46.
29. **Kelvin P., Jarrett J.** 1985 *Unemployment, its social and psychological effects.* Cambridge University Press, pp. 26, 59.
30. Whitehead M. *Inequalities in health.* p. 240.
31. Quoted in **Smith R.** 1985 'Bitterness, shame, emptiness, waste': An introduction to unemployment and health. *British Medical Journal* 12 October **291:** 1025.
32. **Henwood F., Miles I.** 1987 The experience of unemployment and the sexual division of labour. In **Fryer D., Ullah P.** (eds) *Unemployed people: Social and psychological perspectives.* Open University Press, pp. 94–110.
33. **Clarke J.** 1983 Sexism, feminism and medicalism: Decade review of the literature on gender and illness. *Sociology of Health and Illness* **5:** 62–82.
34. Blackburn C. *Poverty and health.* p. 40.
35. **Graham H.** 1984 *Women, health and the family.* Wheatsheaf, pp. 61, 153–9.
36. Clarke J. Sexism, feminism and medicalism: Decade review of the

literature on gender and illness. *Sociology of Health and Illness* **5:** 62–82.

37. This subject is discussed in **Oakley A.** 1986 *The captured womb: A history of the medical care of pregnant women.* Basil Blackwell.
38. **Williams F.** 1989 *Social policy: A critical introduction. Issues of race, gender and class.* Polity Press, p. 193. First published 1984.
39. **Showalter E.** 1987 *The female malady: Women, madness and English culture, 1830–1980.* Virago, pp. 203, 222, 250.
40. **Douglas J.** 1992 Black women's health matters: Putting black women on the research agenda. In Roberts H. (ed) *Women's health counts.* Routledge, pp. 33–46.
41. Ibid. pp. 41–2.
42. **Pearson M., Madden M., Greenslade L.** 1991 Generations of an invisible minority: The health and well-being of the Irish in Britain. Occasional papers in Irish Studies no. 2 Institute of Irish Studies, p. 1.
43. Whitehead M. 1988 *Inequalities in health.* p. 251.
44. **Cooper R.** 1986 Race, disease and health. In **Rathwell T., Phillips D.** (eds) *Health, race and ethnicity.* Croom Helm, pp. 28–9; **Bandaranayake R.** 1986 Ethnic differences in disease – an epidemiological perspective. In Rathwell T., Phillips D. (eds) *Health, race and ethnicity.* Croom Helm, pp. 87–8.
45. **Donovan J.** 1986 Black people's health: A different approach. In Rathwell T., Phillips D. (eds) *Health, race and ethnicity.* Croom Helm, pp. 117–19.
46. **Torkington N. P. K.** 1983 *The racial politics of health: A Liverpool profile.* University of Liverpool, p. 74.
47. **Grant J.** 1987 Getting it right: Health and maternity care in multiracial Britain. *Medicine in Society* **13:** 22.
48. **Brent CHC** 1981 *Black people and the health service.* Brent CHC, p. 14.
49. This seems to be the underlying assumption of **McNaught A.** 1988 *Race and health policy.* Croom Helm.
50. For example, Donovan J. Black people's health: A different approach. p. 134.

BIBLIOGRAPHICAL NOTE

Some of the debates touched upon may be explored in greater depth in the following works. Blaxter M 1990 *Health and lifestyles.* (Routledge) is important for defining 'health' and examining the complex interaction of so many aspects of our lives and our health. The best overall picture of health and historians work on the subject is Berridge V 1990 Health and medicine. In Thompson FLM (ed) *The Cambridge social history of Britain, 1750–1950. vol. 3 Social agencies and institutions.* (Cambridge University Press). In the companion vol. 2 Oddy D 1990 Food, drink and nutrition is also useful. Dwork D 1987 *War is good for babies and other young children: A history of the infant and child welfare movement in England, 1898–1918.* (Tavistock) has a useful chapter which reviews the debate over the quality of the race, government policies and their implications for women. For the First World War and its effects on people's health Winter J 1986 *The Great War and the British people.* (Macmillan) should be read.

The best review of the debates over health in the inter-war years is to be found in Constantine S 1980 *Unemployment in Britain between the wars.* (Longman). Also worth reading is Macnicol J 1980 *The movement for family allowances 1918–45: A study in social policy development.* (Heinemann). Still influential for the Second World War is Titmuss R 1950 *Problems of social policy.* (HMSO). For the post-war years see Allsop J 1984 *Health policy and the National Health Service.* (Longman). For current debates on health and women's issues see Roberts H (ed) 1990 *Women's health counts.* (Routledge) and its sister volume Roberts H (ed) 1992 *Women's health matters.* (Routledge). For the debate over unemployment and health see Smith R 1988 *Unemployment and health: A disaster and a challenge.* (Oxford University Press). On the subject of the health of ethnic minorities, Rathwell T, Phillips D (eds) 1986 *Health, race and ethnicity.* (Croom Helm) has some interesting chapters; however there is a great need for more historical and contemporary research in this field.

Health and society in twentieth-century Britain

For evidence of recent and continuing inequalities in health see Inequalities in health 1988 *The Black report: The health divide.* (Penguin).

Basic statistics relating to health over the course of the century can be found in McPherson K, Coleman D 1988 Health. In Halsey AH *British social trends since 1900: A guide to the changing social structure of Britain.* (Macmillan).

TABLES

TABLE 1   Deaths, 1901–80 England and Wales

Period	Standardised[1] mortality ratios (1950–52 = 100)		
	Persons	Males	Females
1901–05	249	234	264
1906–10	221	208	234
1911–15[2]	205	195	215
1916–20[2]	190	180	199
1921–25	157	147	166
1926–30	145	137	153
1931–35	134	127	141
1936–40[2]	128	123	132
1941–45[2]	112	110	113
1946–50[2]	101	99	102
1951–55	97	98	95
1956–60	91	94	89
1961–65	90	95	87
1966–70	87	92	83
1971–75	85	89	81
1976–80	81	85	78

Notes
[1]The standardised mortality ratio shows the number of deaths registered in the year of experience as a percentage of those which would have been expected in that year had the sex–age mortality of a standard period (1950–52) operated on the sex–age population of the year of experience.
[2]For the years 1915–20 and from 3 September 1939 to 31 December 1949 for males, and from 1 June 1941 to 31 December 1949 for females, the mortality rates are based upon civilians only but, as in other years, the number of deaths include those of non-civilians registered in England and Wales.

Source McPherson K, Coleman D, 1988 Health. In Halsey AH *British social trends since 1900: A guide to the changing social structure of Britain*. Macmillan, p. 401.

Health and society in twentieth-century Britain

TABLE 2   Death rates per million population at ages under 15 years

Period	Scarlet fever	Diphtheria	Whooping cough	Poliomyelitis	Measles
1901–10	271	571	815	–	915
1911–20	123	437	554	13	838
1921–30	64	298	405	11	389
1931–39	46	290	197	11	217
1940–49	7	112	111	11	62
1950–59	neg.	1	17	9	13
1960–64	neg.	neg.	3	1	7
1965	neg.	—	2	2	11
1970	—	—	1	–	3
1975	—	0	1	–	1
1978	—	—	1	–	2

Source McPherson et al. p. 4.

TABLE 3   Expectation of life[1]: by sex and age

	1901	1931	1961	1991	1996	2001
Males						
At birth	45.5	58.4	67.9	73.2	74.0	74.5
At age:						
1 year	53.6	62.1	68.6	72.8	73.5	74.0
10 years	50.4	55.6	60.0	64.0	64.7	65.2
20 years	41.7	46.7	50.4	54.3	54.9	55.4
40 years	26.1	29.5	31.5	35.2	35.8	36.2
60 years	13.3	14.4	15.0	17.8	18.2	18.7
80 years	4.9	4.9	5.2	6.5	6.7	7.0
Females						
At birth	49.0	62.4	73.8	78.6	79.5	79.9
At age:						
1 year	55.8	65.1	74.2	78.1	78.9	79.3
10 years	52.7	58.6	65.6	69.3	70.1	70.5
20 years	44.1	49.6	55.7	59.4	60.2	60.6
40 years	28.3	32.4	36.5	39.9	40.6	41.0
60 years	14.6	16.4	19.0	21.8	22.4	22.7
80 years	5.3	5.4	6.3	8.1	8.6	8.8

Note
[1]Further number of years which a person might expect to live.

Source Central Statistical Office *Social Trends* HMSO 1993.

TABLE 4[1]   Infant mortality, 1900–85, England and Wales[1]

Year	Total live births	Deaths under one year	Rate per 1,000 live births
1900	257,480	142,912	154
1910	267,721	94,579	105
1920	379,982	76,552	80
1930	648,811	38,908	60
1940	607,029	33,892	56
1950	697,097	20,817	30
1960	785,005	17,118	22
1970	784,486	14,207	18
1975	603,445	9,518	16
1980	656,234	7,899	12
1985	656,417	6,141	9

Note
[1]Infant mortality rates are the number of deaths under one year per 1,000 live births occurring in the year, except in the years 1931–56 when they were based on the related live births, that is, combined live births of the associated and preceding year to which they relate.

Source McPherson et al. p. 409.

TABLE 5 Mortality by social class: standardised mortality ratios[1] for men aged 20–64 from all causes, 1910–12 to 1982–83 (percentages)

	1910–12,[2],[3]	1921–23	1930–32	1949–53[4]	1949–53	1959–63 unadjusted	1959–63 adjusted	1970–72 unadjusted	1970–72 adjusted[5]	1979–80 1982–83[6]	1976–81
Class I	88	82	90	98	86	76	75	77	75	66	66
Class II	94	94	94	86	92	81	–	81	–	76	77
Class III	96	95	97	101	101	100	–	99 (IIIN)[7] 106 (IIIM)[8]	–	94 (IIIN) 106 (IIIM)	105 (IIIN) 96 (IIIM)
Class IV	93	101	102	94	104	103	–	114	–	116	109
Class V	142	125	111	118	118	143	127	137	121	165	124

Notes The table excludes non-civilians.

[1] Standardised mortality ratio can be defined as the number of deaths registered in a standard period within a given social class grouping ages 20–64, as a percentage of the number that would have occurred if the death-rates had been the same as in a standard population consisting of all males in England and Wales.

[2] In 1910–12 for ages 25–65 inclusive, other years for ages 20–64 inclusive.

[3] In 1910–12 miners, textile and agricultural workers were not included in the social class groupings. In 1930–32 minor changes were made in the classification of occupations into social class groupings. For the period 1949–53 there were some further changes in assignments of occupations to the social class groupings. The following table shows the 1949–53 figures grouped according to the classification of 1951 and the 1931 classifications.

[4] Corrected figures as published in 'Registrar-General 1971 *Decennial Supplement, England and Wales, 1961: Occupational Mortality Tables*' HMSO: 22.

[5] Occupations in 1959–63 and 1970–72 have been reclassified according to the 1950 classification.

[6] Data from 1979–80, 1982–83 Decennial Supplement, based on 1980 Classification of Occupations. The Decennial Supplement warns that the social class data should not be regarded as reliable, especially for Class V which are exaggerated by bias.

[7] Class III, non-manual workers.

[8] Class III, manual workers.

Source McPherson et al. p. 419.

TABLE 6 Reported long-standing illness or disability: by socio-economic group and condition group, 1989

	Professional	Employers and managers	Intermediate	Skilled manual	Semi-skilled manual	Unskilled manual	Total[1]
Condition group							
Musculoskeletal system	10.0	12.6	13.0	15.5	17.1	20.1	14.5
Heart and circulatory system	6.4	8.1	8.0	9.4	11.8	12.1	9.1
Respiratory system	5.2	5.2	6.8	6.4	7.2	9.6	6.4
Digestive system	2.1	3.3	4.0	3.9	4.8	5.0	3.8
Nervous system	2.5	2.1	3.1	2.7	2.9	4.4	2.8
Eye complaints	1.5	2.2	2.9	2.0	3.0	3.2	2.4
Ear complaints	1.9	1.4	1.9	2.7	2.5	3.1	2.2
All long-standing illness	29.1	32.5	34.9	37.0	41.6	47.8	36.5
Sample size (=100%) (numbers)	1,164	3,557	4,065	5,987	3,190	981	19,562

Note
[1] Members of the Armed Forces, persons in inadequately described occupations and all persons who have never worked are not shown as separate categories but are included in the total.

Source Central Statistical Office Social Trends HMSO 1993.

199

Health and society in twentieth-century Britain

TABLE 7   New addicts notified: by type of drug

Type of drug	1973	1981	1986	1990	1991
Heroin	508	1660	4855	5819	6328
Methadone	328	431	659	1469	2180
Dipianone	28	473	116	154	155
Cocaine	132	174	520	633	882
Morphine	226	355	343	296	185
Pethidine	27	45	33	39	37
Dextromoramide	28	59	97	78	89
Opium	0	0	23	14	12
Others	2	4	4	4	1
Total addicts notified[1]	806	2248	5325	6923	8007

Note
[1]As an addict can be reported as addicted to more than one notifiable drug, the figures for individual drugs cannot be added together to produce totals.

Source Central Statistical Office Social Trends HMSO 1993.

INDEX